"*How to Be an Atheist* is the best ⟨⟩ conflict between science and religion ⟨⟩ well written, well organized, and philosophically sophisticated. Moreover, the author's knowledge of science, the history of science, and the history of 'the conflict between science and religion' is admirably suited to his purpose. Above all, the book is *accessible*. No reader who is interested in questions about the relation between science and religion will have any difficulty in following the author's arguments."

Peter van Inwagen, John Cardinal O'Hara Professor of Philosophy, University of Notre Dame

"How many times has atheistic naturalism appeared to be a charade, like a shell game where you never seem to see all the steps of the process? Or how frequently have you been told that atheists are too soft—that they must be even more rigorously skeptical? But then when they do follow their own system, there is nothing left with which to build their worldview! Get ready—you're embarking on a challenging journey here. In this volume, Mitch Stokes uncovers issue after issue where atheistic naturalism looks more like the king who wore no clothes, and Stokes is the one to give him the message! This is must reading—I recommend it highly!"

Gary R. Habermas, Distinguished Research Professor and Chair, Philosophy Department, Liberty University

"I've been saying for years that professional skeptics are not skeptical enough, that they are selective in their skepticism, and that if they ever turned their skeptical faculties on their own skepticism and the materialist worldview that almost invariably comes attached to it, they would see the house of cards they've built collapse of its own internal inadequacies. Mitch Stokes, in this incisive book, does a wonderful job filling in the details to this charge against skepticism."

William A. Dembski, Senior Fellow, Center for Science and Culture, Discovery Institute; author, *Being as Communion*

"*How to Be an Atheist* is both readable and well documented, both incisive and wide-ranging. It is a wise book that exposes the dead-end reasoning and ultimately antihuman positions of modern skepticism. If you're looking for an accessible book to take you through the host of such skeptical arguments against belief in God, this is it!"

Paul Copan, Pledger Family Chair of Philosophy and Ethics, Palm Beach Atlantic University

How to Be an Atheist

How to Be an Atheist

Why Many Skeptics Aren't Skeptical Enough

Mitch Stokes

Foreword by J. P. Moreland

WHEATON, ILLINOIS

How to Be an Atheist: Why Many Skeptics Aren't Skeptical Enough

Copyright © 2016 by Mitchell O. Stokes

Published by Crossway
          1300 Crescent Street
          Wheaton, Illinois 60187

Cover design: Jeff Miller, Faceout Studio

First printing 2016

Printed in the United States of America

Scripture quotations are from the ESV® Bible (The Holy Bible, English Standard Version®), copyright © 2001 by Crossway, a publishing ministry of Good News Publishers. Used by permission. All rights reserved.

Trade paperback ISBN: 978-1-4335-4298-5
ePub ISBN: 978-1-4335-4301-2
PDF ISBN: 978-1-4335-4299-2
Mobipocket ISBN: 978-1-4335-4300-5

Library of Congress Cataloging-in-Publication Data
Stokes, Mitch.
   How to be an atheist : why many skeptics aren't skeptical enough / Mitch Stokes ; foreword by J. P. Moreland.
      pages   cm
   Includes bibliographical references and index.
   ISBN 978-1-4335-4298-5 (tp)
   1. Apologetics. 2. Christianity and atheism. 3. Atheism. 4. Skepticism. I. Title.
BT1212.S76   2016
239—dc23   2015023759

Crossway is a publishing ministry of Good News Publishers.

VP		26	25	24	23	22	21	20	19	18	17	16
16	15	14	13	12	11	10	9	8	7	6	5	4	3	2

To my parents,
who had to put up with a lot.

I think my ultimate goal would be to convert people away from particular religions toward a rationalist skepticism.

Richard Dawkins, interview by Larry Taunton

Their scepticism about values is on the surface: it is for use on other people's values; about the values current in their own set they are not nearly sceptical enough. And this phenomenon is very usual.

C. S. Lewis, *The Abolition of Man*

Contents

Part 3
MORALITY

Foreword

When Crossway editor Justin Taylor asked me to write a foreword to *How to Be an Atheist*, I was excited to have this opportunity. I felt this way for two primary reasons.

First, I was and am impressed with and encouraged by Professor Stokes's academic pedigree. He has a BS and MS in mechanical engineering (with five patents!), so he understands science well. Then, too, he received an MA in religion at Yale under Nicholas Wolterstorff, and an MA and PhD in philosophy from Notre Dame with Peter van Inwagen and Alvin Plantinga as his dissertation supervisors. When I read this, my head exploded! Having been in the ministry for forty-five years, I am thrilled to see a whole movement arise, typified by Stokes, of well-educated Jesus lovers who can competently address the important issues of the day, and who can lead and teach others to be involved more intelligently.

Second, for a long time I have thought that while atheists claimed to embody the virtue of skepticism and, thus, have rationality on their side, the truth of the matter is that many, if not most, atheists employ a selective skepticism. They are skeptical of anything that supports theism, but they are not skeptical enough of some of their own beliefs as atheists. And now, finally, Professor Stokes has provided us with a book that carefully distinguishes different forms of skepticism and convincingly exposes (many) atheists' skeptical inconsistencies and inadequacies.

When I got the manuscript, I literally could not put it down. I spent the day reading the entire work. Why? The content was so well selected, so intelligently presented, and so accessible that it was a delight to read. Moreover, it is very well crafted. Stokes is a wordsmith in his writing style. (And the guy is funny!)

How to Be an Atheist is, indeed, a model work in philosophical apologetics in the sense that Stokes painstakingly criticizes atheistic views that are raised against Christianity and responds to objections. But it would be a grave mistake to think that this is just another apologetics book. No, this book gives the reader an education in a number of important areas, and it teaches us how to think. Time and time again, Stokes takes an angle on an issue that is different, insightful, and refreshing. And his research is exemplary.

If you are a believer, I urge you to get this book, encourage friends to get it, and form a study group in which you can work through the material slowly and thoughtfully. I promise you, it is well worth the effort. I meet many Christians who wish they could go back to graduate school and get an education relevant to their Christianity, but finances and other commitments present insurmountable obstacles to this move. Well, there is a second alternative: read books like this one and you will get an education.

If you are an atheist who is intellectually open to investigating some of the problems in your worldview, this is the book for you. It has an irenic tone and deals fairly and proportionately with its subject matter.

I thank Mitch Stokes for doing the hard work that made it possible to write a book like this. And I am so happy that *How to Be an Atheist* is being published. Read it, study it, and ponder what it says. You will be the better for it.

J. P. Moreland
Distinguished Professor of Philosophy
Talbot School of Theology
Biola University

Preface

I'm a skeptic by training and temperament. I understand why some people are skeptical about religion. What I don't understand is how naive some atheists are about the rational strength of their position. It's one thing to believe there's no God, but it's quite another to say things like "there exists not a shred of respectable evidence" for God's existence, or "science shows that God does not exist."[1] When atheists make such grand claims, they're either frightfully ignorant of the relevant complexities or else bluffing. In either case, they should stop, if for no other reason than that they're damaging their credibility.

Not all atheists writing today are guilty of such posturing—this should go without saying. Nor am I criticizing atheists for holding their views passionately. The real problem is when unwarranted confidence shows up in their *considered* remarks—for example, when they slow down long enough to write. This goes for all of us, in fact. Intellectual dishonesty is a sin no matter who commits it; über-certainty is a form of lying. No doubt I'm guilty of it too, and if I knew where, I'd stop. But whenever the opportunity arises, we should exercise intellectual restraint.

Part of the solution is to realize and admit that belief and unbelief are each far more than a matter of reason. Although I think that reason tips the scales in favor of belief in God, all things being equal, it also seems to me that all things *aren't* equal. Reason alone won't settle the issue. No one is neutral. This is why debates over God's existence can sometimes seem like making a legal case for your devotion to your spouse: there

---

[1] The first is from Christopher Hitchens's introduction to Christopher Hitchens, ed., *The Portable Atheist: Essential Readings for the Nonbeliever* (Philadelphia: Da Capo, 2007), xxii; the second is from the subtitle to Victor J. Stenger, *God: The Failed Hypothesis—How Science Shows That God Does Not Exist* (Amherst, NY: Prometheus, 2008).

are good objective reasons, but those reasons aren't the whole of it. It's always *logically* possible that your spouse is part of an alien army sent to seduce and distract earth's inhabitants prior to the invasion. Or worse, it's always logically possible that he or she is cheating on you. Reason can get away from us. As Chesterton said in *Orthodoxy* (and he's probably right), some insane people aren't *ir*rational; they're hyperrational, with no way to tap the brakes: "The madman is the man who has lost everything except his reason."[2] Not that we shouldn't marshal reason. Indeed, it should play as much a role as possible in our deliberations. Just no more than that.

Now, one of atheism's virtues is its avowed skepticism. (I cannot, in fact, think of another virtue at the moment.) Yet many unbelievers, it seems to me, don't take their skepticism seriously enough. I find this puzzling. I mean, I identify with their no-nonsense skeptical stance and general distrust of humanity; these appeal to me, probably more than they ought to. What I don't understand is the lack of skeptical follow-through.

Moreover, I'm surprised that science-fueled atheism is often naive about the alleged source of said unbelief, namely, science and its methods. I must admit that I too am enthusiastic about science; you'll see no science bashing in these pages. But I will direct attention to legitimate epistemological questions regarding science. This will help us take science seriously *for the right reasons*. It will also prevent us from taking it too seriously. Ironically, overestimating science in some areas leads to underestimating it in others. For example, many of us don't appreciate how difficult science is and so don't appreciate nearly enough what scientists have actually accomplished.

But if someone *were* to insist on taking science too seriously, believing, for example, that it implies a materialistic and neo-Darwinian view of nature, this would have important implications for that person's views about morality. Morality for that person would be, I'll argue, no more than a matter of taste. If I'm right, then unbelievers should be extremely skeptical of the authority of their own moral beliefs and even about the very concept of morality. The lesson, I claim, is that über-optimism about science leads to moral skepticism—along a path through atheism (or what I will sometimes call *naturalism*, the view that

---

[2] G. K. Chesterton, *Orthodoxy* (1908; repr., San Fransisco: Ignatius, 1995), 24.

the natural world is all there is—"or ever was, or ever will be," according to Carl Sagan's secular Gloria Patri).

We believers have lots of room for improvement too. We also should become more adept at skepticism. After all, the problem in the garden was, to my lights, that we weren't skeptical enough. Never get into a stranger's car, no matter what kind of fruit he offers you. But the believer's skepticism should be a studied one, not an ignorant flinch. We often throw out the baby with the bathwater. There are, for example, overzealous "science deniers" who take their skepticism too far. And even when sane and sober believers doubt science at the right points, we often do a poor job identifying why science went wrong (or we fail to appreciate how reasonable it is for science to end up there).

So both sides should be more skeptical, and about the right things. We should take skepticism as seriously as possible, but no more than that. This is what I will attempt. I've divided this book into three main sections. In the first section, by far the shortest, I lay some of the epistemological groundwork. In particular, I look at the limits of what we can know in general, considering our epistemic abilities with respect to sense perception and reason, our two main cognitive faculties.

Once we've gotten our epistemological bearings, I turn to science and, in particular, to how we should think about its methods and claims. Again, my goal is by no means to denigrate science or to deny that it tells us important and surprising things about the world. But there are also good reasons to remain agnostic or even doubtful about things we cannot directly observe; and we directly observe far less than many people imagine. My main point regarding science is that anyone who takes skepticism seriously should also seriously question whether science gives us the sober truth about fundamental reality, especially about whether naturalism is true.

In these first two sections, much of what I have to say applies to us all, believers and unbelievers alike. That is, we can all agree on much of what I say about our epistemological limitations—including the limitations of science (although the limitations are significantly worse if humans aren't the product of design). But suppose that naturalism *were in fact* true, and further suppose that science largely supports naturalism. What implications does this have for our standard view that there are objective moral standards? In the third section, I'll argue that if naturalism is true, then there are no such standards. Most atheists, however, will be loath to agree. Their reluctance is understandable; but if they're serious about their skepticism—about following reason where'er it leadeth—they'll reluctantly agree.

Or at least I would if I were an atheist.

Acknowledgments

Though I can't say for certain, I'm pretty sure I know what kind of atheist I would be: I'd be darn skeptical about some of the things my unbelieving colleagues held most dear. And for quite a while, I've wanted to speak frankly to atheists—skeptic to skeptic. This book has been a chance to do that and I'm extremely grateful to (now Dr.) Justin Taylor and Crossway for the opportunity. Everyone at Crossway has been very supportive, despite some schedule setbacks due to a temporary downturn in my health. Justin in particular was entirely understanding and wholly gracious.

Speaking of Crossway, my editor, Thom Notaro, was just stellar. He had a preternatural ability to make stylistic improvements while retaining my "voice" (such as it is). He never tried to force me to say things I wouldn't say otherwise but also prevented me from letting it all hang out, metaphorically speaking. Moreover, and just as important, Thom has the theological acumen to help guide substantive content changes whenever necessary. And his attention to detail is unsurpassed. He's a valuable asset to Crossway and to any author whose book he helps craft.

Speaking of my health (which I was doing in the paragraph before last), I want to express my gratitude to New Saint Andrews College for allowing me a leave of absence during the fall of 2014 to finish this book. It was more than I deserve.

As for the book's title (which I wasn't speaking of at all), it will puzzle some folks, so I'd like to mention that it was inspired by Alvin Plantinga's article "How to Be an Anti-Realist." And, all things being equal, anything inspired by Al is ahead of the game simply in virtue of that.

My wife, Christine, proofread the entire manuscript, and though she has done this exact thing for each of my books, her efforts are no less appreciated for their frequency; the opposite in fact. And I never once had to sleep on the couch, no matter how many chapters she had to read in a day.

And lastly, speaking of acknowledgments (which I've been doing this entire time) I must acknowledge that I'm utterly dependent on my agent, Aaron Rench. Without him, this project would never have gotten off the ground.

Introduction

Skepticism and Contemporary Atheism

Science and Morality: The Engines of Atheism

Perhaps the most conspicuous trait of contemporary atheists—besides their atheism—is that they're especially fervent about two things: science and morality. This observation is not a criticism. Science and morality should have everyone's vote. In fact, as I'll point out in a moment, we're hardwired to be enthusiastic about both. But such enthusiasm manifests itself in a special way among atheists.

Consider science. According to unbelievers, belief in God flies in the face of what "we now know" about the world. This is largely because science allegedly shows that there is, in all likelihood, no God. In fact, the two most famous scientists of our generation—Stephen Hawking and Richard Dawkins—are atheists. (Dawkins was even voted the world's top thinker in 2013.)[1] Is it merely a coincidence that both scientists, at the pinnacle of their respective fields, don't believe in God? Is there something about science that encourages, suggests, or even slightly hints that God doesn't exist? It would seem so: Dawkins's and Hawking's atheism is largely driven by what they think science tells us about reality. And they aren't isolated examples.

But why think that science and God are incompatible? Let's consider

---

[1] John Dugdale, "Richard Dawkins Named World's Top Thinker in Poll," *The Guardian*, April 25, 2013, http://www.theguardian.com/books/booksblog/2013/apr/25/richard-dawkins-named-top-thinker.

an anecdote. Around 1800, French physicist Pierre-Simon Laplace presented Napoleon with a copy of his monumental work on celestial mechanics.[2] When Napoleon asked Monsieur Laplace why this massive work made no mention of the Creator, Laplace is said to have replied, "I had no need of that hypothesis."

This little exchange, said Christopher Hitchens, just might mark the moment in history when God became superfluous.[3] It also illustrates the prevalent sentiment born during the Enlightenment: science has shown that the universe's staggering order and complexity, which we once attributed to God's meticulous care, is actually the result of entirely natural processes.[4]

We'll look more closely at this line of thinking later, but for now, suffice it to say that most atheists see science as underwriting their unbelief. But according to some atheists, there's something else wrong with believing that God exists. When the current crop of "new atheists" began writing, it was primarily in response to the 9/11 tragedy. Belief in God, they said, is not merely false; it is morally wrong. It places humanity's future in jeopardy, and we therefore have a moral responsibility to eradicate it. We are also told that religious violence isn't limited to acts of terrorism, but includes telling innocent children paralyzing stories of eternal damnation and dinosaurs on the ark. According to Dawkins, such indoctrination is worse than "ordinary"

---

[2] Stephen Jay Gould, *Dinosaur in a Haystack: Reflections in Natural History* (New York: Three Rivers, 1995), 25.

[3] Christopher Hitchens, *God Is Not Great: How Religion Poisons Everything* (New York: Twelve, 2007), 66. Laplace's famous quip is popular among unbelievers. The director of the Stanford Institute for Theoretical Physics, Leonard Susskind (also one of the founders of string theory), places it squarely on the opening page of his book *The Cosmic Landscape: String Theory and the Illusion of Intelligent Design* (New York: Little, Brown, 2006).

[4] As an interesting aside, the facts surrounding this anecdote may be somewhat different. For one thing, it's not entirely clear that Laplace actually uttered these words, although he may have said something that could be taken to imply them. For example, Daniel Johnson says that the source of this story was the English astronomer William Herschel. In his diary, Herschel says:

> The first Consul [Napoleon, who had not yet crowned himself emperor] then asked a few questions relating to Astronomy and the construction of the heavens to which I made such answers as seemed to give him great satisfaction. He also addressed himself to Mr. Laplace on the same subject, and held a considerable argument with him in which he differed from that eminent mathematician. The difference was occasioned by an exclamation of the first Consul, who asked in a tone of exclamation or admiration (when we were speaking of the extent of the sidereal heavens): "And who is the author of all this!" Mons. De la Place wished to shew that a chain of natural causes would account for the construction and preservation of the wonderful system. This the first Consul rather opposed. Much may be said on the subject; by joining the arguments of both we shall be led to "Nature and nature's God."

In any case, from Herschel's comments, it sounds like Laplace could have believed that he could account for the prevailing order of the cosmos—and perhaps even its origin—with all-natural explanatory ingredients. See Johnson's article, "The Hypothetical Atheist," *Commentary*, June 18, 2007, https://www.commentarymagazine.com/2007/06/18/the-hypothetical-atheist.

child abuse.[5] And Hitchens said that religion in general poisons *everything* and that Christianity in particular is a "wicked cult." For anyone desiring moral progress, the abolition of religion will be an important first or second step.

It's Only Natural

Science and morality, then, are the drivers of contemporary atheism and thus "sweet spots" in the debates between believers and nonbelievers. In fact, the most popular arguments against God's existence come from science and morality, the latter in regard to evil and suffering. (Of course, many believers will think that science and morality show us just the opposite: nature looks suspiciously like it was designed, and morality seems to require a divine Lawgiver.)

But we shouldn't be surprised that these two topics are central to the debate. In the case of science—the study of the natural world—humankind has concentrated an immense amount of resources toward understanding the cosmos. If humans were to ever get an A for effort, it would be here. On the other hand, man cannot live by facts alone. Morality tells us how we ought to behave, how we should live. Notice then, that science and morality fall along the all-important fact/value divide. Science tells us what *is* the case; morality tells us what we *ought* to do, although some atheists believe that science also tells us what we ought to do, as we'll see.

Humans seem to be hardwired to contemplate both conscience and cosmos. Even the Bible suggests this. In the first chapter of Paul's letter to the Romans, he says that something in us is triggered by the created order, causing us to just "see" that God exists (cf. 1:19–20). There seems to be something like a built-in faculty that causes immediate belief in God (or would cause it, were it not for sin). In his next chapter, Paul suggests that humans come equipped with a built-in *moral* faculty or, as he puts it, a moral law "written on their hearts" (2:15).

In any case, we seem specially attuned to the wiles of nature and the commands of morality. And these propensities were not lost on the great Enlightenment philosopher Immanuel Kant, who famously said, "Two things fill the mind with ever new and increasing admiration and awe, the more often and enduringly reflection is occupied with them: the

---

[5] Richard Dawkins, *The God Delusion* (Boston: Houghton Mifflin, 2006), 356.

r heavens above me and the moral law within me."[6] Kant has inspired more than his share of skepticism about God's existence, whether he intended to or not.[7] He was also, not unrelatedly, the culmination of the eighteenth-century Enlightenment and was wildly impressed by the Scientific Revolution of the previous century, a revolution in which Aristotle was overthrown by Newton. Although there was no doubt in Kant's mind (or anyone else's) that Newton's mathematical physics was correct, it wasn't clear how creatures with such limited cognitive faculties could be privy to such knowledge. So in his famous (and immensely difficult) *Critique of Pure Reason*, Kant developed an excruciating epistemology meant to underwrite our mathematical and scientific knowledge.

The situation depicted by the new physics also made it difficult to see how we might account for morality. For one thing, if the world behaves according to deterministic physical laws—and humans are simply parts of that world—then how might we be held responsible for our actions? Aren't our actions entirely dictated by the laws of physics (or some similarly natural laws)? "See God, 'twasn't my fault I ate the fruit; it was the physics that thou gavest me."

Kant's overall philosophical project then was a monumental attempt to reconcile the new scientific picture with the traditional one that we're morally responsible beings, that is, to reconcile the laws of nature with the laws of morality. Ever since the Enlightenment, this has been a pressing goal. And the problem is even stickier for atheists: if there's no divine Lawgiver, then even the very concept of morality changes—or so I'll argue in part 3, where we'll look at the prospects of this reconciliatory project.

In any case, none of this would have been a problem for Kant had science not suggested it. Today we're familiar with science telling us strange things about us and the world. But it can be disturbing nonetheless. And it was much more disturbing for folks living immediately downstream of the Scientific Revolution.

Skepticism and a New Enlightenment

Yet these folks also felt an exhilarating sense of freedom, which was at a premium during the Enlightenment. We might even summarize the

---

[6] Immanuel Kant, *Critique of Practical Reason*, trans. Werner S. Pluhar (Indianapolis: Hackett, 2002), 203.
[7] No doubt his intentions weren't entirely pure, but as far as skepticism about God goes, he says that he had destroyed knowledge (of God) in order to make room for faith.

Enlightenment the way philosopher Karl Popper did: as *liberation*, that is, "self-emancipation through knowledge."[8] But what exactly were the shackles? In a word, religion. Not that all Enlightenment thinkers were atheists; many were deists (of course, many were still Christians). But a sizeable portion of them saw organized religion as oppressive and over-bearing, an intellectual dictatorship, and so they sought the freedom to think for themselves. In fact, people who bucked the religious consensus were called *freethinkers*. It was a second revolution in as many centuries: this time religion overthrown by reason.

But, allegedly, our shackles were in some sense our own fault, due to a kind of immaturity and cowardice. Kant memorably put it this way in his 1784 essay "What Is Enlightenment?"

> Enlightenment is man's release from his self-imposed tutelage. Tutelage is man's inability to make use of his understanding without direction from another. Self-incurred is the tutelage when its cause lies not in lack of reason but in lack of resolution and courage to use it without direction from another. *Sapere Aude!* [Dare to know!] "Have courage to use your own reason!"—that is the motto of enlightenment.[9]

The Enlightenment, then, was an intellectual coming of age, a coming into one's majority; and this required a stout heart and moral resolve. Who could fail to be moved?

The connection between knowledge and freedom was certainly not new to the Enlightenment. The ancient liberal arts were a curriculum for the liberated man, as opposed to the slave. In one sense, this is getting things backward. It is not so much that only free people should be educated (although that was true), but that education makes one free. As Epictetus—himself once a slave—said in his *Discourses*, "We must not believe the many, who say that only free people ought to be educated but rather believe the philosophers who say that only the educated are free."[10] Anyone who doesn't appreciate educational freedom, or the freedom that genuine education provides, probably already has it.

---

[8] Karl Popper, "Emancipation through Knowledge," in *Challenges to the Enlightenment: In Defense of Reason and Science*, ed. Paul Kurtz and Timothy J. Madigan (Buffalo, NY: Prometheus, 1994), 71.
[9] Immanuel Kant, "What Is Enlightenment?," in *The Portable Enlightenment Reader*, ed. Isaac Kramnick (New York: Penguin, 1995), 1.
[10] Quoted in Carl Sagan, *The Demon-Haunted World: Science as a Candle in the Dark* (New York: Ballantine, 1996), 354.

The Enlightenment's revolution continues. Some of today's most influential atheists are part of the Freedom from Religion Foundation (FFRF), the largest atheist advocacy group. The group's purpose is to protect "the constitutional principle of the separation of state and church" (and one of the ways you can support this cause is to buy a bumper sticker with their slogan "In Reason We Trust"). Honorary board members of FFRF have included such intellectual luminaries as Richard Dawkins, Daniel Dennett, Jerry Coyne, Steven Pinker, Rebecca Goldstein, and the late Christopher Hitchens.

Another group, the Academy of Humanism, is an organization of unbelievers who, among other things, "are devoted to free inquiry in all fields of human endeavor" and "committed to a scientific outlook and the use of scientific methods in acquiring knowledge."[11] Laureates of the academy (past and present) include Richard Rorty, Lawrence Krauss, Dawkins, Pinker, Dennett, A. C. Grayling, Hitchens, Antony Flew, J. J. C. Smart, and Philip Kitcher.

These groups continue the Enlightenment's emphasis on reason and freedom. It's no coincidence then that Christopher Hitchens ended his searing attack on religion *God Is Not Great* with the chapter "In Conclusion: The Need for a New Enlightenment."[12] Hitchens characterizes this coming age with heroic phrases like "unfettered scientific inquiry," "the path of skepticism," and "doubt and experiment" (as opposed to "dogma and faith"). The idea seems to be that we should be wary of what others tell us, particularly if those "others" are religious. We should be skeptical of authority and think for ourselves. *Sapere aude!*

Sober Skepticism

If knowledge unlocks freedom, then whither the notions of doubt and skepticism that Hitchens so highly valued? Knowledge and skepticism seem to be polar opposites of one another. A full-blown skeptic is someone who doubts that we can have knowledge about anything whatsoever.

There are, of course, kinder, gentler versions of skepticism. According to these, we do not (or cannot) have knowledge merely about specific topics. For example, we can be skeptics about God's existence, in

---

[11] Paul Kurtz and Timothy J. Madigan, eds., *Challenges to the Enlightenment: In Defense of Reason and Science* (Buffalo, NY: Prometheus, 1994), 9.
[12] Hitchens, *God Is Not Great*, 277.

which case we don't believe—or at least we doubt very seriously—that there is any such divine being. (In fact, were you to randomly tell someone that you're a "skeptic," this is most likely the version of skepticism she would attribute to you.) But we can be skeptics about all manner of things. We might be skeptics about a physical world outside our minds (which we'll consider in part 1), about unobservable scientific entities like electrons, quarks, and gravitons (part 2), or about objective moral laws (part 3). People can also be skeptics about events, like a worldwide flood, or evolution, or the Big Bang, or the moon landing.

But "skepticism" can also refer to something much less controversial, something more mundane and practical. This kind of skepticism is an overall epistemological stance, a kind of "safety first" attitude toward what one believes, an intellectual caution. This even kinder, even gentler skepticism merely says that we shouldn't be unduly credulous, that we should filter our beliefs using a sufficiently fine doxastic sieve (*doxa* is the Greek word for "belief"). Let's call this *sober skepticism*. Sober skepticism can obviously be embraced by believer and unbeliever alike (at least it's obvious to *me*). In fact, most of us will want to say that we're sober skeptics. After all, such skepticism is *sober* in that it is in accord with reason and intellectually sophisticated: it doesn't take skepticism *too* seriously, charging recklessly into cynicism. But it's serious about epistemic standards all the same: the *skepticism* part suggests that we're epistemologically savvy and streetwise, that we've been around the intellectual block more than once. Even better, it's cool, hip, and a little dangerous. Or we skeptics see it this way.

Skepticism about God

Unfortunately, the two main kinds of skepticism we'll consider in this book—sober skepticism and skepticism about God—are often conflated. Of course, unbelievers will explain that this is no accident: if we take sober skepticism seriously, we'll also be skeptics about God's existence. General epistemic wariness (i.e., sober skepticism) implies that we'll reject things that others all too eagerly accept.

Consider, for example, the Committee for Skeptical Inquiry (CSI), which publishes *Skeptical Inquirer* magazine.[13] CSI's founding mem-

---

[13] The group's Twitter bio says, "Promoting scientific inquiry, critical thinking, science education, and the use of reason in examining important issues with our magazine, *Skeptical Inquirer*."

bers include the famous atheists Carl Sagan, Isaac Asimov, and Paul Kurtz. The committee's mission is "to promote scientific inquiry, critical investigation, and the use of reason in examining controversial and extraordinary claims."[14] The idea seems to be that in addition to exercising epistemic restraint, they expose those bent on deceiving us. Typical of "controversial and extraordinary" topics are the usual suspects: astrology, UFO sightings, alien abductions, Bigfoot, ghosts, and ESP; but they also include miracles, creationism, and intelligent design. Many of these subjects are categorized as *pseudoscience*, that is, questionable endeavors trying to pass themselves off as credible inquiry (i.e., as science).

Putting it this way, however, implies that there's something incompatible between sober skepticism and belief in God (as well as between belief in God and science). This is a real shame and in any case seems to me misguided. Epistemic caution does not (or does not obviously) require skepticism with respect to God's existence. But I am leaving that topic for another time. My concern in this book—part 2, in particular—is to look at the implications of sober skepticism for our general view of science. That is, my goal here isn't to show that there are good reasons for a sober skeptic to believe in God (though I heartily believe there are); instead I will try to make a decent case that there is conflict between sober skepticism and science-induced atheism.

Avoiding the Ditches

In any case, believers and unbelievers can agree that we should temper our credulity. Consider, for example, some of the characteristics described in Sagan's seminal article "The Burden of Skepticism" (which was, by the way, published in CSI's *Skeptical Inquirer*).[15] This article is dear to contemporary unbelieving skeptics[16] and, indeed, has much to commend it. Sagan points out that skepticism, as he means it, is noth-

---

[14] "About CSI," http://www.csicop.org/about/about_csi.
[15] Carl Sagan, "The Burden of Skepticism," *Skeptical Inquirer* 12 (Fall 1987), http://www.csicop.org/si/show/burden_of_skepticism.
[16] For example, Michael Shermer (whom we'll meet in a moment), in the dedication to his book *Why People Believe Weird Things*, says this about the lecture version of the article:

> To the memory of Carl Sagan, 1934–1996; colleague and inspiration, whose lecture on "The Burden of Skepticism" ten years ago gave me a beacon when I was intellectually and professionally adrift, and ultimately inspired the birth of the Skeptics Society, *Skeptic* magazine, and this book, as well as my commitment to skepticism and the liberating possibilities of science.

Shermer, *Why People Believe Weird Things* (New York: MJF, 1997).

ing esoteric and that most of us are skeptics in the everyday business of life, for example, when we are afflicted with a used-car salesman: "If you don't exercise some minimal skepticism, if you have an absolutely untrammeled credulity, there is probably some price you will have to pay later."[17] And this is just plain good sense. You should keep your guard up.

Of course, as Sagan points out, we can take skepticism too far, turning it into the nonsober kind: "If you are only skeptical, then no new ideas make it through to you. You never learn anything new."[18] So there's a tension, a balancing act, a happy medium between fanatical omni-acceptance and incredulity run amok. In the one ditch are gullible folks who swallow everything whole, who are undiscerning epistemological vacuum cleaners. In the other ditch are hyperskeptics, cynical folk who miss out on important truths and harbor a constant fear of appearing uneducated. This latter group turns the volume of Ben Franklin's slightly paranoid "Distrust and caution are the parents of security"[19] up to eleven.

Scientists: The Exemplars

It's not easy to stay on the road; sometimes the ditches are separated by little more than a footpath; and even when they are a respectable distance apart, the shoulders may not be clearly marked. But this is where scientists can help us as examples, advises Sagan. A good scientist manages to avoid the extremes of gullibility and incredulity. In *The Demon-Haunted World: Science as a Candle in the Dark*, Sagan says that the trick to being a good scientist is to combine skepticism with wonder. After all, scientists realize that nature can surprise us. Science has repeatedly altered our view of reality, and so scientists keep an open mind to even the craziest ideas. But they fully accept these ideas only after subjecting them to the most stringent scrutiny.[20] This kind of epistemological stance—which has become known as "scientific skepticism"—is one we all should take, says Sagan. And of course, taken at face value, it seems that scientific skepticism is little more than sober skepticism as practiced by scientists.

---

[17] Sagan, "The Burden of Skepticism."
[18] Ibid.
[19] *Poor Richard's Almanack*, 1733.
[20] Sagan, *The Demon-Haunted World*, 306.

Atheist Michael Shermer, columnist for *Scientific American*, founder of the Skeptics Society, and editor of *Skeptic* magazine, also believes that science is the paradigmatic example of skeptical propriety. "Modern skepticism is embodied by the scientific method. . . . The key to skepticism is to navigate the treacherous straits between 'know nothing' skepticism and 'anything goes' credulity by continuously and vigorously applying the methods of science."[21] Adding to this testimony is the great physicist Richard Feynman, who says that "science is the organized skepticism in the reliability of expert opinion."[22] Again, the thought is that we should do as scientists do if we want to be sober skeptics. And there is nothing objectionable about any of this, supposing that scientists are generally good examples of sober skepticism, a skepticism that is neither too hot nor too cold. My only point here is that there are strong associations between science and sober skepticism. And though there are good reasons for this association, there's room for improvement, as we'll see later.

The Real Work

Regardless of whether scientists are professional skeptics, sober skepticism is a virtue. But despite its appeal, our view of such skepticism is still incomplete. When it comes to actually *being* sensibly skeptical, we haven't really been given much direction. After all, You-Know-Who is in the details, and it's not clear that we've said anything more than a commendation to take our mental hygiene seriously. There's a reason for this coyness. Sober skepticism is nothing more than the view that we should properly manage our epistemic household; we should think clearly and well, operating our cognitive faculties with propriety.

This isn't very exciting, unfortunately. I wish sober skepticism were flashier. The luster that many people see in skepticism—that it's iconoclastic, heroic, and antiauthoritarian—is really not part of skepticism proper. If I'm skeptical about something simply because I don't like someone telling me what to do or because I fancy myself a modern Prometheus, I'm simply being childish. Anyone who wishes to be thought of as an independent thinker is usually neither.

---

[21] Shermer, *Why People Believe Weird Things*, 16.
[22] Lee Smolin, *The Trouble with Physics: The Rise of String Theory, the Fall of a Science, and What Comes Next* (Boston: Houghton Mifflin, 2006), 307.

But skepticism—the sober kind—is no less important for its lack of sex appeal. Our society needs sober skeptics more than ever, people who think clearly and carefully. The pressing question then is this: what does a good skeptic look like, particularly when it comes to science and morality? I'm afraid there's no simple answer, beyond learning some philosophy and carefully studying the issues.

So let's do this.

Part 1

SENSE AND REASON

1

Hume Exhumed

Hume's Legacy

In the introduction I mentioned that the Scientific Revolution led to the Enlightenment's skeptical distemper. The great David Hume provides us with the best example of this science-induced skepticism. If we want to understand the link between atheism, skepticism, science, and morality, we can hardly do better than begin with Hume's philosophy. In it we find the ingredients for a thoughtful, robust skepticism, combined with a particularly antireligious rancor. His writings were generally sophisticated, iconoclastic, and Promethean, and he has been a champion of skeptical unbelievers ever since.[1]

Not that Hume was always consistent. But who is? Let him who is without sin cast the first stone. Hume was, however, more consistent

---

[1] It isn't clear what exactly Hume believed with regard to God. He had rejected Christianity early on, but there are a few times when he seems to be sympathetic to deism. In any case, it seems that he made attempts to ward off encroaching doubts. Writing to a friend in 1751, he says:

> And tis not long ago that I burn'd an old Manuscript Book, wrote before I was twenty; which contain'd, Page after Page, the gradual Progress of my Thoughts on that head [i.e., religious belief]. It begun with an anxious Search after Arguments, to confirm the common Opinion: Doubts stole in, dissipated, return'd, were again dissipated, return'd again; and it was a perpetual Struggle of a restless Imagination against Inclination, perhaps against Reason.

J. Y. T. Greig, ed., *The Letters of David Hume*, vol. 1, *1727–1765* (New York: Oxford University Press, 2011), 154.

James Fieser notes:

> Although his manuscript book was destroyed, several pages of his study notes survive from his early twenties. These show a preoccupation with proofs for God's existence as well as atheism, particularly as he read on these topics in classical Greek and Latin texts and in Pierre Bayle's skeptical *Historical and Critical Dictionary*.

James Fieser, "David Hume," *Internet Encyclopedia of Philosophy* (2011), http://www.iep.utm.edu/hume.

than most who avow skepticism today. Many of today's skeptical atheists don't understand the real significance of Hume's philosophy, despite their admiration. They typically ignore his radically pessimistic assessment of our cognitive faculties and what that implies. More specifically—and we'll see this later—they don't usually follow Hume in his skepticism about causation, induction, the material world, personal identity, and morality.

But some try, or at least go further than others. One of these is Duke University philosopher of science Alexander Rosenberg. In his book *The Atheist's Guide to Reality*, Rosenberg—who has been called a "mad dog naturalist"[2]—credits Hume with helping him answer the questions that kept him up at night.

Rosenberg had initially turned to physics for answers and was quickly disappointed. The answers physics provided just didn't scratch Rosenberg's "itch of curiosity."[3] So he switched to philosophy. Unfortunately, he says, philosophy pointed him right back to science.

> Imagine how troubling it was for me to discover quite soon that the history of philosophy was mainly a matter of great minds wrestling with science! At least from the beginning of the seventeenth century onward, the agenda of every one of the great philosophers has been set by advances in physics and chemistry and later also biology.[4]

He eventually found his way. "It took a few years, but by reading David Hume (1711–1776), I was able to figure out the mistake preventing science from satisfying me. The mistake, as Hume showed so powerfully, was to think that there is any more to reality than the laws of nature that science discovers."[5] But once Hume showed Rosenberg that science tells us all there is, the pieces of his atheistic worldview fell into place.

So science really had given him the correct answers, but it took some time for Rosenberg to accept them. Here are some of the answers science gives, he says:

---

[2] See, for example, Richard Marshall, "The Mad Dog Naturalist," interview with Alexander Rosenberg, *3:AM* magazine, July 19, 2013, http://www.3ammagazine.com/3am/the-mad-dog-naturalist.
[3] Alexander Rosenberg, *The Atheist's Guide to Reality: Enjoying Life without Illusions* (New York: W. W. Norton, 2011), xiii.
[4] Ibid.
[5] Ibid.

Is there a God? No.

What is the nature of reality? What physics says it is.

What is the purpose of the universe? There is none.

What is the meaning of life? Ditto.

Why am I here? Just dumb luck . . .

Is there free will? Not a chance.

What is the difference between right and wrong, good and bad?
There is no moral difference between them.

Why should I be moral? Because it makes you feel better than
being immoral.

*Is abortion, euthanasia, suicide, paying taxes, foreign aid, or
anything else you don't like forbidden, permissible, or
something obligatory?* Anything goes.[6]

Many of these answers are usually resisted by even the most hard-nosed atheists. But I agree with Rosenberg. I think he gets the right *naturalistic* answers. We disagree, however, about whether the naturalistic answers are right.

Most atheists, on the other hand, think that Rosenberg gets things right when he says that science tells us there's no God. But as I alluded to, few follow him to the conclusion that atheism leads to an "anything goes" morality. Almost all of them believe that atheism is entirely consistent with objective moral laws. I think things are just the opposite: I do not think science shows that there is no God, nor do I think that atheism is consistent with an objective ethical standard. So, as I said, I'll give reasons for doubting that science implies naturalism in part 2, while in part 3 I'll argue that if naturalists persist in their unbelieving ways, they should seriously doubt the existence of objective moral standards.

"The Experimental Method"

Like most intellectuals of his time, Hume was wildly impressed with Newton's "new philosophy" (today we would call it *science*). There were two main aspects of this new philosophy, both of which attested to the uncanny cognitive powers of the human mind. One was the use of mathematics in the formulation of nature's laws. What made this

---

[6] Ibid., 2–3.

astounding was that mathematics is something you do with only your mind—perhaps with heuristic help from paper and pen—and yet it tells you something *true* about the world outside your mind. When you add, for example, a group of 1,375,228 people to a group of 3,245,672 people, you can predict (using addition) that the total number of people will be 4,620,900. But we're now so familiar with addition that it has lost much of its luster. In fact, familiarity has bred contempt.[7] Still, we would begin to discover the power and strangeness of mathematics if we were to carefully look at the details of how, say, calculus enables us to describe—and predict—much of the world's behavior, or at least more than it ought to. It really shouldn't work.[8]

But mathematics can't remain in the mind; its use in science must ultimately answer to the world. It simply isn't free to roam the conceptual landscape without alighting on physical reality at some point. At least if it's going to tell us physical truths about the world. Mathematics must describe and predict behavior that we can *observe*, and creatures like us need sense perception to do this. Mathematics, then, must ultimately earn its keep by matching observations. Math can say all it wants, but seeing is believing, and the only way to know whether the mathematics is telling the truth is to check the world.[9]

Hume was well aware of all this and saw how the new philosophy had succeeded where the old philosophy (Aristotelian science) had failed. And though the mathematics was a substantive part of the new philosophy, it was only through its connection with the sensible world that Newton revealed its true power.[10]

But Newton had done so only for the inanimate world. Hume wanted to extend this method beyond natural philosophy—to what was called *moral philosophy*, which included epistemology and meta-

---

[7] That will happen when you have been browbeaten for twelve or more years by a mathematical pedagogy that seems to have been carefully designed for ineffectiveness. I will step down off my soap box now.

[8] For a bit more explanation, see Mitch Stokes, *A Shot of Faith to the Head: Be a Confident Believer in an Age of Cranky Atheists* (Nashville: Thomas Nelson, 2012), chap. 17.

[9] This is slightly controversial. Do we really need to check the world to see whether addition works? This is a vexing question. Some philosophers—empiricists especially—are prone to answer yes. Of course, once you *trust* addition, you need not check the world; but that is a psychological point, not an epistemological one.

[10] Newton, in addition to his mathematical acumen, was the most ingenious and meticulous experimenter of his generation (and perhaps any other). It is one thing to watch the world go about its business, but quite another to make it perform for you in ways amenable to measurement. Newton constructed elaborate experiments that revealed the behavior of the physical world that he wouldn't have seen had he not coaxed it out.

physics as well as ethics. In particular, Hume wanted to apply the "experimental method" to *humans*, to the knowing subjects themselves. So he launched a program of "scientifically" studying human cognitive abilities.[11] He called it the "science of man."

> *'Tis evident*, that all the sciences have a relation, greater or less, to human nature; and that however wide any of them may seem to run from it, they still return back by one passage or another. Even *Mathematics, Natural Philosophy, and Natural Religion*, are in some measure dependent on the science of *Man*; since they lie under the cognizance of men, and are judged of by their powers and faculties.[12]

For Hume, knowledge of the world must be grounded in experience. Science had turned him into an empiricist. And he wasn't the last convert: Rosenberg calls empiricism the official epistemology of science.[13]

Of course, when it came to the "science of man," Hume couldn't really perform experiments in any strong sense of the word. But, he said, we can extend the experimental method to our intellectual capacities by paying careful attention to how we actually think, reason, and perceive. And so he did.

Skepticism about Sense Perception

Suppose you're hiking through the mountains near your house, enjoying the way the green conifers stand out against the gray, craggy cliffs in the distance. You see a strangely twisted tamarack tree about ten feet away.

In actuality, you're really seeing only an *image* of that tree, an image that is behind your eyes and beneath your skin. The tree itself isn't in your head—you'd be the first to know if it were. But the *image* is in your head, it must be admitted, for if your head went out of existence (we need not get graphic), so too would the image. Of course, it seems for all the world that what you're *seeing* is the tree itself, out there, but that's only because our optical faculties, including the mind and

---

[11] The subtitle to his monumental *Treatise of Human Nature* is *An Attempt to Introduce the Experimental Method of Reasoning into Moral Subjects.*
[12] David Hume, *A Treatise of Human Nature* (Oxford: Clarendon, 1978), xv.
[13] Alexander Rosenberg, *The Philosophy of Science: A Contemporary Introduction*, 3rd ed. (New York: Routledge, 2012), 142.

its construction of the image, are remarkably advanced. The movie of the world playing in your head is very convincing, so convincing that we rarely think of it as a movie. Rather, we take the images to be the objects themselves.

But the most we can say about your "tree idea" is that it is merely a representation of the tree. We call this view of sense perception—which is our contemporary view—*representationalism*. The idea in your head stands for or represents the tree itself. But it is not the tree.

There's something further we believe about your "tree idea," namely, that it *resembles* the tree in important respects; it "looks like" the tree. Now why think that? Is there a good reason for thinking that your idea of the tree resembles or is similar to the tree itself? Well, that depends on what we mean by "a good reason." If we're asking whether we have an *argument* for our "resemblance assumption," then no, there's no good reason. One way to see this is to realize that you couldn't distinguish between actually standing in front of the tree and simply experiencing a remarkably vivid dream, or being a "brain in a vat" that's electrochemically stimulated by a vast network of computers (a BIV, as it's known to philosophers).[14] Your experience would be identical whether you were a BIV or really in front of a tree.[15]

You might object that you're pretty certain your ideas resemble the world "out there" because your senses have (so far) kept you alive: they've kept you from falling over cliffs, from walking out in front of cars, from stumbling into open flames.[16] Unfortunately, this objection won't work. The only way you "know" that you've done all these things is through the very senses you're trying to vouch for. You're arguing for the credibility of your senses while using their own credentials. As Thomas Reid (one of Hume's contemporaries) said, this would be like asking a man whether he's telling the truth when you suspect him of lying.

Suppose, however, that you're undaunted: "Look," you reply, "perhaps I can't know for certain that I'm not a BIV, but what's more likely: that I'm a BIV or that I'm really in front of a tree?" Unfortunately, this reply won't work either. After all, you judge which scenario is more

---

[14] Philosophers came up with this scenario prior to the appearance of *The Matrix*.
[15] This goes for your other senses too. Experience is all in your head. Literally.
[16] Victor Stenger uses this argument. See Victor J. Stenger, *The New Atheism: Taking a Stand for Science and Reason* (Ahmherst, NY: Prometheus, 2009), 60.

likely based on other things you know. And for all you know, you're a BIV. To be sure, we have a lifetime of experience that powerfully conditions us to believe that there's a world "out there" and that this world resembles our ideas. But this very conditioning is being called into question.

Of course, you'd be insane to believe you're a BIV, but that is much different from arguing that you aren't. Worse still, what's wrong with believing you're as likely a BIV as not, logically speaking? If you threw in your epistemic lot with reason alone, would it be *unreasonable* to believe that each is equally likely? *Reason* doesn't decide which is more likely. After all, it may be that you've been a BIV all these years, and the evil geniuses in charge of your simulation have been slowly adjusting your brain to the idea of living in a virtual world. (They don't want you to have a nervous breakdown like all the previous test subjects.) Notice that, slowly, over your lifetime, technology has advanced, movies have portrayed increasingly elaborate Matrix-like scenarios, and you've gradually gotten used to it all. All the experiences they've fed you are simply preparation for the moment when the nefarious scientists reveal their entire plan.

Whatever. The point is that Hume helped us to see that we have no good reason (i.e., no good argument) for believing that our ideas resemble the world outside our minds. In fact, we don't have good *reason* (argument) to believe that there *is* a world outside our minds. Of course, Hume admitted that he *couldn't help but* believe in an external world that matched his ideas; but this was, he said, because nature is simply too strong for philosophical arguments. Nature won't let us follow reason; we believe by instinct.[17] And good thing, too; otherwise humans wouldn't have lasted very long. In any case, nature has ensured that our species has lasted at least long enough to realize our predicament, which Hume called "the whimsical condition of mankind."[18] To echo W. V. Quine, the Humean condition is the human condition.[19]

---

[17] "It seems evident, that men are carried, by a natural instinct or prepossession, to repose faith in their senses; and that, without any reasoning, or even almost before the use of reason, we always suppose an external universe, which depends not on our perception, but would exist, though we and every sensible creature were absent or annihilated" (David Hume, *An Enquiry concerning Human Understanding*, ed. Eric Steinberg, 2nd ed. [Indianapolis: Hackett, 1993], 104).

[18] Ibid., 111.

[19] Cf. W. V. O. Quine, "Epistemology Naturalized," in *Ontological Relativity and Other Essays* (New York: Columbia University Press, 1969), 72.

xkcd.com

Skepticism about Induction

But things get worse, even if our sense experience is as reliable as you please. For, in addition to direct experience, we must often *reason from* that experience. That is, we frequently use our brains to reason from old beliefs about the world to new beliefs about the world. This reasoning process can take many forms, but in general it's called *inference*. We know lots of things by way of inference. For example, I know that if I let go of this coffee cup, it will fall to the floor. And though I know this partly from experience—I'm pretty familiar with how gravity has worked in the past—I've never actually seen that the cup *will* fall. And yet, I know that cups the world over would behave similarly in relevantly similar circumstances because I've inferred this from past sense experience. This kind of reasoning or inference from prior experience is called *induction*. Much of our knowledge of the world rests on induction. Without induction we'd be dead.

Characteristically, Hume noticed something peculiar about the whole induction process. Take a simple example: We all know—or at least seem to have very good reason to believe—that the sun will rise tomorrow. And we have induction to thank for our confidence. But Hume recognized that induction depends on our belief that *the future will resemble the past* (or more generally, that nature is uniform). Now, what reason do we have for believing that the future will resemble the past? Well, it's because in the past, the future has always resembled the past. (You see where Hume is going with this.) The very basis for believing that the future will resemble the past, and therefore the basis for all inductive reasoning, is our belief that the future will resemble the past. But this latter belief is also the result of induction and so relies on itself. We have no (noncircular) reason for trusting induction. Like Hume, then, if we're going to follow the arguments where they lead, we too must be skeptics about induction.

Again, Hume concedes that we can't help but trust induction. But again, we don't trust it because we have reason to; rather we simply can't help ourselves.

Skepticism about All Reasoning

Now in all this arguing for skepticism, Hume is using his reason, and so it had better not be inductive reason, as we've seen. But there are other kinds of reasoning. Why should we trust *these*?

Unfortunately, with respect to any kind of reasoning at all—inductive, deductive, abductive—things look pretty dismal.[20] When it comes to our inferences, there is always, says Hume, the possibility that we've made a mistake. We know this from experience, at least from those mistakes we've recognized. (Assume for the moment that there's no specific problem of induction.) We should therefore afford, says Hume, some measure of doubt to our conclusions, no matter what they are, even if the doubt is minimal. But, he continues, this evaluation of the reliability of our first belief is *also* an inference, and therefore it *too* should be doubted, even if ever so slightly. This could theoretically go on *ad infinitum*, according to Hume, just as we can theoretically add 1 to any number *ad infinitum*. Hume says that our confidence in that original belief should "in this manner be reduc'd to nothing."[21]

Though there may be something to Hume's argument, to my mind it's not very compelling. But there's a much more troubling problem with reason. Even if we ignore the calculus of infinitesimal doubts, we still never have a noncircular argument for reason's reliability. To offer *any* argument for reason is to use it. And to use it, we must first trust it. *Credo ut intelligam*—"I believe so that I may understand."

---

[20] Hume, "Of Skepticism with Regard to Reason," in *A Treatise of Human Nature*, 180ff.
[21] Ibid., 182.

When I reflect on the natural fallibility of my judgment, I have less confidence in my opinions, than when I only consider the objects concerning which I reason; and when I proceed still farther, to turn the scrutiny against every successive estimation I make of my faculties, all the rules of logic require a continual diminution, and at last a total extinction of belief and evidence. (ibid., 183)

The Importance of Safety Inspections

So, according to standard intellectual rules of engagement, we have to take reason at its word, take it on faith. This is one of the most important ideas in all of philosophy, and it is crucial for understanding the inner workings of debates. By definition, we have disagreements because we believe different things. But no two of us have *entirely* different beliefs. We share a host of them, and the game's rules depend on such beliefs. There will be times, however, when we disagree on the rules themselves. And that makes a world of difference.

In any case, we've seen that Hume applied what he saw as the new scientific method to the "study of man." In particular, he tested the limits of human cognitive faculties. Think of it as a kind of epistemological Underwriters Laboratories, where intellectual tools are pushed to their breaking point to ensure that they're safe for everyday use. (I'm probably romanticizing what UL actually does, but this seems like a dream job to my inner twelve-year old.)

Such testing is just plain prudent. If we understand the limitations and actual workings of our belief-forming mechanisms, we'll be less likely to claim more for them than they can deliver. When it comes to philosophy—and indeed when it comes to science—we are often on the skinny branches, where discretion is the better part of valor. This is just the sober skeptic's way, a safety-first mind-set that has a vaunted history.

Hume was right: there are no noncircular arguments for the reliability of the senses or reason (or memory, or any of our other cognitive tools). In the course of this book we'll see other implications of Hume's safety inspections—for science and morality especially. But in this chapter—and in the next—I am focusing on the *foundation* upon which these are built: our cognitive faculties.

There are people who think that these epistemological considerations are mere niceties. But they're not niceties. Any debate about God's existence that ignores them will go well purely by accident. Which is why so many go so poorly. To put it differently, epistemology is our friend.

2

The Believing Primate

The subtitle of Victor Stenger's book *The New Atheism* is *Taking a Stand for Science and Reason*. The book in your hands is an effort, in part, to do just that. We've seen so far that if we're going to take reason seriously, we're justified to question both sense perception and reason. This is a precarious position, one where reason threatens to undermine itself. Sometimes you're your own worst enemy.

But even if we can't support the reliability of our cognitive faculties with faculty-independent arguments, there is *something* we can do. We can at least work toward a *coherent story* of perception and reason, a story that provides soothing relief for our skeptical discomfort, however sober such skepticism may be. We need, then, an *explanation* of how humans came to have reliable cognitive contact with the world. Of course, we can't step outside the explanation to check whether it's correct, and so the best we can do is come up with one that's coherent and keeps all our important beliefs intact.[1]

Hume didn't have an explanation. He was writing a century prior to Darwin, and so there was no plausible alternative to divine design. Other than the truism that we'd be dead if our cognitive faculties weren't dependable (which isn't necessarily true, as we've seen), there wasn't much an unbeliever could say to explain why such faculties

---

[1] That is, we can check our beliefs' coherence with themselves but not their correspondence with the world out there, strictly speaking.

are reliable. (And this truism isn't even an explanation—it's merely a restatement of the very thing that needs explaining.)

But this is no longer the case, we're told. We're living downstream of Darwin, and now unbelievers everywhere have an all-natural explanation for the dependability of sense and reason. As Alexander Rosenberg says, "With the advent of Darwin's theory of evolution the need for . . . theological explanations in biology was completely eliminated."[2] Indeed, Richard Dawkins has notably said that it's finally possible to be an intellectually fulfilled atheist thanks to Darwin.[3]

Let's, then, look at the Darwinian story of our cognitive faculties' origins. I'll suggest that there are decent Darwinian reasons for being skeptical of the standard Darwinian account. Or of our cognitive capacities. Or both.

The Origin and Evolution of Our Cognitive Wetware

According to Darwin's theory (very roughly), life originated at a single location (probably on earth) from inorganic matter, and then, by way of random genetic mutations, evolved from simpler to more complex organisms. Of course, not all mutations or genetic variations were conducive to survival. No doubt many of them were just the opposite, while others neither helped nor hindered. This winnowing of helpful from harmful mutations is called *natural selection* or natural *filtering*.[4] The result is a stupefying array of flora and fauna.

There are really two separate issues here: the *origin* of life and its *evolution*. In the case of life's origins, the question is how did lifeless matter come alive? In the case of life's evolution, the question is, once life appeared in its simplest form, how did organisms of greater and greater complexity develop?

Evolution proper addresses only the latter question; the former question is much more difficult. As Dawkins says, the origin of life is an "extremely improbable event, many orders of magnitude more improbable than most people realize."[5] But there's one consolation, he

---

[2] Alexander Rosenberg, *The Philosophy of Science: A Contemporary Introduction*, 3rd ed. (New York: Routledge, 2012), 104.

[3] Richard Dawkins, *The Blind Watchmaker* (New York: W. W. Norton, 1986), 6.

[4] Alexander Rosenberg, *The Atheist's Guide to Reality: Enjoying Life without Illusions* (New York: W. W. Norton, 2011), 257.

[5] Richard Dawkins, *The God Delusion* (Boston: Houghton Mifflin, 2006), 162.

says: "The origin of life only had to happen once."[6] So at least there's that. But evolution, too, is monumentally improbable. As Stephen Jay Gould put it, if we were to rewind the video of life and "let it play again from an identical starting point," "the chance becomes vanishingly small that anything like human intelligence would grace the replay."[7] (Note: *vanish*: "to pass completely from existence"; "to assume the value of zero.")[8]

Some unbelieving scientists will admit that random mutation and natural selection might not be enough to account for the enormous diversity and complexity of life. Stenger, for example, says that "there may be more to the mechanism of evolution than random mutation and natural selection."[9] But, he continues, the extra something—whatever it turns out to be—"simply isn't intelligent design."[10]

In any case, the overall result of life and its evolution is that there are beings such as you and I who can consider the questions of origins and evolution, beings that arose from inanimate material stuff. As Thomas Nagel puts it, "Each of our lives is part of the lengthy process of the universe gradually waking up and becoming aware of itself."[11] The universe has risen from the dead. And of its own accord.

Life then is a freak accident, and therefore so too our cognitive faculties. For some folks, this is a bit hard to believe, which brings us to the point of this chapter: if this all-natural explanation is correct, then there is reason to doubt the reliability of our cognitive faculties—or else doubt the claim that life arose naturally. If you're an atheist who takes science and reason seriously, there may be reasons to doubt at least one of them. Or so I'll argue.

Skepticism about Evolution

Before we go any further, notice that the problem of prohibitive probabilities doesn't so much as arise if theism is true. Even if we granted

---

[6] Ibid.
[7] Stephen Jay Gould, *Wonderful Life: The Burgess Shale and the Nature of History* (New York: W. W. Norton, 1989), 14.
[8] *Merriam-Webster's Collegiate Dictionary*, 11th ed. (Springfield, MA: Merriam-Webster, 2008), senses 1b and 2.
[9] Victor J. Stenger, *God: The Failed Hypothesis—How Science Shows That God Does Not Exist* (Amherst, NY: Prometheus, 2008), 61.
[10] Ibid. Rather, he says, "Complex systems exhibit a purely natural process called *self-organization* and this appears to occur in both living and nonliving systems" (ibid.).
[11] Thomas Nagel, *Mind and Cosmos: Why the Materialist Neo-Darwinian Conception of Nature Is Almost Certainly False* (Oxford: Oxford University Press, 2012), 85.

that organisms *did* evolve, it seems reasonable to suppose that a being as powerful and knowledgeable as God could have supervised the relevant genetic mutations. Alternatively, as Aldous Huxley—"Darwin's bulldog"—suggested, it's also possible that God arranged the initial conditions of the universe so that organisms appeared and evolved solely through the laws of physics and chemistry (or whatever).[12]

In fact, some people consider any alleged evidence for evolution to be *ipso facto* evidence for design, since rudderless evolution seems unlikely in the extreme. After all, naturalists must believe, as Daniel Dennett says, that "an impersonal, unreflective, robotic, mindless little scrap of molecular machinery is the ultimate basis of all the agency, and hence meaning, and hence consciousness, in the universe."[13] We might think of this as one premise in an evolutionary argument for theism.

But even if we didn't go *this* far, unguided evolution is still hard for most people to believe. As Christian philosopher Alvin Plantinga points out, "Many—theists and others—have found these claims at least extremely doubtful; some have found them preposterous."[14] He asks, "Is it really so much as possible that language, say, or consciousness, or the ability to compose great music, or prove Gödel's incompleteness theorems, or think up the idea of natural selection should have been produced by mindless processes of this sort?"[15]

Recently, Nagel, himself an eminent atheist philosopher, caused a firestorm among fellow unbelievers for writing a book (*Mind and Cosmos*) with the subtitle, *Why the Materialist Neo-Darwinian Conception of Nature Is Almost Certainly False*. He has become an academic pariah for saying things like the following:

> My skepticism is not based on religious belief, or on a belief in any definite alternative. It is just a belief that the available scientific evidence, in spite of the consensus of scientific opinion, does not in this matter rationally require us to subordinate the incredulity of common sense. That is especially true with regard to the origin of life.[16]

---

[12] Alvin Plantinga, *Where the Conflict Really Lies: Science, Religion, and Naturalism* (Oxford: Oxford University Press, 2012), 16. Huxley was agnostic, in fact coining the term (ibid.).
[13] Ibid., 34.
[14] Ibid., 35.
[15] Ibid.
[16] Nagel, *Mind and Cosmos*, 7.

Nagel was once considered one of the top philosophers in the world. But he's now castigated as a heretic, or else pitied as an aged and declining intellect. At least by those who disagree with him.

Nagel is also bothered by scientists who encourage us to abandon our incredulity in favor of an extremely tentative story.

> It is prima facie highly implausible that life as we know it is the result of a sequence of physical accidents together with the mechanism of natural selection. We are expected to abandon this naïve response, not in favor of a fully worked out physical/chemical explanation but in favor of an alternative that is really a schema for explanation, supported by some examples. What is lacking, to my knowledge, is a credible argument that the story has a nonnegligible probability of being true.[17]

And as Plantinga points out, at this stage Darwinians really have only

> some informed guesses as to how, at a high level of abstraction, some of the transitions occurred: examples would be the sorts of guesses made by Dawkins as to the origin and development of the mammalian eye, or the common suggestion that the bones in the mammalian ear developed from the reptilian jawbone.[18]

Moreover, we're speaking not merely about the evolution of organisms with such astonishing features as eyes, but also about creatures with *minds*, for Pete's sake. And so evolution must account for "consciousness, intentionality, meaning, purpose, thought, and value."[19]

So it isn't at all clear that evolution is anything more than a sketch of a theory, even if it is a suggestive sketch. And is this really enough to overcome the mind-breaking improbabilities associated with life's origins and evolution? Should it overcome the sober skeptic's common-sense incredulity?

Skepticism about Our Faculties

We've obviously not given evolution a fair hearing; we've only ever-so-briefly mentioned why someone might be skeptical of it. So let's do

---

[17] Ibid., 6.
[18] Plantinga, *Where the Conflict Really Lies*, 16.
[19] Nagel, *Mind and Cosmos*, 13. Nagel interestingly points out that whereas materialism suggests that matter came first and then mind, theism is the "polar opposite" in that mind—God's mind—preceded matter. On the one hand, mind is "a consequence of physical law"; on the other, physical law is the "consequence of mind" (ibid., 21).

the gracious thing and assume for now that it's true, and that current science can explain, if not fully, then to a reasonable extent, the origins and evolution of organisms. On this assumption, what reason would we have to believe that our cognitive faculties—memory, sense perception, reason—are reliable? That is, what reason would we have to believe that these mechanisms produce (mostly) true beliefs?

Well, the obvious reason is that we're here asking such questions. If your senses had not correctly informed you that the traffic light was red, you might very well have missed this whole discussion. Similar considerations hold for reason. (And even if we're BIVs, *someone* would need reliable senses to inflict such a fate on us. In any case, let's ignore the Matrix-type situations.) So then, survival seems to require true beliefs, and since the aim of natural selection is survival—usually only those genetic mutations that provide survival advantage are allowed through the filter—natural selection ensures that our cognitive faculties are reliable.

But there are reasons to think that survival *doesn't* require true beliefs. Let's begin by noticing the following: What matters for the survival of an organism is the organism's behavior. That is, the organism must avoid threats, find food, and successfully reproduce. But many organisms, perhaps most, can do all this without any beliefs at all, much less true ones. Viruses and bacteria, for example, are remarkably successful at survival, with nary a belief to be found. All that is required is that these organisms track important features of their environment.[20] They merely need sensors, detectors, or indicators, as Plantinga says.

> Indicators, however, need not be or involve beliefs. In the human body there are indicators for blood pressure, temperature, saline content, insulin level, and much else; in these cases neither the blood, nor its owner, nor anything else in the neighborhood ordinarily holds beliefs on the topic.[21]

Much less true beliefs. As the philosopher Patricia Churchland has said:

> Boiled down to essentials, a nervous system enables the organism to succeed in . . . feeding, fleeing, fighting, and reproducing.

---

[20] Plantinga, *Where the Conflict Really Lies*, 329.
[21] Ibid.

The principle chore of nervous systems is to get the body parts where they should be in order that the organism may survive. . . . Improvements in sensorimotor control confer an evolutionary advantage: a fancier style of representing is advantageous *so long as it is geared to the organism's way of life and enhances the organism's chances of survival.* Truth, whatever that is, definitely takes the hindmost.[22]

True beliefs—or any beliefs at all—are a luxury, a superfluous bonus if survival is the real gold standard.[23]

Of course, that's not to say that natural selection couldn't have resulted in faculties that generally produce true beliefs. But is that really probable? Well, who knows? How could we determine the probabilities here? Yet, as Plantinga points out, even if the probabilities are entirely inscrutable, our foregoing considerations still undermine our confidence that evolution would result in reliable faculties.

At least if we're taking skepticism seriously.

Dinosaur Comics, by Ryan North, qwantz.com

---

[22] Patricia Churchland, "Epistemology in the Age of Neuroscience," *Journal of Philosophy* 84 (October 1987): 548–49; emphasis original.
[23] Notice too that some mental illnesses, hallucinogenic drugs, and sleepwalking provide instances where people can successfully navigate the world with wildly false beliefs (or maybe no beliefs at all).

Should Primates Be Good at Science?

But suppose survival really *does* require true beliefs about our surroundings. That is, suppose our cognitive faculties must produce (mostly) true beliefs about matters pertinent to survival. On this assumption, we're reliable about things like the feeding, fleeing, fighting, and reproducing (though, of course, we all know humans who are unsuccessful at one or more of these). But what about highly theoretical realms like quantum mechanics, general relativity, and superstring theory? Should we expect our faculties to be reliable on such topics? According to evolution, our brains evolved solely for the task of survival, not for the construction of complex theories that describe entities and events entirely beyond the realm of observation. Dawkins puts it in his characteristically memorable way:

> Each of us builds, inside our head, a model of the world in which we find ourselves. The minimal model of the world is the model our ancestors needed in order to survive in it. The simulation software was constructed and debugged by natural selection, and it is most adept in the world familiar to our ancestors on the African savannah: a three dimensional world of medium-sized material objects, moving at medium speeds relative to one another.[24]

But the parts of the world uniquely described by general relativity (the very large) and quantum mechanics (the very small) are not at all like our "Middle World," as Dawkins calls it.[25] If unguided evolution is anywhere near correct, then our cognitive faculties were not crafted or calibrated for the unobservable realm.[26] And this realm occupies most of science, as we'll see.

In fact, considerations like these cast doubt on evolution itself. Developing such a story is an enormous task and requires an elaborate theoretical framework. It's not like falling off a log; *that's* natural, after all. But the theory of evolution seems to be something entirely unnatural, especially if combined with naturalism. As Nagel says:

> Evolutionary naturalism provides an account of our capacities that undermines their reliability, and in doing so undermines itself. . . .

---

[24] Dawkins, *The God Delusion*, 405.
[25] Ibid., 407.
[26] There is, says Rosenberg, "lots of evidence that natural selection is not very good at picking out true beliefs, especially our scientific ones." Rosenberg, *The Atheist's Guide to Reality*, 110.

Mechanisms of belief formation that have selective advantage in the everyday struggle for existence do not warrant our confidence in the construction of theoretical accounts of the world as a whole.[27]

Even the great Darwin had his doubts: "With me the horrid doubt always arises whether the convictions of man's mind, which has been developed from the mind of the lower animals, are of any value or at all trustworthy. Would any one trust the convictions of a monkey's mind, if there are any convictions in such a mind?"[28] So even if we grant that unguided evolution has provided us with reliable cognitive faculties, there are good *evolutionary* reasons to think that these faculties are reliable only in the "Middle World"—and only on topics related to survival. Now, it's not *impossible* that unguided evolution went beyond the call of duty, making us reliable about highly theoretical topics. But sober skepticism suggests that we should seriously doubt it.

Saving Hume?

Someone of a skeptical bent, then, has good reasons to doubt that evolution could underwrite the reliability of sense perception and reason. To put it differently, it's reasonable to think that Darwin provided Hume with only minimal help.

And yet the question of cognitive reliability has been quietly swept under the rug. Most naturalists—for all their skeptical drumbeating—aren't interested in this issue. I would have thought that hard-nosed skeptics would be itching to follow reason—along any path. And this particular path seems to lead us to the realization that we have no independent reason to believe reason—other than the fact that we already do and that we couldn't help it in any case. (Maybe possession is nine-tenths of the law.)

Perhaps naturalists see skepticism about our cognitive faculties as pedantic, childish, or a violation of academic propriety—each of which, I agree, should be studiously avoided. In any case, in what follows I'll simply assume that our "intellectual instruments" (as Nagel calls them)[29] have impeccable credentials. Given this magnanimous allowance, let's turn our attention to the reliability of science, and to whether there are any good reasons for doubting that science has shown there's no God.

---

[27] Nagel, *Mind and Cosmos*, 27.
[28] Plantinga, *Where the Conflict Really Lies*, 316.
[29] Thomas Nagel, *The View from Nowhere* (Oxford: Oxford University Press, 1986), 80.

Part 2

SCIENCE

3

Science: Ruining Everything since 1543?

Most people would never have given much thought to whether God exists had there been no Scientific Revolution.[1] But since Copernicus's publication of *De Revolutionibus* in 1543, it seems we just can't help ourselves. The general picture, we are told, is this. In benighted days of yore, when we had no science to guide us, we employed God to explain the wonders of the world, including the existence of the world itself. But now, in the fullness of time, we have seen a great light (hint: it rhymes with *science*), and this light has chased God into the shadows. To this day, science continues to replace God-filled gaps in our understanding with all-natural ingredients. And since we don't need God to explain the existence and nature of the universe, we don't need God, *period*.

Now, the undeniable success of science can make this line of reasoning seem pretty plausible. But there are good reasons to doubt it, many of them scientific. In this part of the book—cleverly designated Part 2—I'll make a case that these kinds of arguments leave a lot to be desired and that those of us who are enthusiastic about science should regard them with healthy suspicion.

To make our discussion less abstract I'll use this chapter to look at two scientists—very good scientists—who argue that we no longer

[1] The title of this chapter comes from a *Saturday Morning Breakfast Cereal* comic strip.

need God to account for the universe's existence and bio-friendly organization.

Life's Toughest Questions

Let's head immediately to the top of the scientific food chain, to the great Stephen Hawking. Although it wasn't much of a surprise, Hawking recently confessed his atheism.[2] His book *The Grand Design*, coauthored with Leonard Mlodinow, is a stirring attempt to answer what he calls the "Ultimate Question of Life, the Universe, and Everything," which is really a triad of questions:

> *Why is there something rather than nothing?*
> *Why do we exist?*
> *Why this particular set of laws and not some other?*[3]

Answering these questions is a lofty goal indeed—they're the toughest problems in philosophy. Unfortunately, says Hawking, we can no longer depend on philosophy for assistance. "Traditionally these are questions for philosophy, but philosophy is dead. Philosophy has not kept up with modern developments in science, particularly physics. Scientists have become the bearers of the torch of discovery in our quest for knowledge."[4] Hawking and Mlodinow then go on to do a lot of philosophy. But no matter; we can at least admit that scientists could have something significant to say about life's big questions. Let's see what that might be.

The Answer

Hawking's overall point is that our triad of questions can be answered "purely within the realm of science, and without invoking any divine beings."[5] He pulls out the big guns, marshaling the latest and most

---

[2] "Before we understand science, it is natural to believe that God created the universe. But now science offers a more convincing explanation. What I meant by 'we would know the mind of God' is, we would know everything that God would know, if there were a God, which there isn't. I'm an atheist" (Stephen Hawking, quoted in Alan Boyle, "'I'm an Atheist': Stephen Hawking on God and Space Travel," NBC News, September 23, 2014, http://www.nbcnews.com/science/space/im-atheist-stephen-hawking-god -space-travel-n210076). As I said, this isn't shocking news, but some people thought Hawking had hitherto been a bit coy about his unbelief.

[3] Stephen Hawking and Leonard Mlodinow, *The Grand Design* (New York: Bantam, 2010), 10.

[4] Ibid., 5.

[5] Ibid., 172. Hawking is, however, willing to believe in highly intelligent extraterrestrial beings. He says, however, that it would be "too risky" to communicate with them: "We only have to look at ourselves to see how intelligent life might develop into something we wouldn't want to meet." (He's got a good point.)

sophisticated theory in physics, M-theory.[6] M-theory—no one knows what the *M* stands for—is a unification of five different string theories and posits eleven dimensions. In fact, says Hawking, M-theory is "a candidate for the ultimate theory of everything,"[7] and "the unified theory Einstein was hoping to find."[8] And if so, he continues, "It will be the successful conclusion of a search going back more than 3,000 years. We will have found the grand design."[9]

Minus a designer.

The only point now is that this new theory of everything is putting us hot on the trail of an answer to the "Ultimate Question of Life, the Universe, and Everything." And this is news fit to print. Here is what we might call The Answer, at least in broad outline:

> According to M-theory, ours is not the only universe. Instead, M-theory predicts that a great many universes were created out of nothing. Their creation does not require the intervention of some supernatural being or god. Rather, these multiple universes arise naturally from physical law. They are a prediction of science. Each universe has many possible histories and many possible states at later times, that is, at times like the present, long after their creation. Most of these states will be quite unlike the universe we observe and quite unsuitable for the existence of any form of life. Only a very few would allow creatures like us to exist. Thus our presence selects out from this vast array only those universes that are compatible with our existence. Although we are puny and insignificant on the scale of the cosmos, this makes us in a sense the lords of creation.[10]

There's a lot going on here, so let's unpack it bit by bit.

First, consider the question *why is there something rather than nothing?* Notice the striking thing Hawking reveals about the "something." The something we're trying to account for is not what we expected; it's not merely the universe we've come to know and love,

---

He goes on to say, "I imagine they might exist in massive ships . . . having used up all the resources from their home planet. Such advanced aliens would perhaps become nomads, looking to conquer and colonize whatever planets they can reach" ("Aliens May Pose Risks to Earth," *NBC News*, April 25, 2010, http://www.nbcnews.com/id/36769422#.VECxqRa_gn4).

[6] Hawking and Mlodinow, *The Grand Design*, 117.
[7] Ibid., 8.
[8] Ibid., 181.
[9] Ibid.
[10] Ibid., 9.

but in fact an incomprehensible number of universes. Hawking says there are perhaps as many as 10^{500} (more than all the atoms in the known universe),[11] all hermetically sealed from each other, yet existing simultaneously.[12]

These universes—collectively called a *multiverse*—originated, Hawking says, "naturally from physical law." Now this is verily a dark saying of the wise. But remember that we're looking for an explanation of the multiverse's existence. This quest can also be thought of as a search for the multiverse's *cause*, that which brought everything into existence. Now, by saying that the multiverse came from physical law, it's doubtful that Hawking means that physical laws literally caused our universe (and its siblings).[13] What he means, more specifically, is that these laws *tell us* that "quantum fluctuations lead to the creation of tiny universes out of nothing."[14] And so, he says, we at least "know that the origin of the universe was a quantum event."[15]

So then, science—with no help from philosophy, thank you very much—has answered why there's something rather than nothing. And there's nary a God to be found: "Spontaneous creation is the reason there is something rather than nothing, why the universe exists, why we exist. It is not necessary to invoke God to light the blue touch paper and set the universe going."[16]

Just as my dad used to say: "Spontaneity is the spice of all the things that have ever existed."

Life in the Multiverse

Let's take Hawking's word for it that current science really does provide decent evidence for a multiverse and that all these universes came from nothing by purely physical means. (We'll question this assumption later.)

---

[11] Lee Smolin, *The Trouble with Physics: The Rise of String Theory, the Fall of a Science, and What Comes Next* (Boston: Houghton Mifflin, 2006), xiv.

[12] "The laws of M-theory therefore allow for *different universes* with different apparent laws, depending on how the internal space is curled. M-theory has solutions that allow for many different internal spaces, perhaps as many as 10^{500}, which means it allows for 10^{500} different universes, each with its own laws" (Hawking and Mlodinow, *The Grand Design*, 118). Remember that 10^{500} is shorthand for a 1 with five hundred zeroes after it (that is, five hundred 10s all multiplied together). Since it is hard for humans to get a feel for what a measly trillion, or 10^{12}, is, we shouldn't kid ourselves that we even faintly understand how large 10^{500} is. By the way, when I say that each universe is "hermetically sealed" from all the others, I mean that you can't travel between universes, nor is there *any* causal interaction between them.

[13] Laws aren't those kinds of things. We'll look at this later.

[14] Hawking and Mlodinow, *The Grand Design*, 137.

[15] Ibid., 131. He says elsewhere, "Bodies such as stars or black holes cannot just appear out of nothing. But a whole universe can" (ibid., 180).

[16] Ibid.

That takes care of how our universe got here. But how exactly does it explain the vast complexity and order we see around us? Our universe isn't just something that can be thrown together willy-nilly. So how does the multiverse explain the existence of complex life forms (especially us)? How does the multiverse help us to answer Hawking's second question, *why do we exist?*

In our previous chapter, we saw that there are two issues regarding the existence of organisms: (1) the *origin* of life and (2) the *evolution* of life (from simpler to more complex forms). We do not currently have a natural mechanism for life's origins, the enormous leap from dead, inert bits of matter to living organisms. But recall that there is allegedly an entirely natural explanation for the evolution of life—from its initial form to the extravagance we see now. The explanation is (roughly) that natural selection sifts through random genetic mutations, keeping those that enhance survival. These mutations can arise from any number of sources—even cosmic rays—but the filtering process is simply the organism's daily routine of surviving in a world bent on killing it.

In any case, let's suppose that the appearance and evolution of all living things occurred naturally, that is, with no supernatural guidance. Notice that these natural processes—even the biological ones—will be ultimately explained by the laws of *physics*, since the laws of physics govern all the fundamental entities out of which the universe is made; and in any case these entities existed long before life of any kind (according to the evolutionary story). Any additional chemical or biological processes are considered reducible to, or at least ultimately dependent on, physics.[17]

So the general answer to the second question *why do we exist?* is this: because the laws of physics make the universe biologically friendly. That is, although the more proximate cause of humans is the process of evolution (and some unknown cause of life's origins), the more remote explanation is that the laws of physics are conducive to the appearance of life.

To be sure, this doesn't get to the heart of the matter, namely, how

---

[17] For example, says Stenger, the double spiral pattern in plants like sunflowers, can be explained in terms of a principle from physics called "the minimization of potential energy" (Victor J. Stenger, *God: The Failed Hypothesis—How Science Shows That God Does Not Exist* [Amherst, NY: Prometheus, 2008], 63). "It might be thought that some biological process, perhaps associated with Darwinian evolution, is taking place. However, it turns out to be simply physics" (ibid., 62–63).

we might account for the felicitous fact that our universe landed in the biological "Goldilocks" zone. But all we need now is the multiverse to complete the explanation. The multiverse, says Hawking, is an all-natural way to tame the staggering improbabilities associated with the universe coming to life. Out of so many universes, one of them was sure to produce life from dead matter. And of course, it was ours—after all, if it weren't, we wouldn't be marveling at our unbelievable luck (don't say you've never won anything).

The only question left is *why this particular set of laws and not some other?* And we've really already answered it. The proliferation of universes makes universes and their laws a dime a dozen, greatly increasing the odds that at least *some* universe or other will have these laws. And if 10^{500} universes aren't enough, there may be more: every *logically possible* world.[18] And perhaps there are infinitely many of these. If so, all we need to stack the odds ever in our favor is the assumption that our universe is logically possible. And I think we can all agree that our cosmic dwelling is a distinct possibility. After all, it's actual.

Dinosaur Comics, by Ryan North, qwantz.com

---

[18] "In this view, the universe appeared spontaneously, starting off in every possible way" (Hawking and Mlodinow, *The Grand Design*, 136).

A Second Opinion

Hawking isn't the only celebrated physicist who believes that science can account for the universe's existence. Lawrence Krauss, in *A Universe from Nothing*, argues much the same thing, though Krauss stays closer to the shore, using relativistic quantum field theory.[19] But like Hawking, Krauss has a low view of philosophy, believing that science has had to relieve it of its regular duties.[20] Despite this, he too—like Hawking—makes a manful attempt at philosophy throughout his entire book (how successfully, we'll see later).

For now, it's enough to point out that Krauss argues that creation *ex nihilo* ("out of nothing") is possible without a Creator, despite widespread opinion that *ex nihilo nihil fit*, "out of nothing, nothing comes."[21] But, says Krauss, it's pretty clear that this so-called metaphysical rule—which, he says, "is held as an ironclad conviction by those with whom I have debated the issue of creation"—has little to commend it, since it "has no foundation in science."[22] That is, science has shown that out of nothing something *can* come: according to physics, the universe was generated spontaneously by quantum fluctuations—again, from nothing whatsoever.[23] This, then, eliminates the "requirement of a creator."[24]

Dr. Krauss's opinion on the issue of why there's something rather than nothing agrees with Hawking's. And as far as the other questions—why are we here, and why *these* laws?—both physicists are again in agreement: the relevant quantum fluctuations result in a multiverse, not

---

[19] See Lawrence M. Krauss, *A Universe from Nothing: Why There Is Something Rather Than Nothing* (New York: Free Press, 2012), 161ff. The following is, as David Foster Wallace would have put it, IYI ("if you're interested"): Actually, Krauss seems to go beyond established quantum field theories like QED, QCD, etc., and speculate what might happen when we combine quantum theory with general relativity and therefore add gravity, to get a theory of quantum gravity. But he adds, since "general relativity is not fully consistent with quantum mechanics, at least as far as we can tell . . . we have to make some guesses in advance based on plausibility and check to see if the results make sense" (ibid., 162–63).

[20] Ross Andersen, "Has Physics Made Philosophy and Religion Obsolete?," *The Atlantic*, April 23, 2012, http://www.theatlantic.com/technology/archive/2012/04/has-physics-made-philosophy-and-religion-obsolete/256203.

[21] The traditional Christian doctrine of "creation *ex nihilo*" is somewhat misleading, at least phrased this way. It doesn't literally mean that there was nothing prior to creation nor that nothing whatsoever caused the universe. Rather, it is a reply to (something like) Plato's popular creation account in which a divine craftsman (the "demiurge") takes some pre-existing material and arranges this material into the cosmos. Christendom has typically frowned upon the idea of there being anything independent of God, much less something that he's just stuck with. That is, God isn't limited by his medium because he creates all the stuff (in addition to arranging it).

[22] Krauss, *A Universe from Nothing*, 174. And even if he's wrong about this, he says that God can't explain the universe's existence: "Moreover, those who argue that out of nothing nothing comes seem perfectly content with the quixotic notion that somehow God can get around this" (ibid., 174).

[23] "In quantum gravity, universes can, and indeed always will, spontaneously appear from nothing" (ibid., 169).

[24] Ibid., 143.

merely our own universe. As Krauss puts it, "Almost every logical possibility we can imagine regarding extending laws of physics as we know them, on small scales, into a more complete theory, suggests that, on large scales, our universe is not unique."[25] Bio-friendly laws are bound to occur in *some* universe. And again, this would surely account for happenstances like me and you.

I mention Krauss's book in part because it has received enthusiastic support from none other than Richard Dawkins. (Krauss costars with Dawkins in the documentary *The Unbelievers*.)[26] In his afterword to Krauss's book, Dawkins announces:

> We can read Lawrence Krauss for what looks to me like the knockout blow. Even the last remaining trump card of the theologian, "Why is there something rather than nothing?" shrivels up before your eyes as you read these pages. If *On the Origin of Species* was biology's deadliest blow to supernaturalism, we may come to see *A Universe from Nothing* as the equivalent for cosmology. The title means exactly what it says. And what it says is devastating.[27]

That's high praise, and if Dawkins is right, we'll be celebrating the centennial of Krauss's book in 2112. Save the date.

Of course, a sober skeptic will want to know a bit more before accepting all this. And again, David Hume is a good place to look for guidance. We'll see in the next chapter that Hume's science-induced skepticism brought even science under suspicion. In spite of himself, Hume was forced to admit that science could do only so much—much less than some would have liked. Or will admit.

---

[25] Ibid., 126.
[26] "'The Unbelievers' follows renowned scientists Richard Dawkins and Lawrence Krauss across the globe as they speak publicly about the importance of science and reason in the modern world—encouraging others to cast off antiquated religious and politically motivated approaches toward important current issues" (promotional copy about the documentary, http://www.unbelieversmovie.com/info.htm).
[27] Afterword to Krauss, *A Universe from Nothing*, 191.

4

Science and the Humean Condition

There's a strong skeptical lineage running from today's scientistic skeptics back to Hume. Hume rightly saw the Scientific Revolution as one of humankind's greatest epistemological feats; and he wanted to get himself some of *that* for his own philosophy. (By the way, this kind of epistemic imitation/flattery had happened before in philosophy, with Euclid playing Newton's role. In fact, this prequel was responsible for Newton. Had there been no Euclid, there would have been no Newton. But that's a story for another time.)[1] Hume focused on the empiricist side of science, its "experimental" side, despite the success that mathematics afforded Newton's physics. (Newton had to invent calculus to capture motion.) And for Hume, knowledge must be ultimately grounded in sense perception—even mathematics must answer to observations. Seeing is believing. To borrow from the old boxing saying, "You can't know what you can't see."

We saw, however, that by taking science so seriously, Hume got more than he bargained for, further encouraging his skeptical temperament, and forcing him to recognize that we have no noncircular arguments for the reliability of sense perception or reason. And even though we don't have real grounds for taking these faculties seriously, we can't help it. Mankind's whimsical condition.

But things got even worse. Science itself, obviously enough, is

---

[1] Then again, there's no time like the present. Go and see Mitch Stokes, *Isaac Newton* (Nashville: Thomas Nelson, 2010).

founded upon sense perception and reason. So Hume had a choice: he could fully accept his skeptical conclusions and reject science (and every other endeavor), or else he could go ahead and trust his cognitive faculties, thereby sustaining his devotion to science. He chose the latter, realizing that true love always requires trust.

Causation: (Merely) One Darn Thing after Another

So Hume ignored his own skeptical arguments while otherwise trusting his cognitive faculties, taking perhaps (some) solace in the fact that this was inevitable. But even though Hume allowed sense and reason back into the fold, problems remained. That is, even though Hume (naturally enough) believed that there *is* an external world and that he could reliably reason about his experiences of that world, not everything in science was returned to him. You can't go home again.

Consider the following event: a cue ball colliding with an eight ball. By coming into contact with the eight ball, the cue ball causes the eight ball to move. What, however, do we actually *see* or *experience* in such a collision? Hume argued that we never see the cue ball *cause* the eight ball's motion. We only see the cue ball coming into contact with the eight ball, hear that satisfying "click," and see the eight ball move in turn. We don't actually see the "necessary connection" (as Hume called it) between the two balls. That is, we don't see that *causal* or metaphysical "glue" that supposedly links the motion of the one to the motion of the other. For all we know—for all we perceive, which is saying the same thing, for Hume—angels or fairies (or academically speaking, *homunculi*, "little men") could cause the eight ball's motion when the two balls get into the proper spatial relation. In such a case the eight ball would move not *because* the cue ball moved it, but *because* the angel or fairy did. Yet the two scenarios would look identical to us, and movies make lucrative use of this experiential limitation.

Of course, Hume didn't actually *believe* that fairies or angels or *homunculi* moved the billiard balls. His only point was to ask what we actually observe. And it's true, we don't observe the necessary connection; all we see in cases of "causation" is one thing happening *and then* another thing happening. We see, in Hume's terms, only a "constant conjunction" of events. That is, every time a ball behaves *this way* around another ball, the other ball behaves *that way*. By seeing countless constant conjunctions over our lifetime, we become conditioned to believe in an underlying metaphysical glue.

Nor can we help *but* believe in this glue. Nature, again, is too strong for us. But the fact that we never *see* an actual causal connection has important implications for Hume's view of scientific explanations, and not merely for those "mechanistic" explanations of the new mechanical physics, but for any explanation that we cannot directly observe.

"Hypotheses Non Fingo"

Hume realized that scientific explanations have serious limitations. Consider gravity. Newton's law of universal gravitation, a mathematical law both uncannily concise and precise, describes the force between objects as diverse as planets and bowling balls. Yet this is "all" it does: it merely describes. That is, Newton's law allows us to calculate (and so numerically describe) the gravitational force between any two objects. But his law doesn't tell us what *causes* the force; it doesn't *explain* the objects' behavior. It doesn't answer the question *why is the force thus?*

Now in light of the stupefying successes afforded by this law, it might seem a bit petty to criticize it for such a minor drawback. But the top scientists of Newton's age saw this as a going concern. Leibniz, especially, thought that Newton (and no doubt Galileo before him) had denigrated the job of science. In fact, this "denigration" is one of the great changes made to philosophy during the Scientific Revolution. Scientists like Galileo and Newton believed that we should stop looking for unobservable explanations or causes. But Aristotelian science had such explanations as its ultimate goal, and mathematical descriptions— as rare as they were—were simply quaint, albeit interesting, results of mere technicians. Mathematical descriptions certainly weren't the work of genuine philosophers.

A paradigmatic example is Aristotle's explanation of why dropped objects fall to the ground. There are, he said, unobservable "natures," an internal essence, something *inside* physical objects that cause them to move toward their "natural" place of rest, namely, the center of the universe (aka the center of the earth). It was literally in the rock's nature to move toward the center of the cosmos; this was what it did *naturally*.

These natures, according to Aristotle (and every natural philosopher until Galileo), were actual *things*. But of course, no one had ever seen an internal nature or essence. Natures were unobservable. Yet they were part and parcel of an elaborate—and amazingly coherent—story of what goes on behind the scenes in the cosmos. And again, this un-observed, behind-the-scenes story was the very point of Aristotelian science. Any old clod could *look* at things; it took a real philosopher to arrive at the theoretical workings of the world behind the veil. Or so philosophers believed.

You can imagine, then, the uproar Galileo caused when he suggested that natural philosophy should limit itself to what we can "see." But Galileo's success at mathematically describing behavior of physical objects was difficult to overlook, and so he was taken very seriously. Newton even more so: he was seen as the culmination of mankind at the time, a new Adam for a new enlightened race.[2] When Newton spoke, people listened, and so his goal for science is still ours.

Newton realized that his law of gravity didn't specify what *caused* the attractive force between two objects. It was as inscrutable in physics as it is in love, and so Newton didn't try. In fact, he famously said concerning gravity's cause, *hypotheses non fingo*—"I'm not even going to pretend to explain it" (my loose translation).[3] This was considered a huge problem with Newton's physics: there seemed to be no mechanical cause, that is, no cause that depended on direct contact of pushes or pulls. And yet mechanical philosophy was all the rage. Newton's theory of gravity was (ironically enough) out of fashion, which is worse than being wrong.

But it was hard to argue with success.

Taking Science Seriously

Hume inherited Newton's restraint regarding unobservable causes. He realized, however, that when it came to gravity, the problem was even worse than simply divining some hidden cause of the force. We can't

---

[2] Lest ye think that I doth exaggerate, consider this snippet from Lord Byron:

When Newton saw an apple fall, he found
In that slight startle from his contemplation—
'Tis said (for I'll not answer above ground
For any sage's creed or calculation)—
A mode of proving that the earth turn'd round
In a most natural whirl, called "gravitation";
And this is the sole mortal who could grapple,
Since Adam, with a fall or with an apple.

[3] Isaac Newton, "General Scholium," in *Mathematical Principles of Natural Philosophy*, trans. I. Bernard Cohen and Anne Whitman (Berkeley: University of California Press, 1999), 943.

even observe the *forces* themselves.[4] Hume believed we only observe (and feel) the *effects* of these alleged forces, not actual forces: "When we talk of gravity, we mean certain effects, without comprehending that active power."[5] And so, if the new philosophy was going to avoid the problems of Aristotelian essences, natures, and other "occult" powers, we have to reinterpret words like *force, power,* and *energy* if they are to have legitimate meaning.[6] (In fact, one of the criticisms leveled at Newton's theory of gravity was that it made gravity an "occult power.")

So then, Hume was painfully aware of the epistemological problems associated with unobserved causes. We shouldn't ask too much of natural philosophy; we should be cautious, circumspect, skeptical.

> As long as we confine our speculations to *the appearances* of objects to our senses, without entering into disquisitions concerning their real nature and operations, we are safe from all difficulties, and can never be embarrass'd by any question. . . . We are only acquainted with its effects on the senses, and its power of receiving body. Nothing is more suitable to that philosophy, than a modest scepticism to a certain degree, and a fair confession of ignorance in subjects, that exceed all human capacity.[7]

Hume believes, then, that whenever laws seem to refer to forces or gravity—or anything else we don't observe—we should think of them not as referring to actual "causes" or "powers" but simply, as philosopher Eric Schliesser says, "as a way to keep track of the appearances."[8] Rosenberg puts Hume's goal for science in terms that are striking (and to some, depressing): "For Hume, the aim of science cannot be to reveal the intelligible character of the universe, but

---

[4] This problem of action at a distance is what partly led to the development of "field" theories. But fields are unobservable as well, objects posited by the mathematics. See, for example, Mary B. Hesse, *Forces and Fields: The Concept of Action at a Distance in the History of Physics* (Mineola, NY: Dover, 1962).
[5] David Hume, *An Enquiry concerning Human Understanding*, 2nd ed. (Indianapolis: Hackett, 1993), 48n32.
[6] Eric Schliesser, "Hume's Newtonianism and Anti-Newtonianism," in *Stanford Encyclopedia of Philosophy*, ed. Edward N. Zalta (Stanford, CA: Metaphysics Research Lab, CSLI, Stanford University, 2007).
[7] David Hume, *A Treatise of Human Nature* (Oxford: Clarendon, 1978), 638–39. He also says:

> Nothing is more requisite for a true philosopher, than to restrain the intemperate desire of searching into causes, and having establish'd any doctrine upon a sufficient number of experiments, rest contented with that, when he sees a farther examination would lead him into obscure and uncertain speculations. In that case his enquiry wou'd be much better employ'd in examining the effects than the causes of his principle. (ibid., 13)

[8] Schliesser, "Hume's Newtonianism and Anti-Newtonianism."

simply to catalogue the regularities that causal sequences reflect."[9] (We'll meet this view of the scientific endeavor again.) In any case, Hume and Newton both believed that we should limit the domain of science to what we can observe, although Newton still held out some hope that it is possible to go behind the scenes. Hume, however, moved the empiricist ball down the skeptical field. Again, Rosenberg: "All explanatory theories must consist in what Hume called 'obscure and uncertain speculations'—hypotheses in the pejorative sense that Hume sometimes shared with Newton, and which they both stigmatized as superfluous to the aims of science."[10] Hypotheses, whether in a pejorative sense or not, are *unobserved* explanations. I cannot overemphasize this. We'll look at this in more detail later, but the distinction between what we observe and what we *infer from* these observations is crucial; otherwise all manner of folly ensues. And for Hume, keeping this straight is appropriate for anyone holding a "modest scepticism to a certain degree."[11]

And yet Newtonian science combined modest aims with astounding achievements, showing that less is more. Hume followed suit, keeping safely within the confines of direct experience but hoping to push philosophy out of its two-thousand-year torpor.

This epistemological restraint, however, quickly diminished the credentials of our cognitive faculties. The limits of sense experience undermined common sense, threatening to take science with it. We do not see that there is an external world, that reason is reliable, and that the cue ball causes the eight ball to move. And even if we ignore these skeptical results, science, according to Hume, is still limited to merely cataloging and describing what we can directly observe. The success of science—for example, the ability of Newton's theory of gravity to predict observable phenomena—ironically led to skepticism about gravity itself, leaving only the husk of its effects. For Hume, things came full circle, but like a snake eating its tail.

My point here is that Hume valiantly tried to take science and skepticism seriously, attempting to follow reason wherever it led. His most successful moments were also his most despondent.

---

[9] Alexander Rosenberg, "Hume and the Philosophy of Science," in *The Cambridge Companion to Hume*, ed. David Fate Norton (Cambridge: Cambridge University Press, 1993), 73.
[10] Ibid., 80.
[11] Hume, *A Treatise of Human Nature*, 639.

Where am I, or what? From what causes do I derive my existence, and to what condition shall I return? Whose favour shall I court, and whose anger must I dread? What beings surround me? and on whom have I any influence, or who have any influence on me? I am confounded with all these questions, and begin to fancy myself in the most deplorable condition imaginable, inviron'd with the deepest darkness, and utterly depriv'd of the use of every member and faculty.[12]

Reason could not lead him out of this cul-de-sac; only "nature herself suffices to that purpose, and cures me of this philosophical melancholy and delirium."[13]

For Hume, then, science led to skepticism, which in turn led to wariness about the reach of science. This is taking science and skepticism pretty seriously. And I think Hume is right. But as we will see, Hume's lesson has been lost on today's scientistic unbelievers. If we take science and reason as seriously as, say, the Richard Dawkins Foundation for Reason and Science says it does, we should all show a bit more restraint.

[12] Ibid., 269.
[13] Ibid.

5

Photoshopped Science

Not putting too fine a point on it, science is impressive (über-skeptical concerns notwithstanding). Hume, then, was right to be impressed. Newton's natural philosophy was a dramatic improvement over what was seen as the rickety claptrap of Aristotelian science. The new philosophy was orderly and restrained, and placed tight restrictions on observation and reason. It was simple yet powerful; in fact, its power was due in part to its simplicity. By sticking to cool reason and sober observation, Newton and his colleagues—we can't say *peers*; he had none—seemed to avoid dogmatic speculation while simultaneously eliminating the subjective influences of worldviews and biases. Everyone was on the same scientific page: other scientists could check your experiments and reasoning, and this kept everyone honest.

This was Hume's smooth and shiny picture of science. And we too miss science's earthiness, seeing it as more robotic than human. Not that we ever think it's easy; but even when we recognize how hard it is—and appreciate the technical virtuosity required by its practitioners—science seems more like an elaborate computer program than a sublime work of art. It's *science* after all. But by misunderstanding science this way, we underestimate its impressiveness.

The source of our misunderstanding is Hume, albeit channeled through his influential followers. This received tradition is that of a cold, sterile, steely science; and the story of this tradition is really the story of twentieth-century philosophy, one which has left an indelible mark on today's philosophers and scientists. It begins in the 1920s with a scientistic movement in Vienna, during a period much like Hume's own—only more so, as we'll see. To understand this story we'll need to first discuss an important distinction, one that Hume put to devastating effect in his crusade against tradition. It is important because his twentieth-century disciples will use these same ideas to dish out even more trouble.

Hume's Fork

Remember that all knowledge, according to Hume, must be grounded in sense perception. Anything we can genuinely know must be seen, touched, etc. But things aren't quite as simple as that, and the slight additional complexity is crucial for what comes next.

More specifically, according to Hume, all *matters of fact* must be grounded in sense perception. A "matter of fact" is any contingent truth about the world, anything that's not simply true by definition or otherwise *necessarily* true. *Mom is in the living room* and *Objects near the earth accelerate at 9.8 m/s²* are matters of fact. These statements are "contingent" because they could have been false; there are possible situations—or "possible worlds" as philosophers put it—in which they aren't true. On the other hand, *All red objects are colored objects* and 2 + 2 = 4 are not matters of fact but merely "relations of ideas" (more on these in a moment). Matters of fact make up nearly everything we know about the world around us, including much of what science knows. But to have genuine knowledge of such matters, said Hume, we must be able to check the world—at least in theory. We must be able to verify our ideas—these matters of fact—with sense perception.

Relations of ideas, on the other hand, are things we can know *without appealing to sense perception*. I can know, for example, that bachelors are unmarried males without checking the world; it would be true even if every male happened to be married. Similarly, I need not check the world to know that 1,375,228 + 3,245,672 = 4,620,900. But the epistemic standards for relations of ideas are lower because such statements aren't really about the world, strictly speaking. They merely tell us how concepts are related to one another.

The distinction between matters of fact and relations of ideas is often called *Hume's fork*. And the fork helps us identify the limits of knowledge. All our beliefs must run through Hume's fork (said Hume, though the term came later), and any that don't make the cut—any that aren't either matters of fact or relations of ideas—aren't even candidates for knowledge. That is, if something you believe doesn't fall into one of these two categories, you should forget it and move on.

Doodling with Words

Hume's fork gives us additional information; it's a criterion not merely for what we can *know*, but also for separating *sense* from *nonsense*. Unless a proposition falls into either the matter-of-fact category or the relation-of-ideas category, it doesn't mean anything. It is strict and utter gibberish. It's neither true nor false, never even getting off the ground, linguistically speaking.

So then, according to Hume, all matters of fact have to ultimately connect with the world to be meaningful, much less knowable. Relations of ideas need not submit to this test, but that's only because these are meaningful (and knowable) by definition. We can know that unicorns have a single horn, but only because that's just what *unicorn* means.[1]

Philosophers are often ridiculed for doodling with words. And rightly so; they're prone to analyze language in excruciating detail, getting bogged down in pedantic quagmires. Or sometimes they simply hide their ideas behind sludgy terminology. It's helpful, then, for philosophers to know when they're being "bewitched by language," that is, when they're being misled by the words themselves. Hume's fork offers some help here.

You have probably noticed that Hume's fork directs the traveler along one of two paths in the epistemological/semantic road: into the realm of empirical science (matters of fact) or the realm of mathematics (relations of ideas), with no *tertium quid*. This isn't coincidental, and Hume's followers will pick up on this in the twentieth century. The Scientific Revolution's success was predicated upon the mathematically buttressed "experimental method." The cynical among you might think that Hume's fork was reverse engineered to fit the deliverances of mathematical physics. And I must confess that it looks pretty suspicious.

---

[1] Students of philosophy will recognize the precursor of Kant's analytic/synthetic distinction—but not his a priori/a posteriori distinction, which was Kant's point.

Hume's Agenda

But as important as Hume's fork is to the history of philosophy, like most philosophy, it can seem rather dull and dry—until it's used as a weapon. For example, in Hume's rousing conclusion to *An Enquiry concerning Human Understanding*, see if you can identify how the fork has been weaponized:

> When we run over libraries, persuaded of these principles, what havoc must we make? If we take in our hand any volume of divinity or school metaphysics, for instance, let us ask, *Does it contain any abstract reasoning concerning quantity or number?* No. *Does it contain any experimental reasoning concerning matter of fact and existence?* No. Commit it then to the flames, for it can contain nothing but sophistry and illusion.[2]

Hume is railing against Scholastic theology and philosophy, and one of the things that irks him—understandably—is Scholasticism's use of obscure "jargon."[3] Even a philosopher's patience can be sorely tested by Scholastic philosophy, and Hume, as we saw, hoped to put philosophy on the right track by taking cues from Newton. Indeed, Hume meant to inaugurate a second Scientific Revolution of sorts. As he once said in a letter, "My principles . . . would produce almost a total alteration in philosophy: and you know, revolutions of this kind are not easily brought about."[4]

Nothing New under the Sun

So, Hume had an agenda (don't we all?). Part of this agenda was to remove metaphysics and theology from the list of acceptable academic practices. This has resonated with a lot of people, and it is here that our story again picks up, around the 1920s, with a school of (mainly German-speaking) philosophers and philosophically minded scientists. This school was called the *logical positivists* or *logical empiricists* (I'll explain the name in a moment).[5] An important part of the logical positivists was

[2] David Hume, *An Enquiry concerning Human Understanding*, ed. Eric Steinberg, 2nd ed. (Indianapolis: Hackett, 1993), 114; emphasis original.
[3] He said that "if a proper use were made of it, might render every dispute equally intelligible, and banish all that jargon, which has so long taken possession of metaphysical reasonings, and drawn disgrace upon them" (ibid., 13).
[4] Quoted in Eric Steinberg's introduction to ibid., viii.
[5] There is actually a vague and therefore difficult-to-describe distinction between logical empiricism and logical positivism; this distinction is usually ignored and indeed doesn't make a bit of difference for most purposes, including ours.

the famous "Vienna Circle." In any case, the logical positivists were consciously following Hume's seeing-is-believing canons of intellectual propriety, which is why they sometimes called themselves empiricists. They also set the agenda for all philosophy of science thereafter. Their spirits are found congregating around Hume's ghost, haunting philosophy and science departments worldwide.

Moreover, the logical positivists were as impressed with science as Hume ever was. The latter part of the 1800s and the beginning of the 1900s were heady times for those following science and mathematics. In the 1800s there had been nothing short of a revolution with the discovery of non-Euclidean geometry, followed quickly by Cantor's mind-altering theory of the infinite, which helped establish a rational foundation for the real numbers (which support the entirety of mathematics). There was also the resulting invention of symbolic logic by Frege, Russell, Whitehead, and others, intended to clarify and ground mathematics. This logic also promised sizable dividends for ordinary language, which is why philosophy departments offer courses in symbolic logic to this day. Then, in 1905 and 1915 Albert Einstein arrived at his theories of special and general relativity, respectively, the latter of which employed non-Euclidean geometry (in which space can be *curved*). If that weren't enough, the even stranger quantum mechanics followed close on its heels during the 1920s. Relativity and quantum theory stunned the world by overthrowing Newton, who himself had overthrown Aristotle.

None of this was lost on the logical positivists. Moreover, they couldn't help but compare such mathematical and scientific advancements with philosophy's two-thousand-year stagnation (well, all parts of philosophy except natural philosophy, which had by now become "science"). In contrast to the scientific disciplines, philosophy was a dried husk of historical curiosities. Indeed, Whitehead—not himself a logical positivist, but certainly a beacon of hope—memorably quipped that all of European philosophy was little more than a footnote to Plato.

The logical positivists realized that they were in a historical position not unlike Hume's. Discontent with philosophy was indeed a major factor in the Scientific Revolution, when the greatest minds in Europe turned to mathematics and experiment (in one way or another) for help with renovations. And as you already know, this revolt led immediately to the Enlightenment of the 1700s. And so to Hume.

The logical positivists, believing that philosophy had been circling a cul-de-sac for as long as anyone could remember, looked to the scientific disciplines as models of progress. Perhaps, they proposed, if philosophy became more like science—if it took scientific and mathematical developments seriously—it could finally make headway.

Still Bewitched by Language

A significant part of the problem with philosophy, said the logical positivists, was that philosophers had been bewitched by language. I mentioned this problem earlier and we're now at the place where we see why. Philosophers, said the logical positivists, had become preoccupied with problems that weren't problems at all. They were pseudo-problems and only seemed like substantive issues because they were expressed in ordinary language, with nouns, verbs, and adjectives. It was akin to the king's confusion in *Through the Looking Glass*:

> "I see nobody on the road," said Alice.
> "I only wish *I* had such eyes," the King remarked in a fretful tone. "To be able to see Nobody! And at that distance too! Why, it's as much as *I* can do to see real people, by this light!"

The king mistook the term "nobody" as actually referring to something. Philosophers were doing something similar with terms like *being*, *God*, *essence*, *right*, and *wrong*; these are only empty jargon, just as Hume had warned. One of the most notorious cases is from Heidegger's *What Is Metaphysics?*—and I quote:

> What is to be investigated is being only and—nothing else; being alone and further—nothing; solely being, and beyond being-nothing. What about this Nothing? . . . Does the Nothing exist only because the Not, i.e. the Negation, exists? Or is it the other way around? Does Negation and the Not exist only because the Nothing exists? . . . We assert: the Nothing is prior to the Not and the Negation. . . . Where do we seek the Nothing? How do we find the Nothing. . . . We know the Nothing. . . . Anxiety reveals the Nothing. . . . That for which and because of which we were anxious, was "really"—noth-

ing. Indeed: the Nothing itself—as such—was present. . . . What about this Nothing?—The Nothing itself nothings.[6]

It's hard to resist picking on Heidegger, but it's easy to see he had it coming.

The diagnosis, then, was that much of philosophy was trucking in meaningless language. The obvious cure, said the logical positivists, was to use something like Hume's fork, his criterion of meaning. They said that a statement is meaningful only if (1) it can be empirically checked, or "verified," or (2) it is a matter of definition, or is "analytic."[7] These two conditions correspond to Hume's matters of fact and relations of idea. Again, the first condition underwrites science, while the second licenses mathematics and logic. Nothing else is sanctioned. These two conditions also correspond, respectively, to each term in *logical positivism*. *Positivism* means something like "experience" or "empiricism," emphasizing admiration for science, and *logical* points to enthusiasm for math and logic.

Philosophy as a Weapon

The logical positivists' version of Hume's fork was known as the *verifiability criterion*, and it too became a fearful weapon, wreaking "havoc" (as Hume might say) among philosophy departments throughout Europe and America. The verifiability criterion convinced a significant portion of the academic community that traditional philosophy—what logical positivists derogatorily called *metaphysics*—was dead.

The logical positivists were more philosophically Spartan than even Hume. Take, for example, the problem of the external world. Whereas Hume believed it to be a genuine philosophical problem—one that revealed real and troubling limitations on human knowledge—the logical positivists dismissed it as a pseudo-problem merely disguised as substantive philosophy. After all, there's no *empirical* difference between a Matrix-type scenario and the "ordinary" world we think we're in. So according to empiricism we can't rationally choose between the two scenarios, even in theory. The logical positivist's conclusion, then, is that

---

[6] Roy Sorensen, "Nothingness," in *Stanford Encyclopedia of Philosophy*, ed. Edward N. Zalta (Stanford, CA: Metaphysics Research Lab, CSLI, Stanford University, 2012), http://plato.stanford.edu/entries/nothingness.
[7] "Analytic" isn't really identical with "true by definition," but let that pass. It's close enough for us.

there *is* no problem of the external world. So, instead of solving it, the logical positivists *dis*solved it. You will be excused entirely if you think they merely swept it under the rug.

The logical positivists also convinced most of academic philosophy that any reference to God is literal nonsense. They relegated all moral discourse similarly ("Murder is wrong" merely expresses one's emotions, like "Boo, murder!"). Religious and ethical discourse say nothing true or false about the world. Scientific and mathematical discourse, on the other hand, are not only meaningful, but the surest way to genuine knowledge.

The logical positivists had philosophy and theology in a choke hold for a good portion of the twentieth century.[8] Their negative or destructive project was to clear the academic world of meaningless bramble. Their positive or constructive project was to study the rational methods of science, which included logic and mathematics as tools, in hopes of limiting the pursuit of truth to those methods alone. Philosophy, according to the logical positivists, was limited to these two projects and nothing more.

Things Get Messy

But logical positivism became harder to maintain during the 1950s and 1960s. In fact, there was a problem at its core: the verifiability criterion undermined itself. The requirement that a meaningful statement must be either empirically verifiable or else a matter of definition is itself neither one of these, and so the verifiability criterion doesn't meet its own requirements. It eventually imploded.

There was pressure from outside logical positivism too. One source was actually very sympathetic to the logical positivist's goal of making philosophy more scientific: the Harvard philosopher and logician W. V. Quine—the most influential American philosopher of the twentieth century. Quine questioned the distinction between empirically verified statements and analytic ones.

The other major hit—and the one important for us—came from the historian of science, Thomas Kuhn. In *The Structure of Scientific Revolutions*, Kuhn described some of the ways science works in real life. The

---

[8] See Mitch Stokes, *A Shot of Faith to the Head: Be a Confident Believer in an Age of Cranky Atheists* (Nashville: Thomas Nelson, 2012), xiv ff., for the story of how the logical positivists virtually shut down the philosophy of religion.

result was a disconcerting realization that science cannot live by logic and observation alone. The very nature of our cognitive faculties—combined with the goals of scientific theories—makes science epistemically messy. It usually comes as a surprise to most people that science has a human face and so participates in the Humean condition.[9] The logical positivists' picture of science turned out to be heavily doctored. Their photoshopped version was pristine and perfect. In fact, it was a little too perfect, eerily smooth and plastic-like. Up close, it didn't look human.

The undoctored picture, on the other hand, is most certainly human, as Kuhn and others began pointing out. Humans are half god and half goon, as Devo once pointed out, so the realistic picture of science is much more interesting. Science can rise to rarefied heights but can also reach tragic depths—often simultaneously. Science is one big personal-interest story.

And so the logical positivists' influential view of a sanitized science died along with logical positivism. But many people never received the memo—including most scientists. This might surprise you, but scientists don't normally step back and carefully study scientific methods: they have enough on their plate just *doing* science. This is entirely natural and understandable, but it's also like being too busy driving to get gas.

I'll argue that when we *do* take the time to look closely at scientific methods, those of us who pride ourselves on our no-nonsense skeptical stance will have good reasons to be skeptical about important features of science—and about the status of current scientific theories.

Of course, this claim can be easily misconstrued as saying we should be skeptical of *all* things scientific. But that's not my point (since that isn't my view). Rather, my point in part 2 is that anyone who takes skepticism seriously should also be skeptical about the claim that science is somehow in conflict with God's existence. And the reasons I'll present in the next few chapters are fairly uncontroversial (but downplayed) facts about science.

---

[9] The death of logical positivism also freed the philosophy of religion from the verificationist shackles, resurrecting in the academy traditional discussions about God. Again, see ibid., for a discussion of this.

6

Real Science Is Hard

Credulity is a cardinal sin for skeptics. And belief in God is often considered the clearest instance of this mortal transgression. Such a sin may have been venial in the centuries prior to the Scientific Revolution, but no longer. Anyone today who believes in God—and uses cell phones and computers—is wholly culpable. You can't have it both ways. Science has proven itself trustworthy, as evidenced by its astounding technological gifts. It works and therefore we should believe what it says. And what it says—or at least strongly suggests—is that there's no God.[1] That is, science implies naturalism.

Over the next few chapters, I'll argue that we should be somewhat skeptical of what science says about the fundaments of physical reality, despite the fact that science "works." And if science likely gets things wrong about earthly things, why would we believe it when it comes to heavenly things? Even more to the point: why are devoted skeptics so credulous? Perhaps it's just human nature: the spirit is willing but the flesh is weak.

Whatever the reason, in this chapter, I'll describe some important ways in which the scientific method is much more complicated than we often think. The picture of science that develops won't be photoshopped, but will portray instead a beautifully human subject with all

---

[1] One example: the physicist Victor Stenger says, "I claim that not only is there no evidence for God" but also "science shows that God does not exist" (Stenger, *The New Atheism: Taking a Stand for Science and Reason* [Ahmherst, NY: Prometheus, 2009], 238).

the personality and quirkiness of someone you'd actually enjoy being around.

"It's Just a Theory"

First things first. What makes a scientific theory a *theory*? A lot of confusion could be avoided if this were dealt with up front. A good example of the confusion is when someone objects to evolution by pointing out that it's *only a theory*. The objector's point seems to be that we need not believe the theory of evolution because—by dint of its being a theory—it is less than credible, supported by scanty evidence, or otherwise highly tentative.

But a lack of certainty is not what makes evolution a theory. Evolution does, of course, fall far short of certainty, but that in itself is no condemnation. All theories suffer from this affliction to different degrees, and for a wide variety of reasons. Rather, the main feature of a scientific theory—what *makes* it a theory—is that it is *inferred* rather than observed. No one has ever *seen* a theory—by definition.

The observation/theory distinction falls right along the sense perception/reason divide. Let's look at a nonscientific example to get a better appreciation of both. Imagine you're outside in the rain, running from your car to the office building. You of course believe that it's raining, and good for you: you've seen it raining with your own eyes, felt it with your own skin, etc. You've directly observed that it's raining, and this observation naturally enough causes you to form the belief that it's raining. Now, you come into my office, soaking wet. And though my office has no windows (but at least I'm not working in a cubicle), I too form the belief that it's raining. My belief, however, is formed very differently from yours. I see that you're wet and then *infer* from this observation that it's raining. I don't observe that it's raining but, rather, by way of my reason, come to believe it nonetheless.[2]

Consider a more germane case, the seventeenth-century debate over geocentricity and heliocentricity. Aside from the more recent controversies surrounding evolution, this is the most important scientific,

---

[2] There is a third possibility: you could call me from your car telling me that you'll be late for our appointment because it's raining and you forgot your umbrella. In this case, assuming I believe you, I form the belief that it's raining by way of your testimony. We'll ignore testimony for now since it piggybacks on observation. Testimony, nevertheless, is a crucially important source of knowledge—far more important than most of us realize. We'll see this—and its implications—later.

philosophical, and religious debate in history. Recall that—against the Copernicans—the Aristotelians (or Ptolemaists) believed that the sun revolves around a stationary earth. Now, what's important here is that the debate was *not about observations.* Everyone generally agreed on those—the sun is *over there* at this time of day and *over here* at another time. The heavens appeared the same to everyone; all parties could accurately point to the sun's position in the sky (and a host of more subtle phenomena).

The debate, instead, was over how best to *explain* the appearances, how best to account for the agreed-upon observations. That is, the debate was about *theory.* After all, we don't observe heliocentricity or geocentricity (even today); rather, these theories are our inferred stories about what goes on behind the appearances, about unseen mechanisms. In the Copernican debate, each side had a possible answer to the question *why does the sun move the way it does in the sky?* One possible answer—one possible *explanation*—is that the earth rotates on its axis once every twenty-four hours while revolving around the sun roughly once every 365 days; another is that the sun revolves around a stationary earth every twenty-four hours. An explanation, then, is often an answer to a *why* question (quite generally, *why do things appear this way?*)[3] A theory, then, is an explanation. And the type of inference leading to each theory—*inference to the best explanation*—is as complicated as it is common, as we'll see.[4]

Science, then, is in the business of inferring theories. And scientific theories must agree with observations—past, present, and future. These theories must make contact with the world by answering to the "tribunal of experience." But no matter how well a theory predicts or represents observable phenomena—no matter how well it is supported by this agreement with observation—it is still a *theory,* simply because it is inferred and not observed. Not only is evolution "merely" a theory, but so too are general relativity and quantum mechanics, the most well-attested scientific theories humans have devised.

The real question is this: how good are our reasons for believing them; how good are our inferences?

---

[3] Or similarly, *how did that happen,* or *what caused that to happen?*

[4] In particular, we'll discover that, in addition to uncontroversial beliefs about the observations, these inferences also depended on *highly* controversial theological and philosophical beliefs, with entertaining results.

You'll remember that Laplace didn't need God as a *hypothesis*. We're now in a better position to define *hypothesis*, which we need to do since this term is thrown carelessly about, mucking up discussions of science (and religion, as the Laplace anecdote illustrates).

A hypothesis is simply an *unobserved* explanation. Take a standard gloss of the scientific method, one that can be helpful or harmful, depending how it's used:

1. Observation
2. Hypothesis
3. Prediction
4. Experiment

According to this G-rated version, we first observe the phenomena, that is, those things that appear to us (step 1). (*Phenomenon* comes from the Greek word for *appearance*.) We then construct the best explanation for what we've observed: we come up with a hypothesis (step 2). To put it differently, we come up with a theory that makes sense of the fact that the world behaves *this way*, "this way" being a description of our observations. Our hypotheses, therefore, are really theories—although they're usually mini-theories that are part of larger ones.

But the main point about theories and hypotheses is that we don't observe them. Theories and hypotheses are the stories about the physical drama unfolding behind the scenes. And just so we're clear, hypotheses and theories are also *explanations*. But they're explanations of a specific kind: the *unobserved* kind.[5]

And obviously not all theories (and therefore not all hypotheses) are created equal. And one of the main ways we decide which ones are better than others is by comparing how well they predict the world's behavior (steps 3 and 4). That is, we test them to see if they've prophesied correctly. We typically do this by way of experiments—sometimes extremely simple experiments (incline plane), at other times unbelievably elaborate (particle accelerator).

---

[5] There are observed explanations, but these are not theories/hypotheses. If for example, I have a theory or hypotheses that the butler is the murderer (I didn't actually see him commit the crime), this is an unobserved (and presumably possible) explanation. But suppose I check the security camera footage and see him actually kill my parakeet. I still have an explanation of the parakeet's death—namely, that the heartless butler killed her—but it is no longer a hypothesis or theory: I've observed it. (We could complicate things, though, as my students are wont to do, by pointing out that I didn't directly observe that the footage wasn't doctored or that I'm not a BIV or that . . . and believe me, it can get pretty tedious. But it's my own fault.)

Remember what we're ultimately after here. We're considering whether science tells us—or even hints—that God's existence is unlikely, whether naturalism is most likely true. And we're in a much better position to consider this claim now that we have in hand the observation/ theory distinction. We'll turn next to an important fact about the relationship between observations and theories, after which we'll look at the requirements for a successful scientific theory. (Spoiler alert: successful theories require much more than matching observations and making the right predictions.)

Lots of Models to Choose From

So then, to construct a scientific theory (also called a *model*), we first carefully consider our observations and then tell a plausible story that might explain them. But the considerable gap separating observations from theories can make arriving at a decent theory quite an ordeal. And even once we've constructed a theory, we can never *observe* that it's correct. Never ever.

One major complication in all this is that there's usually more than one theory or hypothesis that will match the observations; that is, two (or more) theories can be "empirically adequate."[6] As I said, during the debate between helio- and geocentricity, each theory matched observations; each of them *worked*. But at least one of them was wrong.

In such a case (to generalize), the observations alone can't settle the disagreement. And this poses a legitimate problem for the "seeing is believing" approach to things, which, again, is the official approach of science. As Rosenberg explains:

> Science does not accept as knowledge what cannot be somehow subject to the test of experience. But at the same time, the obligation of science to explain our experience requires that it go beyond and beneath that experience in the things, properties, processes, and events it appeals to in providing these explanations. How to reconcile the demands of empiricism with the demands of explanation is the hardest problem for the philosophy of science, indeed for philosophy as a whole.[7]

---

[6] See, for example, Bas C. van Fraassen, *The Scientific Image* (Oxford: Clarendon, 1980).

[7] Alexander Rosenberg, *The Philosophy of Science: A Contemporary Introduction*, 3rd ed. (New York: Routledge, 2012), 146–47.

So experience alone can't adjudicate between equally empirically adequate theories. Other criteria have to play that role: for example, simplicity, ontological and conceptual economy, aesthetic considerations, suggestive mathematical symbolism, how well a theory fits in with the rest of what we believe, and a host of other hard-to-characterize factors.[8]

But the point now is that there can be more than one possible theory that empirically matches a given set of observations. Or as philosophers of science put it, the observations *underdetermine* the theories. Observation alone—which is where the theoretical rubber meets the empirical road—cannot fully *determine* or "nail down" a unique theory. Indeed, as Quine famously said, there are an infinite number of empirically adequate theories for any given set of observations (though, of course, some will be more plausible than others).

Consider the following analogy (it's really more an example than an analogy). Imagine an *x–y* graph on which you've plotted two data points. Each data point represents some physical data you've measured in a laboratory: say, pressure and temperature. Now suppose your goal is to discover a general relation—that is, a formula or equation—between temperature and pressure so that you don't always have to *measure* pressure. You'd like to be able to just plug the temperature into an equation and *calculate* pressure. To do this, though, you have to determine the shape of the pressure-temperature curve that runs through the two points. Or, algebraically speaking, you need to find the equation that relates temperature and pressure, given all the data at your disposal (in this case, two measly points). Well, given the paucity of your data, you have considerable flexibility in how to connect these two points—from the very simple (a straight line) to the very complex (put your pencil on one of the points and vigorously scribble around the page, eventually touching the other point).[9] In fact, there are an infinite number of ways to connect your points. And the data alone cannot make that decision for you. You'll need additional temperature-pressure data or some other criteria or both.

Our imagined pressure-temperature example is complicated enough, but it's extraordinarily simple compared to full-blown theory construc-

---

[8] By the way, in the Copernican debate, Copernicanism was simpler than its competitors, but it also eventually accounted for new observations (e.g., phases of Venus and the moons of Jupiter).

[9] Forget about other mathematical niceties, such as whether this is a function (passing the vertical-line test), etc.

tion. In our pressure-temperature case we're "only" looking for some mathematical shortcut for calculating. (By the way, it's curious that we expect there to be *any* rhyme or reason between pressure and temperature—much less a discoverable mathematical formula; after all, the world need not be so accommodating. And yet we now feel entitled to it.) In any case, in the pressure-temperature example, we're not aiming at an entire story for how the unobservable particles are behaving (if there even are such particles). To construct such a story is a much more daunting task, and no matter how many observations we make, all we ever observe is the tip of the iceberg, which underneath could be nearly *any* shape. To change the metaphor, constructing an explanatory theory (a redundant phrase) is like "trying to figure out the workings of a closed watch."[10] As Einstein said about anyone in the theory-making business:

> If he is ingenious he may form some picture of a mechanism which could be responsible for all the things he observes, but he may never be quite sure his picture is the only one which could explain his observations. He will never be able to compare his picture with the real mechanism, and he cannot even imagine the possibility or the meaning of such a comparison.[11]

And coming up with a single theory is difficult enough, but to the sensitive scientist, it can be disheartening to know that there are probably countless more.

Some Examples of Inference to the Best Explanation

So, when constructing a theory, we have to sift through all the possible explanations (at least those we can think of, which drastically reduces the pool of contenders), looking for the best one. This process is called, as I mentioned, *inference to the best explanation*, although it's not clear exactly what kind of "inference" it is, technically speaking. In any case, inference to the best explanation isn't unique to science. Sherlock Holmes does it every time he solves a case. He gathers facts during his investigation and then arrives at the best explanation of those

---

[10] Arthur Fine, *The Shaky Game: Einstein, Realism, and the Quantum Theory*, ed. David L. Hull, 2nd ed., Science and Its Conceptual Foundations (Chicago: University of Chicago, 1996), 93.
[11] Quoted in ibid., 93.

facts, a hypothesis that answers *why are things this way?*, the answer being, say, *because Moriarty is the killer*. The hypothesis that Moriarty is the killer best explains all the relevant things that Sherlock believes.

A more mundane but oh so much more important example is when your doctor tells you that you have, say, a staph infection. She sees the redness and swelling, feels that the skin's temperature is higher than normal, hears your complaint of fatigue, etc. Now, she never observes that you have a staph infection. These same symptoms, let us suppose, could be cutaneous lupus. But she thinks that staph is a better explanation, given everything she believes, like how frequent staph infection is versus the rarity of lupus, the fact that you have a history of staph, and so on.

Even you are guilty of making inferences to the best explanation. Suppose you arrive home from work and see the mail on the kitchen table, even though no one else is home (the other cars being gone). You absent-mindedly wonder who brought in the mail and then notice dirty dishes in the sink, dishes that weren't there when you left this morning (and you were the last one out of the house). It is reasonable for you to assume that your spouse came home for lunch and put the mail on the table. Of course, there may be other explanations: perhaps your daughter came home after school to get her volleyball uniform and *she* put the mail on the table.

There are also possibilities you don't even consider: your neighbor brought the mail in (you forgot to lock your front door); your dog brought in the mail—or a strangely conscientious burglar, or an alien. None of these are impossible, but *all things considered* they're unlikely, which is why they don't occur to you.

One last example. You are an astronomer in the early 1800s and notice that the planet Uranus is not following the path predicted by current astronomical theory (you made the calculations yourself). The planet's orbit is every-so-slightly off where it "should" be. There are various possible explanations, you realize. Perhaps you calculated the orbit incorrectly or made careless observations. Or perhaps current theory about planetary orbits is just plain wrong. But after much toil and trouble you arrive at another hypothesis or theory: perhaps there's an unseen planet affecting Uranus's orbit. After a painstaking search, you find that there is indeed another planet—exactly where you calculated it should be. You call it *Neptune* and check "Discover new planet" off your bucket list.

How Do *You* Know What's Best?

Again, sense experience alone is often not enough to determine the best explanation in many cases. Other factors have to come into play. Recall that the doctor believed staph infection to be the best explanation of your symptoms (i.e., of the observations) *all things considered.* This phrase is really disguised hand waving over a remarkably complex web of beliefs that the doctor brought with her to the examination. That is, what determines *best* is a complicated matter that depends on a whole host of beliefs—many of them implicit. You typically think that the best explanation for the fact that there appears to be a tree directly in front of you is that there really *is* a tree directly in front of you. But there are other explanations, as we saw: maybe you're just a brain in a vat being fed electrical signals, making it only *seem* like there's a tree in front of you. Why then do you think the former explanation is better? After all, the observational input would be *identical* regardless of which scenario is true. And "best" in this case, as we saw earlier, is conditioned by what you already believe about the world and the way it works.

The same holds for any inference to the best explanation. Your idea of what constitutes a good scientific theory will also depend on your beliefs about what the physical world is like, which has been shaped by a lifetime of experience, some of which appears to have no relation to science. In the debate over heliocentricity, many factors other than observation played a role in the debate on both sides: beliefs about Neoplatonism, the nature of Scripture, the authority of Aristotle, the authority of the Catholic Church, expectations about how God would have created the world, the reliability of mathematics and of optics, and so on.

A particularly famous example of how worldviews influence theory choice is Einstein's resistance to quantum theory, with its indeterminacy and other weirdness. For example, not only is there a built-in uncertainty in quantum mechanics, but this uncertainty about, say, when a radioactive particle will decay, is the result of there *being* no definite time when the particle will decay. There is nothing physical about the particle that dictates that it will decay at this particular time rather than some other. The same *exact* physical state can produce two entirely different results. But Einstein believed that the world simply isn't like this; he expressed his distaste for such a world by objecting that God doesn't play dice. But he agreed that quantum theory accounted for the relevant observable phenomena. And so Einstein's *worldview* got in the way of his acceptance of quantum theory. He had preconceived notions about what physical reality is like. And so does everyone else.

Einstein also disagreed with some of the founders of quantum theory about what a scientific theory should *do*. When confronted with the counterintuitive world that quantum theory seems to depict, Niels Bohr, for example, said that a good scientific theory need not tell us the truth about the unobservable world; it merely need be a useful tool or instrument for predicting things that we can observe. This attitude toward scientific theories is called *instrumentalism* or *scientific antirealism* or *scientific nonrealism*. The alternative view is known as *scientific realism*, according to which, the entities, properties, and events posited by scientific theories really exist/occur. But Einstein vehemently disagreed with Bohr's instrumentalism, believing that the goal of science is to get at the *truth* about reality, not merely develop tools to manipulate the observable world.[12]

Suppose you and I are arguing over whether Newtonian physics or general relativity is a better account of the nature of space. This argument will be difficult to sort out because each theory assumes up front an entirely different concept of space. So, of course, I'll think that Newtonian physics makes more sense of the concept that Newtonian physics assumes. The nature of space is itself colored by the theory. And this is often the case generally: we must stand on theories to argue for them; there's sometimes nowhere else to stand.[13] Beliefs about the theories are themselves soaked in theories, sometimes the very same ones.

So then, the beliefs *we have* strongly influence the beliefs *we form*. Old beliefs shape new beliefs. New knowledge always builds on background knowledge. This is just another feature of science's human face.[14]

---

[12] James Ladyman, *Understanding Philosophy of Science* (New York: Routledge, 2002), 104.

[13] Mitch Stokes, *A Shot of Faith to the Head: Be a Confident Believer in an Age of Cranky Atheists* (Nashville: Thomas Nelson, 2012), 78.

[14] For a nice introduction to the human face of science, see Thomas S. Kuhn, *The Structure of Scientific Revolutions*, 3rd ed. (Chicago: University of Chicago Press, 1996).

The Education of a Scientist

It often goes unnoticed or at least unmentioned (so I'll mention it now) that scientists undergo a particularly intense kind of indoctrination.[15] This training is extremely formative and very effective, preparing students for membership in a unique culture. Ever after, scientists tend to look at the world differently, through a different set of lenses.

Consider textbooks, for example. Of course, the content of textbooks is important, but just as important is the way textbooks present the material. They depict science as a relatively neat and hygienic accumulation of knowledge, with very little discussion of the historical messiness—its dead ends, misfires, and failures. And rightly so: the volume and difficulty of contemporary science is immense and prohibitive. It is a herculean task to simply take in the main features of a theory. There's little time and energy for asking the big questions, for looking at the history and philosophy of science and mathematics.

Even if you're not a scientist, you've experienced something like this in miniature. Consider how you learned mathematics in high school: it was quite enough to learn how to *do* mathematics. There was no time at all to look at its development or discuss *why* mathematics works, and so on. In fact, most people don't know that there *is* more to mathematics than merely doing problems. Undergraduate and graduate mathematical training is typically more of the same, just at a higher level.

Scientific education also teaches students what kinds of authorities to trust. This is crucial, because most of what a scientist knows—indeed most of what each of us knows—is by way of testimony, from what others tell us.[16] An individual scientist makes only a tiny fraction of the possible calculations, observations, and theory choices that are part of his or her narrow sub-discipline. Sanctioned sources for the additional information include course lectures, journals, books, conferences, and even the most casual discussions with advisors and directors. All of these hone the student's ability to identify community-accepted sources of knowledge.

Even though this is necessary and good, it's also ironic. Remember that Kant challenged us not to trust the authority of others but to believe for oneself—dare to know. Also remember that this sort of skepticism

---

[15] This goes for most STEM (Science Technology Engineering Mathematics) disciplines.
[16] See Stokes, *A Shot of Faith to the Head*, chap. 4.

is supposed to be characteristic of scientists. There's something to this claim, but it's also hopelessly naive—at least in the form it's usually pandered.

In any case, scientists have a special kind of deeply ingrained world-view, one that tells them which kinds of rationality are valuable, which kind of theories count as successful, and so on. Scientists get a "feel" for which kinds of hypotheses are even worth considering. These values become a powerful guide and are usually learned implicitly, which is to say, very effectively. As parents learn (often to their horror), values are more readily caught than taught. Applying this to our discussion of theory choice, to choose the best explanation *just is* to choose your *favorite* explanation. And favorites are always determined by values. (More on values in the last part of the book.)

Theory-Laden Observations

Surprisingly, our scientific theories strongly influence what we *observe*, not just what we believe. For one thing, our current beliefs about what the world is like—largely influenced by what scientific theory we hold—determine what sorts of features we wish to test and the kinds of experiments we use to test them. But this severely restricts the part of the physical world that we'll actually observe. As philosopher of science Peter Kosso explains:

> We cannot look at everything. Nor can we waste time by looking haphazardly at one damn thing after another. Scientific observation must be selective and methodical to be sure we see what is important and relevant to our interests. And any determination of relevance will be directed by the current theoretical understanding of nature. Theories, after all, tell us what is relevant to what by describing how nature is put together and what causes what.[17]

Our theory also tells us which sorts of observations are acceptable, which experiments count as reliable or successful. Again, Kosso explains: "We must know the right conditions from wrong, and here again is a role for background knowledge, this time regarding how the observation itself happens. . . . At least part of that checking will call

---

[17] Peter Kosso, *Appearance and Reality: An Introduction to the Philosophy of Physics* (Oxford: Oxford University Press, 1998), 20.

on a conceptual understanding of how the observation ought to be performed."[18] Background knowledge also tells us "what a particular observation means" and even what counts as evidence for or against a theory.

> To function as evidence, an observation must be of something that is relevant to a theory. The streaks of vapor in a cloud chamber or bubble chamber are of no interest at all unless they can be linked to the passage of elementary particles. . . . The evidence must be of particles, not just streaks, and to make the connection some theoretical understanding of how particles produce streaks is required. . . . So here again, the elevation of observation from the brute physical event of sensation to the useful epistemic event of evidence will be done under the influence of background theory.[19]

James Ladyman gives an example of how a theory can influence what physicists see:

> Another case . . . is the failure of physicists to notice the tracks in cloud chambers caused by positrons before the theoretical postulation of these particles (in 1928) by Paul Dirac. When particle physicists look back at the experiments conducted in the years before Dirac's work they see clear evidence of positrons that seems to have been completely missed by their predecessors.[20]

Theory influences observation, which influences theory, which influences observation. We have here a kind of scientific hermeneutic circle, even for something as apparently objective as *seeing*.[21] Seeing is believing, but the converse is true too.

It's Hard to Kill a Theory

So, deciding which observations count for—or against—a theory isn't at all straightforward. Suppose you're experimentally testing a theory, general relativity, say, and the theory has told you (via calculations) that you should expect to find that light bends as it travels through empty space. Now, suppose you perform your experiment, and lo, light *does*

---

[18] Ibid., 20–21.
[19] Ibid., 21.
[20] Ladyman, *Understanding Philosophy of Science*, 112.
[21] See Kuhn, *The Structure of Scientific Revolutions*, for alarming examples.

bend. This counts—if anything does—as support for general relativity. But underdeterminism implies that this result is also consistent with any number of possible theories.

Surely, though, the fulfillment of such scientific prophecies counts as *some kind of support*. After all, if you *didn't* observe what general relativity predicted (under the appropriate circumstances), then you'd know immediately that the theory wasn't true.[22]

But even on that score things aren't so simple. To be sure, it seems reasonable to think that it's easier to kill a theory than to support it. One failed prediction should do the job. You discover that light doesn't bend. Well then, general relativity is obviously wrong. After all, this is one way in which theories in fact die: they fail to match observations. But recall the process by which you discovered Neptune. This, as it turns out, is just how Neptune was actually discovered. If the Newtonian theory predicted that Uranus should have an orbit that it clearly *didn't have*, why didn't these astronomers conclude that Newtonian physics is wrong? After all, the proof of the pudding is in the observation; the minimum requirement for theories is that they match what we see.

Well, scientists don't immediately give up on a theory the moment trouble arises; there are usually heroic attempts to save it. And this is a good thing. If scientists threw away a theory the instant it didn't agree with observations, *no* theory would get off the ground (or even out of the hangar). As Ladyman explains:

> Scientists are often quite committed to their theories, and sometimes they will adopt all manner of strategies to save them from apparent refutation, rather than simply giving them up. . . . They won't give up the paradigm just because it conflicts with some of the evidence. Perhaps this is justifiable. . . . As Kuhn says, "The scientist who pauses to examine every anomaly he notes will seldom get significant work done"[23]

---

[22] There are other problems, which turn out to be further problems with induction, problems that Hume didn't consider, but that have kept philosophers of science up at night. One is Carl Hempel's "Raven Paradox." Let's say we reasonably believe that all ravens are black because all of the many ravens we've seen have been black. Moreover, each time we observe a black raven, our generalization *All ravens are black* gains further support. *All ravens are black* is logically equivalent to the (rather awkwardly worded) statement *If something is a raven, then it is black*. But according to standard laws of *deductive* logic, this statement is equivalent to *If something is not black, then it is not a raven*. Now, consider my white truck. It is neither black nor a raven, so it counts as support for the generalization *If something is not black, then it is not a raven*. But this generalization is logically equivalent to *All ravens are black*, and so my truck counts as support for the truth of *All ravens are black*. Weird.

[23] Ladyman, *Understanding Philosophy of Science*, 101.

You try to make things work before you file for divorce. No theory matches all observations ever made, and there may be different reasons for any given mismatch. Perhaps the experiment was performed incorrectly, or the wrong simplifying assumptions were made, or the calculation was wrong. In fact, when there's a mismatch between theory and observation, the scientist is usually the first to blame, not the theory.

Theories Are Never Tested by Themselves

But there can be another, more fundamental reason for a prediction's failure. This is because we never test a theory by itself; every experiment is really a test of an entire web of beliefs, a web including far more than the theory. The sentence *If theory T is true, then we will get observation O* contains hidden complications. The antecedent of the conditional—which is just logic-speak for the "if" part of the sentence—is really a conjunction or collection of assumptions, not merely "if theory *T* is true." We're really assuming something more like *If T is true and we've performed the experiment correctly (then we'll get observation O)*. This additional belief or condition is called an "auxiliary hypothesis."

Take a simple example: *If the sample in the beaker is ethanol, then the sample will boil at 78.5 degrees Celsius.*[24] This is actually something closer to *If the sample in the beaker is ethanol, and the thermometer is working properly, and my glassware is clean, and the sample is not contaminated, and the air pressure in the lab is normal, and so on, then the sample will boil at 78.5 degrees Celsius.*[25]

And there are yet more auxiliary hypotheses hidden in the "and so on." For one thing, obviously enough, the laws of logic must hold. And other things must be true too: there must be a world that behaves consistently; mathematics must be a reliable way to arrive at truths about the world; supernatural beings can't be intervening in the world willy-nilly; the future must resemble the past; scientific laws must hold at all times and everywhere throughout the universe; we aren't hallucinating or under the influence of psychotropic drugs, and on and on. All these beliefs are of a piece and confirmed or disconfirmed together.

So then, we never test theories in isolation. When we test theories, we're really testing them with all the relevant background beliefs

---

[24] Richard DeWitt, *Worldviews: An Introduction to the History and Philosophy of Science*, 2nd ed. (Oxford: Wiley-Blackwell, 2010), 43.
[25] Ibid.

simultaneously. Or to put the same point differently, our "theory" is more than the scientific theory. As Einstein wrote, "No one of the assumptions can be isolated for separate testing."[26]

This all-inclusive view of testing is called *conformational holism*. And to complicate matters, when we get a theory-observation mismatch, we often don't know *which* belief is the bad apple or whether the entire batch is spoiled.

In Theory, Any Theory Can Be Saved

As Quine famously taught, we can always save a theory from counterevidence. We can tweak the theory, to be sure, but that's not the half of it. We can also modify nearly any other belief, assuming we're willing to go far enough. And when it comes to which beliefs we modify, Quine says that "no statement is immune to revision."[27]

But is it really possible to modify, say, the laws of logic in the face of "recalcitrant experience"? Quine answers that, yes, "revision even of the logical law of the excluded middle has been proposed as a means of simplifying quantum mechanics."[28] And philosophers of science Martin Curd and J. A. Cover explain:

> Quantum logic was first proposed by the mathematicians Garrett Birkhoff and John von Neumann in 1936 as a solution to the paradoxes of quantum mechanics. . . . To its supporters, the attraction of quantum logic is that it does not permit inferences to any conclusion that quantum mechanics and experiment reveal to be either false or unverifiable. . . . To its detractors, quantum logic does not solve any paradoxes—it simply shifts the mystery from physics to logic.[29]

So we can alter even the laws of logic to make a theory fit observations. Again, it's harder to kill a theory than many people realize.

Skepticism and the Scientific Method

Now nothing in this chapter is an argument that science isn't an extremely impressive human achievement. Nor does anything in this chap-

[26] Quoted in Fine, *The Shaky Game*, 88–89.
[27] W. V. Quine, "Two Dogmas of Empiricism," in *Philosophy of Science: The Central Issues*, ed. Martin Curd and J. A. Cover (New York: W. W. Norton, 1998), 297.
[28] Ibid.
[29] Curd and Cover, *Philosophy of Science*, 380.

ter, by itself, compel us to think that science doesn't get at the truth behind the scenes of appearances. Rather this chapter is an opening salvo against the über-optimism that often accompanies contemporary atheism (Dawkins, Dennett, Stenger, Hitchens, Coyne, and Sam Harris come immediately to mind). My goal is to encourage a calm, level-headed appreciation of science. And this chapter gives us some insight into its workings—in particular, pointing out factors that tell against the naive view that science is nothing more than a matter of cool reason and sober observation. Philosopher of science Arthur Fine goes so far as to call the construction of theories "shaky games":

> These are games insofar as they involve elements of free construction and play. These are shaky because, without firm foundations or a rigid superstructure, their outcome is uncertain. Indeed not even the rules of play are fixed. It follows that at every step we have to be guided by judgment calls.[30]

To be sure, reason and observation are key players, but to think that science is more objective than it is would be to court trouble. And it certainly isn't in accord with a robust and proper skeptical stance. Über-optimism takes neither skepticism nor science seriously. Sober skepticism appreciates both.

But there's the other ditch, and I want us to avoid that too. We should not be über-*skeptics* about science; nor should any skepticism about science be for the wrong reasons. Unfortunately, these are common problems—and usually travel together. As with most things, we should avoid extremes. It's neither simple nor easy, but it's necessary.

---

[30] Fine, *The Shaky Game*, 2.

7

Arguing with Success

"Science Will Win"

In the previous chapter we saw that the scientific method is variegated and not nearly as straightforward as we often believe. Not that science is ever considered easy. Rather, the source of its difficulty is often misidentified; or better, its difficulty is *limited* to its calculations and concepts. But science is also an art. There's no recipe for finding the best theory that will adequately explain the observable phenomena. The process is rife with uncertainty, ambiguity, and subjectivity. Finding a workable theory is nothing at all like falling off a log—despite the countless possible theories that could fit the known data. Even a single theory is hard to find.

All of this makes success in science a matter of an enormous amount of hard work, ingenuity, and creativity—and no small amount of luck. Scientists are legitimate heroes, and it's their hero status that seems to give them the credentials to be our final arbiters of truth. When science speaks, people listen. Again, it's hard to argue with success.

So when we hear that science and religion are at odds, it's all too easy to think *Then so much the worse for religion.* Again, this line of reasoning is predicated on the success of science; science puts its money where its mouth is. There are sizable scientific dividends that we can actually point to: airplanes, computers, lasers, cell phones, atomic weapons, X-rays, MRIs, and all manner of modern conveniences that border on miraculous. If we have to choose, as we are told we must, why believe in the religious miracles we've never actually seen, over those scientific miracles we see every day? Richard Dawkins, when asked why we should believe what science says, responded, "It works, b*****s."[1] Science, after all, "can fly you to Saturn, slingshotting you around Venus and Jupiter on the way. We may not understand quantum theory (heaven knows I don't), but a theory that predicts the real world to ten decimal places cannot in any straightforward sense be wrong."[2] This can be strong testimony coming from the most famous atheist in the world, and the world's top intellectual of 2013.[3] And the world's most famous *physicist* says something similar. Stephen Hawking tells *ABC News*'s Diane Sawyer that in the war between science and religion, "science will win because it works."[4]

The thought, then, seems to be this. Science and religion tell us conflicting things about reality, and so we're forced to make a decision about which source we're going to trust. Again, it's pretty clear that we can trust science since it allows us to actually *do* things, to manipulate the physical world in ways that astound even the most jaded modern. Even when we use the results of science to inflict unimaginable suffering on our fellow humans, it's because science tells us the truth about how the physical world works. If the fundamental properties of matter or light or spacetime weren't what our scientific theories tell us they are—if our theories lied about them—would we really expect them to result in lasers, satellites, and computers? After all, we don't expect astrology to pan out this way, and for good reason: it generally lies about the fundamental workings of the physical universe. As does religion—at least according to Dawkins and Hawking.

Now, we can all agree that science "works." Let's also agree for the moment that our scientific theories really do provide significant evidence against God's existence. That is, let us agree that science says—or implies or proposes or suggests—that naturalism is true, that there's no God (or anything like God). With such generous concessions—along with the undeniable fact that science works—do we *now* have a good argument to the effect that science has shown that God doesn't exist?

Clearly not. We would need at least one other important premise,

---

[1] Aaron Souppouris, "Richard Dawkins on Science: 'It Works, Bitches,' *The Verge*, April 2, 2013, http://www.theverge.com/2013/4/2/4173576/richard-dawkins-on-science-it-works-bitches.
[2] Richard Dawkins, afterword to Lawrence M. Krauss, *A Universe from Nothing: Why There Is Something Rather Than Nothing* (New York: Free Press, 2012), 190.
[3] "World Thinkers 2013," *Prospect*, April 24, 2013, http://www.prospectmagazine.co.uk/features/world-thinkers-2013.
[4] Ki Mae Heussner, "Stephen Hawking on Religion: 'Science Will Win,'" ABC News, June 7, 2010, http://abcnews.go.com/WN/Technology/stephen-hawking-religion-science-win/story?id=10830164.

namely, that what science tells us about the physical world is *true* (in particular, those parts of science that are relevant to any argument leveled at belief in God). And there are very good reasons to doubt this, reasons that align with a sober skeptic's stance toward matters intellectual. To put it differently, there are good reasons to doubt the connection between the *truth* of a scientific theory and its ability to *work*, to accurately describe the observable world.

To put this differently, there are good reasons to be an instrumentalist, to think that theories need only be empirically adequate to be counted as successful. And if you can't manage instrumentalism, then there are good reasons for thinking that our scientific theories aren't successful, since *success* would include—on a rejection of instrumentalism—that science give us the truth about the unobservable parts of the world. In either case, my point is the same: we should be skeptical of what science says about those parts of the world we cannot observe.

The Pessimistic Induction

One of the reasons to be skeptical is that, as we saw in the last chapter, theories are underdetermined by observations. That is, there are many possible theories for any set of data. Observations are the crucial contact point between a theory and the physical world, and while this point of contact anchors a theory to reality, everything else the theory says can float free of the truth.[5] After all, different, equally empirically adequate theories can say conflicting things about what goes on behind the scenes.

But even though there may be any number of empirically adequate scientific theories *in principle*, is it really very likely? Underdeterminism seems like something that would worry only the most pedantic philosopher. Of course, if there were real-life examples of observational evidence being susceptible to more than a single interpretation (i.e., in consonance with more than one theory), then perhaps we might have reason to take underdetermination as a going concern.

Well, we've already seen one example: Copernicanism and geocen-

---

[5] But as I alluded to, there's an important difference between underdeterminism and instrumentalism. Whereas the former is a fact on which everyone can agree, instrumentalism is a person's attitude toward a theory, a view about what makes a theory successful. There are obviously people who do not take an instrumentalist attitude toward theories, and so require that successful theories be literally true. These people believe that—since we're currently saddled with literally false theories that merely match observations—it is a lamentable situation in which our current scientific theories do not meet the criteria of a "successful" or "good" scientific theory.

tricity. Both theories matched the observable data for decades before Galileo turned his telescope toward the heavens. That is, there was a time when the set of data could be explained by both theories. (There was a third too: the Tychonic theory, which was also *mathematically* identical to the Copernican theory, but kept the earth stationary.) Moreover, they matched observations to theretofore unheard of accuracy. (Lee Smolin points out that the geocentric theory, with its Rube Goldberg level of complexity, matched predictions to 1 part in 1000.)[6] During this time, proponents of each theory had to appeal to virtues other than empirical adequacy, virtues such as simplicity and conservativeness (that is, how well it remained in accord with previous beliefs).

But there are many more examples of real-life underdeterminism. The history of science is littered with the remains of successful-but-false theories, theories that matched the available observations, contributed to technological advancements, and even made novel and surprising predictions. Philosopher of science Larry Laudan lists some of the more famous ones:

- the crystalline spheres of ancient and medieval astronomy
- the humoral theory of medicine
- the effluvial theory of static electricity
- the phlogiston theory of chemistry
- the caloric theory of heat
- the vibratory theory of heat
- the vital force theories of physiology
- the electromagnetic aether
- the optical aether
- the theory of circular inertia
- theories of spontaneous generation[7]

(We might add Newtonian physics.) These theories referred to entities or events that neither existed nor occurred. Moreover, these theories were not merely empirically adequate; some of them were nearly beyond question during the height of their popularity. Consider aether theories. As Laudan tells us:

---

[6] Lee Smolin, *The Trouble with Physics: The Rise of String Theory, the Fall of a Science, and What Comes Next* (Boston: Houghton Mifflin, 2006), 21.
[7] Larry Laudan, "A Confutation of Convergent Realism," *Philosophy of Science* 48, no. 1 (1981): 33.

It would be difficult to find a family of theories in this period which were as successful as aether theories; compared to them, 19th century atomism (for instance), a genuinely referring theory (on realist accounts), was a dismal failure. Indeed, on any account of empirical success which I can conceive of, non-referring 19th-century aether theories were more successful than contemporary, referring atomic theories. In this connection, it is worth recalling the remark of the great theoretical physicist, J. C. Maxwell, to the effect that the aether was better confirmed than any other theoretical entity in natural philosophy![8]

In this case, false theories were more successful than true ones. Laudan says that "optical aether theories had also made some very startling predictions, e.g., Fresnel's prediction of a bright spot at the center of the shadow of a circular disc; a surprising prediction which, when tested, proved correct. If that does not count as empirical success, nothing does!"[9] So then, we have examples of theories that were well confirmed—they matched available observations and even predicted new ones—and yet got it wrong when it came to what goes on behind the scenes.

Not only that, but aether theory worked so well that there were excellent reasons to think we had finally "arrived." The great Lord Kelvin said in 1884 that aether is "the only substance we are confident of in dynamics."[10] That is, he continued, "one thing we are sure of, and that is the reality and substantiality of the luminiferous ether."[11] Philosopher P. Kyle Stanford points out that "defenders of past scientific theories occupied at one time just the same position that we do now: they thought the evident success in prediction, explanation, and intervention afforded us by, say, Newtonian mechanics rendered it impossible or extremely unlikely that the theory was false."[12] He asks, therefore,

If the history of science really consists of a succession of increasingly successful theories making radically and fundamentally different claims about what there is in the world and how it works, why on earth would we suppose that this process has come to an end with the theories of the present day?[13]

---

[8] Ibid., 27.
[9] Ibid.
[10] Stephen Hawking and Leonard Mlodinow, *The Grand Design* (New York: Bantam, 2010), 95.
[11] Ibid.
[12] P. Kyle Stanford, *Exceeding Our Grasp: Science, History, and the Problem of Unconceived Alternatives* (Oxford: Oxford University Press, 2006), 7.
[13] Ibid.

So, given what we know about the history of science, it seems that we should at least be wary about how much stock we put in current theories, given the frequency with which theories are overturned. In fact, this argument, called the *pessimistic induction*, seems a wholly appropriate stance for the sober skeptic. As Stanford reminds us, there was always the possibility that Lucy *wouldn't* pull the ball out of Charlie Brown's way, but Charlie Brown had good reason to be skeptical.[14]

Unconceived Alternatives

There are actually two related arguments for scientific skepticism from the history of science. The first is the pessimistic induction, which says that in the past our best and well-confirmed theories turned out to be false, and therefore there's the distinct possibility that our current theories might too. The second argument is this: not only do we have examples of two or more competing theories that matched the same data, but we also have examples where the alternative theory was something we hadn't even dreamed of. Stanford calls this the *problem of unconceived alternatives*. "For example, in the historical progression from Aristotelian to Cartesian to Newtonian to contemporary mechanical theories, the evidence available at the time each earlier theory was accepted offered equally strong support to each of the (then-unimagined) later alternatives."[15]

Consider the avalanche of evidence that accumulated over the centuries during which Newtonian physics reigned supreme. This evidence convinced people not only that Newtonian physics was correct, but also that the Newtonian theory was the final step in mankind's attempts to understand the physical world (with the remaining scientific task "simply" a matter of applying Newtonian physics to more and more areas of reality). We now know that general relativity can also explain that same data, but we obviously didn't know this prior to Einstein, during the latter part of the nineteenth century. Before Einstein, relativity was an unconceived alternative. But it was still an empirically adequate possible alternative to Newtonian physics—just an alternative we didn't know about. This is pretty much the same situation for any succession of theories that progressively accounts for more and more observations: the evidence for the previous theories is also evidence for subsequent

---

[14] Ibid., 25n2.
[15] Ibid., 19.

ones. And perhaps it is the same for our theories now: there are unconceived alternatives.

Moreover, there may be countless alternatives, though we're aware
of a mere handful. After all, science is hard, and arriving at even a single
theory is a chore. Perhaps for beings with our physical and intellectual
limitations, we can really only imagine a few of the billions of (infinitely
many?) logically possible alternatives. It might be tempting to think
that we've got this science thing pretty much dialed in and that we're
near the end of the journey toward understanding fundamental physical
reality. But why think that? The ancient Egyptians could have thought
something similar; after all, they could build pyramids and make beer.
"What else is left?" Immortality? Light bulbs? Perhaps we're only near
the beginning of the scientific story, with yet millions of years left. Perhaps we're at a laughably primitive stage. And perhaps this partly explains why most attempts at formulating successful explanations of the
observable realm are just plain wrong.

The Skinny Branches

Worse yet, we must admit that we're really on the skinny branches
when it comes to, say, the subatomic realm and the structure of space
and time. And yet science-oriented arguments against God's existence
depend on such enigmatic topics. Stanford elaborates:

> And it is when we theorize about such matters as the constitution
> of matter itself, the remote history of the Earth and its inhabitants,
> the most minute workings of our bodies, and the structure of the
> farthest reaches of the universe that we would seem to be in the
> greatest danger of failing to conceive of serious alternative possibili-
> ties or even of what the space of such possibilities might look like,
> and I suggest that as a matter of historical fact this is just what we
> have repeatedly failed to do. . . . [The] evidence for the significance
> of the problem of unconceived alternatives is strongest just where
> the problem would matter most and just where it poses the most sig-
> nificant challenge to our scientific conception of the natural world:
> in our efforts to theorize about the most fundamental aspects of the
> constitution and dynamics of the various domains of nature.[16]

---

[16] Ibid., 32–33.

The fundamental nature of reality—the philosophically important stuff—may be forever beyond our ken. And in any case, it currently is.

It is clear then that a false theory can "work" and, moreover, it's possible we're in such a situation now. And this possibility isn't merely an abstract one: the history of science provides us with many examples of false theories that accurately represented observable phenomena and allowed humans to develop useful technologies.

But These Are the Best Theories *Ever*!

But there's obviously *something* to contemporary science, particularly the two pillars of physics: general relativity and quantum mechanics. (Quantum theory tells us about the domain of the extremely small world of subatomic particles, while general relativity tells us about everything else, particularly about the very large and very fast—about reality on a cosmic scale.) The success of both theories is far beyond that of Newtonian physics (which is no slouch itself: it allows us to hit a distant moving planet—or miniscule comet[17]—with a tiny satellite). Consider Richard Feynman's famous description of quantum theory's accuracy: it's as if we were to measure the distance between New York and Los Angeles within the tolerance of a single human hair.[18] If this kind of hyperbolic-sounding accuracy doesn't surprise us (and it's hard to be surprised these days), it should.

Both quantum mechanics and general relativity have been subjected to ridiculously rigorous testing—far more than any previous theory—and have passed with flying colors. Could it really be that such theories could get it wrong about the fundamental nature of the subatomic realm? That's hard to swallow. Perhaps our *previous* theories got it wrong—as surprising as that was—but it seems we have reached a whole new level of empirical adequacy, so much so that "adequate" seems a monumental understatement.

To put it differently, our current theories work in spades, and it would be a miracle if they didn't give us accurate descriptions of what is going on behind the scenes. In fact, this latter sentiment is the most powerful argument for *scientific realism*—the view that our current theories tell the truth when it comes to the unobservable world—and was memorably

---

17 "Touchdown! Rosetta's Philae Probe Lands on Comet," ESA, November 12, 2014, http://www.esa.int/Our_Activities/Space_Science/Rosetta/Touchdown!_Rosetta_s_Philae_probe_lands_on_comet.
18 Richard Phillips Feynman, *QED: The Strange Theory of Light and Matter* (Princeton, NJ: Princeton University Press, 2006), 7.

put to us by the distinguished Harvard philosopher Hilary Putnam: "The positive argument for realism is that it is the only philosophy that doesn't make the success of science a miracle."[19] And, says Stanford, this simple argument "has always been the strongest consideration in support of the realist position."[20] It's so powerful that the eminent philosopher of science Bas van Fraassen calls it "the ultimate argument," despite the fact that he's an instrumentalist and therefore doesn't believe it.[21]

Twentieth-Century Physics: As It Was in the Beginning

But the ultimate argument—the claim that only the truth of our scientific theories keeps their success from being a miracle—isn't nearly as strong once we consider the instrumentalist views of the *founders* of general relativity and quantum theory.

Consider relativity. Ironically, its founder, Einstein, is famous for his scientific realism, for his view that the goal of science is to get at the truth, not merely to match observations. Yet in his early years, while developing his theories of relativity (both special and general), he "acknowledges the influence of [Ernst] Mach and Hume, especially that of Hume whose *Treatise* he studied during his early years in Bern."[22] Both Hume and Mach were famously skeptical about the truth of unobservable scientific explanations (Mach being another progenitor of logical positivism).

Einstein's conversion to scientific realism occurred around 1920, only *after* he had developed both theories of relativity. But prior to his conversion he actually presented an argument in his 1916 paper "The Foundation of the General Theory of Relativity," in which he says that general relativity "takes away from space and time the last remnants of physical objectivity."[23] That is, space and time are not real entities, according to this paper. In fact, Einstein's early instrumentalist position was an important part of the philosophical framework responsible for the development of relativity.[24] And today, as Fine claims, "Most

---

[19] Bas C. van Fraassen, *The Scientific Image* (Oxford: Clarendon, 1980), 39.

[20] Stanford, *Exceeding Our Grasp*, 6.

[21] Van Fraassen, *The Scientific Image*, 34.

[22] Arthur Fine, *The Shaky Game: Einstein, Realism, and the Quantum Theory*, ed. David L. Hull, 2nd ed., Science and Its Conceptual Foundations (Chicago: University of Chicago Press, 1996), 15n3.

[23] The English translation was published in H. A. Lorentz et al., *The Principle of Relativity*, trans. W. Perrett and G. B. Jeffery (London: Methuen, 1923). This quotation is from p. 117.

[24] Arthur Fine, "The Natural Ontological Attitude," in *Philosophy of Science: The Central Issues*, ed. Martin Curd and J. A. Cover (New York: W. W. Norton, 1998), 1194–95. With respect to special relativity, Fine says, "Without the 'freedom from reality' provided by his early reverence for Mach, a central tumbler necessary to unlock the secret of special relativity would never have fallen into place" (Fine, *The Shaky Game*, 123).

[scientists] who actually use [general relativity] think of the theory as a powerful instrument, rather than as expressing a 'big truth.'"[25]

An instrumentalist or nonrealist position is even more pronounced in the founders of quantum mechanics. Consider Werner Heisenberg, a cocreator of quantum theory and the man responsible for his eponymous "uncertainty principle." Fine points out that

> Heisenberg's seminal paper of 1925 is prefaced by the following abstract, announcing, in effect his philosophical stance: "In this paper an attempt will be made to obtain bases for a quantum-theoretical mechanics based exclusively on relations between quantities observable in principle." In the body of the paper, Heisenberg not only rejects any reference to unobservables, he also moves away from the very idea that one should try to form any picture of a reality underlying his mechanics.[26]

Other founding fathers of quantum mechanics agree. Although Erwin Schrödinger originally tried to visualize what his famous (and eponymous) equation said about the unobservable realm, he quickly demurred from any realistic interpretation.[27] Niels Bohr is famous for his ongoing debate with Einstein about whether quantum theory should be interpreted realistically. It is Bohr's notion of complementarity—a kind of uneasy agree-to-disagree situation between what seem to be contradictory aspects of the subatomic world—that further emboldened the instrumentalist interpretation of quantum mechanics. Fine explains:

> This nonrealist position was consolidated at the time of the famous Solvay Conference, in October 1927, and is firmly in place today. Such quantum nonrealism is part of what every graduate physicist learns and practices. It is the conceptual backdrop to all the brilliant successes in atomic, nuclear, and particle physics over the past fifty years. Physicists have learned to think about their theory in a highly nonrealist way, and doing just that has brought about the most marvelous predictive success in the history of science.[28]

If this is right, then today's two main physical theories had instrumentalist or nonrealist foundations.

---

[25] Fine, "The Natural Ontological Attitude," 1194–95.
[26] Ibid., 1195.
[27] Fine, *The Shaky Game*, 124.
[28] Ibid.

The Copenhagen Interpretation and Quantum Cookery

In quantum theory, the mathematics or formalism is relatively straight-forward in that it's clear how to *do* the math. John Gribbin calls this "quantum cookery": scientists can readily follow the mathematical recipes.[29] What isn't clear, however, is how the mathematics should be *interpreted*, that is, what the math *says* about the unobservable realm. And this is why quantum theory is so often interpreted instrumentally. There's simply no consensus on such matters, even today. Physicist Lee Smolin says, "It is true that there is only one mathematical formalism for the quantum theory. So physicists have no problem with going ahead and using the theory, even though they do not agree what it means."[30] Moreover, says Smolin, this seems to be a sensitive topic, dirty laundry that physics would rather not air in public.

> While many leading physicists admit private misgivings about quantum mechanics, their public stance is that its problems were settled back in the 1920s. A scholarly account of the later work on its foundations does not exist, but I know that since at least the 1950s, the leading journals have only very selectively published papers on this subject, while several journals have excluded such papers by stated policy.[31]

But when pressed for an interpretation of quantum mechanics, most physicists will likely retreat to the so-called Copenhagen interpretation. But this interpretation paints a picture of the quantum world that violates many of our views of what reality could even be like. For example, we normally visualize atoms as Bohr's "solar system" model, where planetary electrons orbit the solar nucleus. This is a helpful heuristic, but also entirely misleading. Gribbin says, "It isn't just that Bohr's atom with its electron 'orbits' is a false picture; *all* pictures are false, and there is no physical analogy we can make to understand what goes on inside atoms. Atoms behave like atoms, nothing else."[32] He continues with these ominous words: "*Nobody* understands what 'really' goes on in atoms."[33] Sir Arthur Eddington

---

[29] John Gribbin, *In Search of Schrödinger's Cat: Quantum Physics and Reality* (New York: Bantam, 1984), 118.
[30] Lee Smolin, *Three Roads to Quantum Gravity* (New York: Basic Books, 2001), 34.
[31] Smolin, *The Trouble with Physics*, 323.
[32] Gribbin, *In Search of Schrödinger's Cat*, 92.
[33] Ibid., 94.

once put it this way: in the atom, "something unknown is doing we don't know what."[34]

One problem is that, according to quantum mechanics, subatomic particles like electrons do not *have* a definite position and momentum prior to our measuring them. A *single* particle isn't really a "particle" as we understand the term, but instead can act like a wave (while not being a wave either). "Particles" are smeared, ghostly entities unlike anything we can visualize or even imagine. Indeed, as Gribbin says, "A fundamental entity such as an electron is neither a particle nor a wave . . . (really, of course, it is a slithy tove)."[35] Bohr is famous for saying that anyone not shocked by quantum mechanics hasn't understood it.[36] (And don't even ask about Schrödinger's cat.)

xkcd.com

So the Copenhagen interpretation does the work of a battlefield medic—it staunches the bleeding, but only so the patient can survive

---

[34] Ibid., 92.

[35] Ibid., 118.

[36] The context of the quotation is relevant to our discussion of skepticism, especially to the lack of skepticism toward science that the logical positivists sometimes exhibited. According to Werner Heisenberg, in the summer of 1952, Bohr recalled a lecture he gave in Copenhagen, saying:

> Some time ago there was a meeting of philosophers, most of them positivists, here in Copenhagen, during which members of the Vienna Circle played a prominent part. I was asked to address them on the interpretation of quantum theory. After my lecture, no one raised any objections or asked any embarrassing questions, but I must say this very fact proved a terrible disappointment to me. For those who are not shocked when they first come across quantum theory cannot possibly have understood it.

Werner Heisenberg, *Physics and Beyond: Encounters and Conversations*, ed. Ruth Nanda Anshen, World Perspectives (New York: Harper & Row, 1971), 205–6.

long enough to receive proper care. For now, at least, the interpretation allows "any competent physicist to solve problems involving atoms and molecules, with no great need for thought about the fundamentals but a simple willingness to follow the recipe book and turn out the answers."[37] It's safe to say that no one understands quantum mechanics (safe because Feynman himself said this),[38] and so we're almost *compelled* to take an instrumentalist view of it. In fact, Fine says that instrumentalism is "the accepted outlook on quantum theory":

> What I have in mind is the easygoing pragmatism of the quantum theory. For the theory is most often seen as merely a coherent framework for the deduction (or "prediction") of experimental consequences and a framework whose principle justification lies in its uncanny success in this enterprise.[39]

Does Quantum Theory Explain?

Another way of putting all this is that quantum theory isn't an explanation of the physical world; it doesn't tell us what's really going on at the subatomic level behind the observable scenes. When pressed on this issue in an interview, physicist John Bell (of Bell's theorem fame) responded:

> Well, it [quantum theory] does not really explain things; in fact the founding fathers of quantum mechanics rather prided themselves on giving up the idea of explanation. They were very proud that they dealt only with phenomena: they refused to look behind the phenomena, regarding that as the price one had to pay for coming to terms with nature. And it is a fact of history that the people who took that agnostic attitude towards the real world on the microphysical level were very successful.[40]

In fact, this is just how the logical positivists viewed science, and even Bell suggests a Humean strain in all this. "If you go back to, say, David

---

[37] Jan Faye, "Copenhagen Interpretation of Quantum Mechanics," in *Stanford Encyclopedia of Philosophy*, ed. Edward N. Zalta (Stanford, CA: Metaphysics Research Lab, CSLI, Stanford University, 2014), 121.
[38] "I think I can safely say that nobody understands quantum mechanics" (Richard Phillips Feynman, *The Character of Physical Law* [Cambridge: M.I.T. Press), 1965], 129).
[39] Fine, *The Shaky Game*, 22.
[40] J. R. Brown and P. C. W. Davies, eds., *The Ghost in the Atom: A Discussion of the Mysteries of Quantum Physics* (Cambridge: Cambridge University Press, 1995), 51.

Hume, who made a careful analysis of our reasons for believing things, you find that there is no good reason for believing that the sun will come up tomorrow, or that this programme will ever be broadcast."[41] Again, our study of Hume was no coincidence or philosophical nicety. The founders of quantum mechanics consciously took a Humean attitude toward the theory. Listen for Hume's ghost in Fine's statement about this foundational period: "The quantum theory that developed in 1925 to 1927 was quickly interpreted . . . as providing *no more than* a device for coordinating the outcomes of all conceivable experimental procedures."[42] And as we saw, this Hume-inspired instrumentalism is popular even among today's physicists.

Hawking and Instrumentalism

Let's return to the world's top physicist. It may not be surprising to learn that Hawking is a type of instrumentalist when it comes to physics. In his book *The Grand Design*, which we've met, he identifies his attitude toward scientific theories (or models) as "model-dependent realism," which turns out to be no realism at all. He says that "a physical theory or world picture is a model (generally of a mathematical nature) and a set of rules that connect elements of the model to observations."[43]

> According to the idea of model-independent realism . . . our brains interpret the input from our sensory organs by making a model of the outside world. We form mental concepts of our home, trees, other people, the electricity that flows from wall sockets, atoms, molecules, and other universes. These mental concepts are the only reality we can know. There is no model-independent test of reality. It follows that a well-constructed model creates a reality of its own.[44]

Notice that Hawking is playing off the representationalist theory of perception, which, you'll recall, says that we never come into direct epistemic contact with the external world. When we see a table, for example, we really have only cognitive contact with the idea, the (alleged) representation of that table outside our minds. We don't ever directly

---

[41] Ibid.
[42] Fine, *The Shaky Game*, 94; emphasis original.
[43] Hawking and Mlodinow, *The Grand Design*, 43.
[44] Ibid., 172.

perceive that there's an external world or that we're not brains in vats or that we're not hooked up to the Matrix.[45]

The view that our scientific theories give us the sober truth about the unobservable world, says Hawking, is simply one we can no longer rationally accept.

> Though realism may be a tempting viewpoint . . . what we know about modern physics makes it a difficult one to defend. For example, according to the principles of quantum physics, which is an accurate description of nature, a particle has neither a definite position nor a definite velocity unless and until those quantities are measured by an observer.[46]

In the case of geocentricity and heliocentricity, Hawking says that "although it is not uncommon for people to say that Copernicus proved Ptolemy wrong, that is not true."[47] He explains:

> One can use either picture as a model of the universe, for our observations of the heavens can be explained by either the earth or the sun to be at rest. Despite its role in philosophical debates over the nature of the universe, the real advantage of the Copernican system is that the equations of motion are much simpler in the frame of reference in which the sun is at rest.[48]

In fact, he says, "These examples bring us to a conclusion that . . . *There is no picture- or theory-independent concept of reality.*"[49]

Hawking's instrumentalism isn't limited to scientific theories. Representationalism means that nonrealism infects all our beliefs about the external world. "We make models in science, but we also make them in everyday life. Model-dependent realism applies not only to scientific models but also to the conscious and subconscious mental models we all create in order to interpret and understand the everyday world."[50] That is, everyday objects like "home, trees, other people" are really only ontological posits that make our "theory" of the external world coherent

---

[45] Ibid., 42.
[46] Ibid., 44. By "an accurate description of nature" he presumably means "an accurate description of *observable* parts of nature."
[47] Ibid., 41.
[48] Ibid.
[49] Ibid., 43; emphasis original.
[50] Ibid., 46.

and relatively simple. This view is similar to Quine's uncompromising (and influential) version of empiricism. The following quotation from him is historically important:

> As an empiricist I continue to think of the conceptual scheme of science as a tool, ultimately, for predicting future experience in light of past experience. Physical objects are conceptually imported into the situation as convenient intermediaries—not by definition in terms of experience, but simply as irreducible posits comparable, epistemologically, to the gods of Homer. For my part I do, qua lay physicist, believe in physical objects and not in Homer's gods; and I consider it a scientific error to believe otherwise. But in point of epistemological footing the physical objects and the gods differ only in degree and not in kind. The myth of physical objects is epistemologically superior to most in that it has proved more efficacious than other myths as a device for working a manageable structure into the flux of experience.[51]

So then, we're back to taking our Humean condition seriously, where even garden-variety objects like tables, chairs, and people aren't directly observed. The reason to believe in these things seems to be merely pragmatic for empiricists like Quine, Hume, and Hawking. That is, the "story" of physical objects provides an explanation for a large swath of sensory experience. Hawking says that "the model in which the table stays put [and doesn't disappear when we leave the room] is much simpler and agrees with observation. That is all one can ask."[52]

But Hawking goes further. His model-independent "realism" becomes not only an *epistemological* position about what we're justified to rationally believe, but a borderline *metaphysical* position about the nature of reality itself. Not only can't we *know* for certain whether our theories are true, but, suggests Hawking, there *is no* fact of the matter which of these theories is true.

> Model-dependent realism short-circuits all this argument and discussion between the realist and anti-realist schools of thought. According to model-independent realism, it is pointless to ask whether a model is real, only whether it agrees with observation. If there are

---

[51] W. V. Quine, "Two Dogmas of Empiricism," in Curd and Cover, *Philosophy of Science*, 298.
[52] Hawking and Mlodinow, *The Grand Design*, 47.

two models that both agree with observation . . . then one cannot say that one is more real than another.[53]

This can sound like full-blown metaphysical *anti*realism, and in any case, sounds like Hume-inspired logical positivism. Hawking even goes so far as to say that although the Big Bang model of the universe's origin is more useful than the Genesis account, "neither model can be said to be more real than the other."[54] This is pretty surprising coming from an avowed atheist.

What Does Success Prove?

My point is to argue against the view that success equals truth. That is, just because a theory matches all the available data doesn't mean that it's true. Let's face it: science is hard and truth is a high bar. You can't always get what you want; but you find that sometimes you get what you need. The question is, what *do* we need scientific theories for? Well there's no consensus on that; it depends on who you ask. But we've seen that we at least need theories to match observations. And perhaps, given that we can't be sure that our theories tell the truth about unobservable reality, we should rest content with empirical adequacy. That is, maybe we shouldn't insist that a theory tell us the truth about unobservable subatomic particles or gravitational fields, as long as the world behaves *as if* there are such entities. In other words, we may need to lower the bar to meet the standards we can achieve. Perhaps to ask for anything more is to cry for the moon. But again, it's really a matter of temperament and entirely up to you.

That's not to say that instrumentalists wouldn't prefer a theory that tells the truth about what goes on backstage, about posited-but-unobservable entities like electrons and quarks (sometimes called *theoretical entities*); it's just that this further requirement isn't necessary for a theory to be counted a success. Moreover, it's useful, instrumentalists say, to play along with the theory, to speak and behave *as if* there really are quarks. But we need not—in our contemplative moments—literally believe in quarks. The theory need not be true: it need only work.

Instrumentalism might seem to some like a radical, subversive, or even backward view, embraced only by those who wish—for one reason

---

[53] Ibid., 46.
[54] Ibid., 51.

or another—to discredit science in the face of its undeniable success. Isn't it simply postmodern silliness or modern religious obscurantism?

Well, we've already seen that the world's most famous physicist says he's a radical instrumentalist. But in fact instrumentalism goes all the way back to the beginning of Western science. In ancient Greece, the great Plato challenged his academy to come up with a mathematical description of the heavens' complex pattern of motions. His pupil and friend, the mathematician Eudoxus, was the first to provide such a theory: an intricate combination of twenty-seven spheres. Neither Plato nor Eudoxus considered these spheres to be real physical structures, the actual mechanical causes propelling planets about the skies.[55] Rather, the system was only a mathematical (geometrical) tool for describing and predicting the motion of the planets, sun, moon, and stars. As long as the theory "saved the phenomena," that is, accurately captured the appearances or observations, Plato deemed it a success.[56]

Plato's student Aristotle complicated things—as he usually did—disagreeing with his mentor, supposing the spheres of Eudoxus's system to be actual, solid crystalline spheres composed of a fifth element, aether or quintessence ("fifth essence"). Nevertheless, as the mathematical system of spheres became more and more convoluted over the centuries, with the addition of epicycles and eccentric circles, the likelihood that these intersecting mathematical devices were solid spheres became more remote. And even the great Ptolemy himself—through whom Europe inherited geocentric astronomy—seems to have taken an instrumentalist attitude toward his canonical theory laid out in the *Almagest* (which means "the greatest" in Arabic).

As science became more and more mathematical, scientists became increasingly cautious about the epistemological status of unobservable phenomena. Galileo, as we saw, eschewed the invisible and mysterious Aristotelian natures that had been posited as the cause of an object's fall to the ground. And remember that Newton himself even expressed skepticism about the cause of "gravity," refusing to speculate on what gravity might actually be.

So then, we measure success in science largely by evaluating how well

---

[55] The renowned historian of mathematics Sir Thomas Heath said that Eudoxus "wouldn't indulge in vain physical speculations on things which were inaccessible to observation" (Thomas Heath, *A History of Greek Mathematics*, vol.1, *From Thales to Euclid* [Mineola, NY: Dover, 1981], 323).

[56] See the seminal work by Pierre Duhem, *To Save the Phenomena: An Essay on the Idea of Physical Theory from Plato to Galileo* (Chicago: University of Chicago Press, 1969).

the theory saves the phenomena or matches what we can observe. To put it differently, the dramatic success of science is primarily measured in terms of what we can observe, including technological applications. And as we've said, insofar as scientific theories match observations—insofar as they are empirically adequate—they're wildly successful. But this doesn't prove that they're true. So Dawkins's claim that science works doesn't get him as far as he'd like.

The Miracle of Science

There are, therefore, decent reasons for being skeptical about scientific realism, about whether our current scientific theories give us the sober truth about the world ever-beyond observations. In the previous chapter we saw that developing scientific theories takes more than logic and observation, requiring also creativity and judgment calls. In this chapter we saw that matching past, present, and future observations through experiments and technology doesn't necessitate that a scientific theory get the story about unobservables correct. But there is another power-ful bit of evidence for thinking that our best theories in physics aren't *true*. As we'll see in the next chapter, important aspects of relativity and quantum theory will probably go the way of all flesh. That is, there is reason to believe that science itself thinks that our contemporary theo-ries are headed for that great laboratory in the sky. And so, though it seems highly improbable that such well-confirmed theories could get the fundamental picture of (unobservable) reality so wrong, there are further reasons for thinking that miracles happen.

8

The Current Crisis

In the last chapter we considered reasons to think that science might not tell the sober truth about the world beyond observation. Science, if those considerations are anywhere near correct, may not be an entirely reliable source of knowledge about the *fundamental* structure of the cosmos, despite its reliability about more proximate matters.

But maybe you're not convinced. Even if it's *possible* that science gets it wrong about the fundamental makeup of physical reality, science may in fact get it right for all we know. This is certainly an excusable view, but it is probably wrong, and for a reason we haven't yet considered: according to science itself, important aspects of our current physical theories are false.

A Brief History of Physics

Modern science was born during the Scientific Revolution of the 1600s, the culmination of which was Newtonian physics.[1] It was a *revolution* because Newton ended Aristotle's two-thousand-year scientific reign. One of the main achievements of Newtonian physics was the mathematization of motion: Newton invented calculus to describe the seemingly chaotic behavior of physical objects, and in uncanny detail. Even today we view the world through Newtonian physics. Indeed, it is such an

---

[1] Physics, by the way, describes the most basic constituents of physical reality: matter, energy, space, and time. The study of such constituents began in earnest in ancient Greece. Indeed, this was really the beginning of Western philosophy, and it came to be called *natural philosophy*. In fact, the Greek word for "physics" is *physis*, which means "nature."

inextricable part of our worldview that it seems no more than common sense, whereas at the time it was anything but.

During the seventeenth and eighteenth centuries, scientists applied Newtonian physics to ever-more phenomena, predicting and describing the world so stunningly that other disciplines—for example, chemistry and biology—tried to ape physics' method. Indeed, the Newtonian picture was so successful and comprehensive that in 1900 Lord Kelvin announced that physics was complete, with only some mopping-up operations needed, perhaps to deal with two "dark clouds" on the horizon. But these clouds, Lee Smolin explains, "turned out to be the clues that led us to quantum theory and relativity theory."[2]

General relativity and quantum mechanics shocked the world with their appearance in the first three decades of the 1900s, and together they account for the entire universe, including nature's four fundamental forces and all the elementary particles out of which the universe is made—whether these particles are entirely at rest or approaching the speed of light.[3] Although Newtonian mechanics is an excellent approximation for medium-sized dry goods at velocities far below the speed of light, when we address the most fundamental aspects of physical reality—when the universe "red lines"—physics becomes an extreme sport and we need quantum mechanics and general relativity.

And they need one another. Neither of them can account for physical reality alone, and so there's a division of labor between them.[4] Quantum mechanics takes care of the subatomic world; general relativity handles everything else. General relativity also treats gravity, which doesn't exist in the eyes of quantum theory. Like spouses, each completes the other.

A Strained Relationship

But the marriage has been rocky from the start. In fact, it began with a shotgun wedding. The division of labor, despite its practical success, was forced upon physicists, really. Our two pillars of physics are logi-

---

[2] Lee Smolin, *The Trouble with Physics: The Rise of String Theory, the Fall of a Science, and What Comes Next* (Boston: Houghton Mifflin, 2006), 13.

[3] Physicist Michio Kaku explains, "Remarkably, these two theories together embody the sum total of all human knowledge concerning the most fundamental forces of Nature" (Michio Kaku, *Introduction to Superstrings and M-Theory*, 2nd ed., Graduate Texts in Contemporary Physics [New York: Springer, 1999], 3).

[4] There are two theories of relativity, both developed by Einstein: the special theory of relativity and the general theory of relativity. *Special* in this case, means "specific" or "narrow" or "species," while *general* means, well, "general" (i.e., from *genera*).

cally incompatible with one another, and so at least one of them is wrong. They tell different stories about the unobservable world. As physicist Brian Greene writes, "When the equations of general relativity commingle with those of quantum mechanics, the result is disastrous. The equations break down entirely."[5] Michio Kaku says that "the great mystery of the past five decades . . . has been the total incompatibility of these two theories."[6]

But they've stayed together through the years just for us kids. We need both of them because so much of our lives are built upon each. They each work astoundingly well in their respective realms, despite always arguing when together.

Although this is common knowledge among family members— among physicists—few outsiders have heard of the irreconcilable differences between general relativity and quantum mechanics. Greene says that the reason for this is not hard to find:

> In all but the most extreme situations, physicists study things that are either small and light (like atoms and their constituents) or things that are huge and heavy (like stars and galaxies), but not both. This means that they need use only quantum mechanics *or* only general relativity and can, with a furtive glance, shrug off the barking admonition of the other.[7]

But it's not as if the fundamental inconsistency has been entirely ignored, and it couldn't have been, in any case. Physics needs a theory that can combine or unify these disparate phenomena. For example, there are physical situations where physicists would really like to use *both* theories simultaneously. There are, Greene points out, "extreme physical situations that are both massive and tiny."[8] Two such extreme cases are, he says, "the center of a black hole, in which an entire star has been crushed by its own weight to a miniscule point, and the big bang, in which the entire observable universe is imagined to have been compressed to a nugget far smaller than a single atom."[9] Normally, in the

---

[5] Brian R. Greene, *The Fabric of the Cosmos: Space, Time, and the Texture of Reality* (New York: Vintage, 2004), 15.
[6] Kaku, *Introduction to Superstrings and M-Theory*, 3.
[7] Brian R. Greene, *The Elegant Universe: Superstrings, Hidden Dimensions, and the Quest for the Ultimate Theory* (New York: W. W. Norton, 2003), 3–4.
[8] Greene, *The Fabric of the Cosmos*, 17.
[9] Ibid.

quantum realm, the force of gravity is negligible because it's so weak, being vastly overpowered by the other three[10] (e.g., even a small magnet can overcome the force of gravity when it lifts a paper clip off the desk). But when the mass of a star or a universe is packed into a volume smaller than an atom, we have to take gravity into account along with quantum effects. In other words, we need a theory of *quantum gravity*.

Unfortunately, this is the one thing we *don't* have. So physics is radically incomplete: there are two fundamental and incompatible theories, and each can be applied only within its respective realm. It would be really nice to have a single theory, a unified theory of everything, but we don't. Physics, says Smolin, is in a genuine state of crisis: "Presently we are in a crucial period during which the laws of physics are being rewritten—just as they were between 1890 and 1910, when the revolutions in twentieth-century physics that led to relativity and quantum physics began."[11] The good news is that these are exciting times in physics; the bad news is that such times also try men's souls.

String Theory

So then, the top item on physicists' to-do list is to develop a quantum theory of gravity, since our current theory of gravity—general relativity—is incompatible with quantum mechanics. Thankfully, physicists have a wildly popular candidate for this theory: *superstring theory* (or sometimes just *string theory*).[12] The theory took off in 1984, during the *first superstring revolution*, with a fervor that has yet to subside.

String theory requires us to (yet again) radically change our views about fundamental reality. We get to retain our current zoo of particles, like electrons, quarks, and other more exotic species, but these particles are no longer considered *elementary* or fundamental; instead, they're composed of strings.

According to superstring theory, every particle is composed of a tiny filament of energy, some hundred billion billion times smaller

---

[10] The other three forces, you ask? The electromagnetic force, the weak nuclear force, and the strong nuclear force.

[11] Lee Smolin, *Three Roads to Quantum Gravity* (New York: Basic Books, 2001), 96.

[12] String theory's full name is *supersymmetric string theory*, often shortened to *superstring theory*. And though its close friends call it *string theory*, all three names refer to the same thing. To complicate matters, however, there was a very early ancestor from the early 1970s called simply *string theory*. No *super* was ever attached to it, even though Super Fly was a popular name at the time. This early string theory's full Christian name was *bosonic string theory* (Greene, *The Fabric of the Cosmos*, 354–55).

than a single atomic nucleus (much smaller than we can currently probe), which is shaped like a little string. And just as a violin string can vibrate in different patterns, each of which produces a musical tone, the filaments of superstring theory can also vibrate in different patterns. These vibrations, though, don't produce different musical notes; remarkably, the theory claims that they produce different particle properties.[13]

String theory unifies all the elementary particles into a single kind. Such unification makes string theory extremely attractive, since with unification comes understanding. String theory therefore *explains why* particles like electrons, quarks, and leptons have the characteristics they have. Moreover, in addition to being a theory of quantum gravity, the theory accounts for all four forces, making it a *theory of everything*, a single theory that elegantly unifies all of physics.[14]

Just as general relativity overhauled our view of space and time—with its melding of the two into a single entity (spacetime) that can warp and bend—our view of the universe's dimensions must again change. String theory says that our universe is actually composed of nine spatial dimensions along with a single time dimension. If string theory is correct, then our universe has ten dimensions instead of the four we currently observe.[15]

Let me pause just a moment to point out how philosophically and historically coincidental it is that the elementary particles are *strings*. The Western agenda to describe the cosmos mathematically began with strings. The first humans to take seriously the idea that the cosmos is mathematical in nature were the Pythagoreans of ancient Greece. And the discovery that alerted them to our fundamentally mathematical world was that the intervals of vibrating strings could be represented as ratios of whole numbers (i.e., octave, fifth, fourth, etc.). After that, the fire would not be put out. And although the entire discipline of physics is a testimony to the Pythagoreans, with string theory everything has come full circle.

---

[13] Ibid., 17–18.
[14] Smolin, *The Trouble with Physics*, xiii–xiv. There's another, less popular candidate for a theory of quantum gravity: loop quantum gravity. This theory, however, is not a full unified theory of everything but merely focuses on the much more modest (yet still nearly impossible) task of combining gravity with quantum theory.
[15] Greene, *The Fabric of the Cosmos*, 18.

M-Theory: The Mother of All String Theories

As it turns out, though, there are five different kinds of string theories, each with characteristics working in its respective domain. Michio Kaku—one of the contributors to string theory—says that "for a theory that makes the claim of providing a unifying framework for all physical laws, it is the supreme irony that the theory itself appears so disunited!"[16] That is, he says, "*The theory itself is not unified.* To someone learning the theory for the first time, it is often a frustrating collection of folklore, rules of thumb, and intuition. At times, there seems to be no rhyme or reason for many of the conventions of the model."[17] So string theory may not be the final theory we were looking for. But there are hopes for combining these various string theories into a single theory. In 1995, physicist Edward Witten—also part of the initial string-theory push—gave a talk that started the *second superstring revolution.* In this lecture, he suggested that there might be a unifying theory, which he called "M-theory" (without indicating what the *M* might stand for, since his proposal was only of a possible-but-unknown theory).[18]

We met M-theory when Hawking and Mlodinow employed it in their argument for a universe spawned from nothing. M-theory, recall, is "the unified theory Einstein was hoping to find,"[19] the one that will, after three thousand years, show us the "grand design."[20] In any case, Hawking and Mlodinow explain that M-theory is a "network of theories" in which each theory "is good at describing phenomena within a certain range."[21] Of course, this sounds very much like our current situation, where general relativity and quantum mechanics each adequately deals with its respective domain, yet in some ways worse. Instead of merely two patches in the theoretical quilt, we now have five.

But maybe it's not as bad as it sounds. Let's assume so. And with this newfound (albeit forced) optimistic mind-set, we can agree that M-theory is a patchwork of mathematical models that, taken together, gets us close to a unified theory of everything. The different theories—the individual patches—tell stories about different physical realms, but each is suited to its individual job. We might call this "situational physics."

---

[16] Kaku, *Introduction to Superstrings and M-Theory*, 5.
[17] Ibid.; emphasis original.
[18] Smolin, *The Trouble with Physics*, 129, 136.
[19] Stephen Hawking and Leonard Mlodinow, *The Grand Design* (New York: Bantam, 2010), 181.
[20] Ibid.
[21] Ibid., 58.

Though M-theory is still a form of string theory and so includes one-dimensional strings, there are also higher-dimensional entities. The next entity in the hierarchy is a two-dimensional *membrane*, or a *two-brane*. (Maybe we can think of the *M* as standing for *membrane*.)[22] Strings, by the way, are called *one-branes*; and three-dimensional entities, *three-branes*. You can see the pattern here. All entities generally are called *p-branes*. I didn't make that up.

M-theory also requires an additional spatial dimension over the individual string theories, bringing the total dimensions to eleven.[23]

Not Enough Evidence

But there are very serious problems with all forms of superstring theory, including M-theory. A particularly troublesome one is that there isn't any empirical evidence for them—nor, perhaps, can there be. This is a pretty dismal situation for *empiricism*, "the official epistemology of science." One of the problems related to this lack of empirical support is that there are a lot of individual string theories within the five classes of string theories, as many as 10^{500}. And this is one of those cases where more isn't better, as Smolin explains:

> With such a vast number of theories, there is little hope that we can identify an outcome of an experiment that would not be encompassed by one of them. Thus, no matter what the experiments show, string theory cannot be disproved. But the reverse also holds: No experiment will ever be able to prove it.[24]

So then, when it comes to experimentally verifying any form of string theory, Smolin says, "we face a paradox."[25] "Those string theories that we know how to study are known to be wrong. Those we cannot study are thought to exist in such vast numbers that no conceivable experiment could ever disagree with all of them."[26] Peter Woit at Columbia University agrees: "Many string theorists have become convinced that superstring theory inherently must allow an astronomically large number of possibilities, so many that it is difficult to see how the theory

---

[22] Smolin, *The Trouble with Physics*, 135.
[23] Walter Wilcox, *Quantum Particles and Principles* (Boca Raton, FL: CRC, 2012), 476.
[24] Smolin, *The Trouble with Physics*, xiv.
[25] Ibid.
[26] Ibid.

can ever be tested."[27] Also, says Woit, string theory "is at the moment unarguably an example of a theory that can't be falsified, since it makes no predictions."[28] Kaku too points out problems regarding experimental evidence for string theories:

> It is impossible experimentally to reach the tremendous energies found at the Planck scale. Therefore, the theory is in some sense untestable. A theory that is untestable is not an acceptable physical theory. . . . [Moreover,] not one shred of experimental evidence has been found to confirm the existence of supersymmetry, let alone superstrings.[29]

The situation is deliciously ironic. British atheist Bertrand Russell once said that if God were to ask him in the afterlife why he wasn't a believer, he would respond, "Not enough evidence, God! Not enough evidence!"[30] Russell's reply nicely summarizes every unbeliever's creed. Recall, for example, Hitchens's uncharacteristically dull-witted claim that there's not a shred of respectable evidence for God's existence.

Not enough evidence indeed.

Beauty and Elegance

You might wonder why physicists would be so enthusiastic about a theory that has no empirical confirmation (as yet). Well, one reason is that string theory promises to be extremely elegant and beautiful.

---

[27] Peter Woit, *Not Even Wrong: The Failure of String Theory and the Search for Unity in Physical Law* (New York: Basic Books, 2006), xi.

[28] Ibid., 207.

[29] Kaku, *Introduction to Superstrings and M-Theory*, 17.

[30] At least this is how it's usually phrased. In *Mind, Language and Society* philosopher John Searle recounts the following story of Russell's celebrated quip:

> The impatient reader may well wonder when I am going to take a stand on the existence of God. Actually, I think the best remark on this question was made by Bertrand Russell at a dinner I attended as an undergraduate. Since this incident has passed into legend, and since a similar incident occurred on another occasion when I was not present, I think I should tell the reader what actually happened as I remember it.
>
>   Periodically, every two years or so, the Voltaire Society, a society of intellectually inclined undergraduates at Oxford, held a banquet with Bertrand Russell—the official patron of the society. On the occasion in question, we all went up to London and had dinner with Russell at a restaurant. He was then in his mideighties, and had a reputation as a famous atheist. To many of us, the question seemed pressing as to what sort of prospects for immortality Russell entertained, and we put it to him: Suppose you have been wrong about the existence of God. Suppose that the whole story were true, and that you arrived at the Pearly Gates to be admitted by Saint Peter. Having denied God's existence all your life, what would you say to . . . Him? Russell answered without a moment's hesitation. "Well, I would go up to Him, and I would say, 'You didn't give us enough evidence!'"

John R. Searle, *Mind, Language and Society: Philosophy in the Real World* (New York: Basic Books, 1998), 36–37.

And there's good precedent that these virtues indicate that a scientific theory is true. After all, Einstein developed his theories of relativity long before he had any empirical support, guided largely by aesthetic considerations.

But some physicists see this as a bad thing. João Magueijo places much of the blame for superstring's high enthusiasm-to-evidence ratio at Einstein's feet:

> Unfortunately, Einstein himself bears a lot of the responsibility for having brought about this state of affairs in fundamental physics. . . . He became more mystical and started to believe that mathematical beauty alone, rather than experimentation, could point scientists in the right direction. Regretfully, when he discovered general relativity—employing this strategy—he succeeded! And this experience spoiled him for the rest of his life.[31]

Of course, one could do worse than taking Einstein as one's example in physics. But then again, not everyone is an Einstein. Not even the later Einstein.

Do String Theories Exist?

There's actually an even more fundamental problem with all variations on the string-theory theme. Smolin says that "many string theorists talk and write as if the existence of those extra dimensions and particles were an assured fact, one that no good scientist can doubt."[32] Even more, they talk as if there *are* these string theories, which can be a little misleading. But unfortunately there *is* no mathematical formulation of string theory.

> The story of string theory is not easy to tell, because even now we do not really know what string theory is. We know a great deal about it, enough to know that it is something really marvelous. We know much about how to carry out certain kinds of calculations in string theory. . . . But we do not have a good definition of it, nor do we know what its fundamental principles are.[33]

---

[31] Woit, *Not Even Wrong*, 191.

[32] Smolin, *The Trouble with Physics*, xvi.

[33] Smolin, *Three Roads to Quantum Gravity*, 149. Smolin isn't an outsider, either. He has worked on string theory: "There have been periods when I avidly believed in string theory and devoted myself to solving its key problems. While I didn't solve them, I wrote eighteen papers in the subject; thus, the mistakes

One famous proponent of string theory—Leonard Susskind—jokes that the theory is elegant in the extreme:

> Elegance requires that the number of defining equations be small. Five is better than ten, and one is better than five. On this score, one might facetiously say that String Theory is the ultimate epitome of elegance. . . . The number [of equations] at present count is zero. We know neither what the fundamental equations of the theory are nor even if it has any.[34]

Now, it may be that superstring theory—in the form of M-theory or some future descendent—will confirm that patience and hard work are still virtues. But the situation in contemporary physics is unique and therefore calls for a certain amount of caution, even if it's of the hopeful kind. As Woit puts it:

> No matter how things turn out, the story of superstring theory is an episode with no real parallel in the history of modern physical science. More than twenty years of intensive research by thousands of the best scientists in the world producing tens of thousands of scientific papers has not led to a single testable experimental prediction of the theory.[35]

And indeed it has now been several decades since the first superstring revolution. And though, as we saw, scientists aren't going to give up at the first sign of trouble, it's safe to say that we're past the first few signs. But if you love a theory, it's hard to put it down. Call it the "Old Yeller Syndrome."

Scientific Skepticism?

The situation in physics is obviously vastly more complicated than anything we could look at here. But we can reasonably say this: physics is

---

. . . are my mistakes as much as anyone else's" (Smolin, *The Trouble with Physics*, xviii). Smolin is now a proponent of loop quantum gravity. As noted above, this theory isn't as ambitious as superstring theory: it's "merely" an attempt at a quantum theory of gravity and not a potential "theory of everything." Brian Greene says, "In fact, the mathematics of string theory is so complicated that, to date, no one even knows the exact equations of the theory" (Greene, *The Elegant Universe*, 19). And see Carlo Rovelli's remarks in John Horgan, "Quantum Gravity Expert Says 'Philosophical Superficiality' Has Harmed Physics," *Scientific American*, August 21, 2014, http://blogs.scientificamerican.com/cross-check/2014/08/21/quantum -gravity-expert-says-philosophical-superficiality-has-harmed-physics/.
[34] Woit, *Not Even Wrong*, 199.
[35] Ibid., 203.

in a bit of a jam.[36] We have decent reasons for thinking that our two best theories—general relativity and quantum mechanics—are false in important ways and that the best candidates for a replacement theory are inchoate, untested, and maybe untest*able*. Perhaps the future will show that the bets on string theories were well placed.

But given the tentativeness in contemporary physics, why would anyone trumpet claims about what science has shown about God's existence? If we have reason to be skeptical about what our scientific theories tell us about the unobservable parts of *physical* reality, why would we believe what they imply about a nonphysical reality? Why believe what false theories (allegedly) imply about topics even further removed from the topics they get wrong? Good skeptics will be wary of both.

So why aren't they?

---

[36] While writing this, I came across an article by George Ellis and Joe Silk, "Scientific Method: Defend the Integrity of Physics," *Nature*, December 16, 2014, http://www.nature.com/news/scientific-method-defend-the-integrity-of-physics-1.16535. The article summary says, "Attempts to exempt speculative theories of the universe from experimental verification undermine science, argue George Ellis and Joe Silk."

9

Physics-Based Metaphysics

Let's take stock. We've been looking at reasons to cool our jets when it comes to thinking science has things dialed in. We've seen, I hope, that a decent case can be made that science doesn't tell us the truth about the fundamental nature of reality, despite its spectacular successes regarding the parts of the world we can observe.

Let's land the plane on this whole discussion and turn to the question of whether science has shown that God doesn't exist (or, more modestly, that it provides at least some good evidence that he doesn't). It seems to me that we can say with a modicum of confidence that if science doesn't get it right about the basic elements of nature—the constitution and behavior of matter, energy, and spacetime, for example—then there are good reasons to doubt what it says about such "unobservables" as God, angels, demons, the soul, and the afterlife. Even if none of these existed, science wouldn't necessarily be the most reliable source of this gloomy news. To say that science has shown that naturalism is true seems to overstate the case.

That Goes for Us Too

So then, it seems to be a bit premature to use scientific premises to account for the origin of the universe. In fact, this is a time for circumspection regarding *any* "physics-based metaphysics" (as philosopher of science Bradley Monton calls it).[1] Of course, this goes for *religious*

---
[1] Monton wrote his dissertation at Princeton under the great Bas van Fraassen.

physics-based metaphysics too. We should be cautious when using, say, quantum mechanics to garner support for the doctrine of the Trinity, as attempted in this example:

> According to Christian doctrine, God is fundamentally relational. God is one, yet God is also Trinity; God is three persons enfolded in a relationship of perfect love. Moreover, each of the persons is fully God. The persons are distinct yet inseparable and interrelated. According to the doctrine of perichoresis formulated in the early Church, the three persons are bound together in a kind of mutual indwelling.
>
> Quantum holism, as demonstrated by the EPR thought experiment, is analogous to this. The electron and positron, though distinct and widely separated, yet form a unified quantum system.[2]

Another example of religious physics-based metaphysics is William Lane Craig's famous marshaling of the Big Bang to support the cosmological argument.[3] This marshaling obviously depends on there *being* a Big Bang, which in turns depends on general relativity being true.[4] But, as we've already seen, now is probably not a good time to hitch any metaphysical wagons to physics. Or if we do, says Monton, we should make sure we emphasize the "if" part of the argument: "If there was a Big Bang, then . . ."[5]

---

[2] Rodney D. Holder, "Quantum Theory and Theology," in *The Blackwell Companion to Science and Christianity*, ed. Alan G. Padgett and J. B. Stump (Oxford: Blackwell, 2012), 229.

[3] Bradley Monton, *Seeking God in Science: An Atheist Defends Intelligent Design* (Peterborough, ON: Broadview, 2009), 98.

[4] Monton explains:

> The Big Bang hypothesis holds that the universe, including space and time itself, came into existence a finite amount of time ago, and shortly after the universe came into existence it was in a state of large energy density, and the energy density in the various regions of the universe has been decreasing overall. General relativity has an infinite number of models of spacetime, and in some of the models there is a Big Bang, whereas in others there isn't. Based on the empirical data we have about our universe, the models of general relativity that best describe our universe are models where there is a Big Bang.

Bradley Monton, "Prolegomena to Any Future Physics-Based Metaphysics," in *Oxford Studies in Philosophy of Religion*, vol. 3, ed. Jonathan L. Kvanvig (Oxford: Oxford University Press, 2011), 150. Unfortunately the term "Big Bang" is ambiguous, as physicist Sean Carroll points out:

> Confusingly, the phrase "Big Bang model" refers to the entire history of the expanding universe that began in a hot, dense state, whose broad outlines are established beyond reasonable doubt. In contrast, the "Big Bang event" is not really an event at all, but a placeholder for our lack of complete understanding.

Sean Carroll, "Does the Universe Need God?," http://preposterousuniverse.com/writings/dtung/, also published in Padgett and Stump, *The Blackwell Companion to Science and Christianity*.

[5] "This can be thought of as counterfactual metaphysics: what metaphysical claims would be true, were general relativity true? . . . This would be an interesting and important philosophical result, but we have to recognize what the limitations of the result are" (Monton, "Prolegomena to Any Future Physics-Based Metaphysics," 157).

Or we could base our metaphysical arguments on those parts of physics that we can actually observe, or those parts of physics we think will survive *any* scientific revolution. In the case of the former, it will take some serious self-control to keep metaphysical pronouncements within these evidential constraints. As for the latter option: if Yoda taught us anything, it's that the future is difficult to see; always in motion it is.

Another option is to become despondent, conceding that philosophy and science are hopelessly difficult and that science will probably never be able to answer our most important philosophical questions. After all, says Monton:

> The history of science is full of seemingly insoluble gaps in our understanding that have never been filled in naturalistically. For example we don't know what the nature of consciousness is, or how conscious mental activity arises out of physical brain activity. We don't know why the universe exists—we don't know why there is something rather than nothing. We don't know why the universe has three spatial dimensions and one time dimension. We don't know what the nature of mass is. We don't know what the universe is made of (most of it seems to be "dark matter," but we don't know what dark matter is). We don't have a single fundamental theory of physics (the two theories we do have, general relativity and quantum theory are incompatible). The list could go on. . . . Thus, it's reasonable to be cautious in assuming that any new gap we discover will be naturalistically filled in as well.[6]

And even if it's not impossible to infer metaphysical conclusions from scientific premises, it *is* a risky business, especially at our level of scientific knowledge.

Of course, philosophy *isn't* easy, which is why philosophical questions persist. They land us in treacherous waters, waters that creatures like us may not be good at navigating. And it's tempting to turn to science for answers since science seems to chart similar waters. But if the blind lead the blind, both shall fall into the ditch.

It's not that we shouldn't ask questions that land us in deep waters; nor do I think we should refrain from trying to answer them. And there

---

[6] Monton, *Seeking God in Science*, 116.

may be some cases where science can help us. Not all science is on the same epistemic footing. Moreover, science has pushed back the veil of our understanding, even if it hasn't removed it. Maybe there are important aspects of the quantum world that we really *have* discovered, aspects that will remain from here on out because we've finally alighted on a precious truth. It's hard to tell. Really the point is that we should be skeptical of any attempt to answer the big questions, especially those relying on physics.[7]

So, when *is* it proper to use science to help us answer philosophical questions? I wish there were an easy answer. Perhaps the best we can do is take it case by case. But perhaps there's *something* we can say here. We might be able to identify the general whereabouts of the cliff's edge. When it comes to the laws of the universe, it simply isn't within the purview of science—not even cosmology and particle physics—to explain the *origin* of these laws. We can say that the universe behaves *this* way or *that* way, but just *why* it behaves this way is something that science isn't equipped to handle. Of course, science can give us proximate explanations and causes—but never ultimate ones. Or so it seems to me. I'll say more about this in a bit.

What about Design Arguments?

There has been a recent upsurge in the popularity of what are known as design arguments—or *teleological* arguments—for God's existence. Design arguments are not new, of course; in 1802 William Paley presented his famous suppose-you-found-a-watch argument, which plays on our natural inclination to think that complexity and order require a designer. Today, the more we learn about biology and physics, the more complex, orderly, and improbable life seems to be. Yet in all design arguments some aspect of nature is (allegedly) best explained by intentional design.[8]

But haven't my remarks about physics-based metaphysics taken much of the teleological wind out of our sails? That depends. It might be that particular design arguments—those that depend on the very

---

[7] Of course if we were to be given some of the answers by, say, God, then we'd have back-of-the-book answers to the big questions. This is exactly what we Christians claim we have. Of course, we're not the only ones.

[8] Often, then, these arguments are taken to be in the form of an inference to the best explanation. But there are other possibilities, as Hume, for example, pointed out: they can also be reasonably thought of as arguments from analogy.

specific details of our best contemporary theories—are substantially vitiated. That is, if they depend on quantum fluctuations, strings, or *p*-branes, then maybe we shouldn't pay them much mind. But there may be other, more general considerations about the cosmos that might still require explaining. No matter what the current theories, maybe there will always be some 'splaining to do. This possibility, however, is complicated by the fact that what counts as requiring explanation is in the eyes of the beholder. People will often disagree about where the line of explanations comes to an end, despite the fact that, as Wittgenstein reminded us, explanations must come to an end somewhere.

In any case, minus these rather subjective aspects of explanations, there are some people who believe that the natural order—its unreasonable rationality and profligate variety and complexity—will require a nonnatural explanation. I am one of these people. That is, I think that no matter how far we push back the natural veil on physical phenomena, there will always be good reason to think that the whole shebang requires a divine designer. Einstein said that "the most incomprehensible thing about the universe is that it is comprehensible."[9] Maybe a divine designer is required to make this nonnegotiable fact comprehensible.

But something important is overlooked by both sides. Though some sort of general design argument might be counted as evidence for a divine designer, I don't think that such an argument is nearly as strong as our *intuition* or *instinct* that the cosmos has been designed. Alvin Plantinga puts it this way:

> I encounter something that looks designed and form the belief that it is designed: perhaps this isn't a matter of argument at all (anymore than in the case of perception or other minds). In many cases, so the thought goes, the belief that something or other is a product of design is not formed by way of inference, but in the basic way; what goes on here is to be understood as more like *perception* than like *inference*.[10]

In the case of perceiving that there is a table before me, and of forming the belief that there is indeed a table before me (as opposed to, say, that I'm hallucinating or merely imagining a table before me), I do not make

---

[9] Brian R. Greene, *The Elegant Universe: Superstrings, Hidden Dimensions, and the Quest for the Ultimate Theory* (New York: W. W. Norton, 2003), 385.
[10] Alvin Plantinga, *Where the Conflict Really Lies: Science, Religion, and Naturalism* (Oxford: Oxford University Press, 2012), 145.

a quick-and-dirty inference *from* things appearing to me "table-wise" (plus from the fact that in the past my perception has generally been reliable about such matters) *to* the conclusion that there is indeed a table before me. Rather I just find myself believing that there's a table. And this belief is so automatic that it's merely tacit.

So my belief about the table is formed not by way of inference but in what Plantinga calls the "basic way": the belief is immediately caused by my *experience* rather than by an inference from previous beliefs (i.e., premises). Theologians like John Calvin and Thomas Aquinas have suggested that belief in God can be similarly instinctual. That is, belief in God may be naturally triggered by a wide variety of stimuli, from the nagging pangs of guilt, to the siren's song of a starry night, to the apparent fine-tuning of various cosmological constants. That is, humans have a kind of built-in cognitive faculty that automatically forms belief in God. Calvin called this the *sensus divinitatis*. Of course, this cognitive faculty—if such there be—has been damaged by the ravages of sin (which is why we believe in all manner of vague and variegated notions of God—or in nothing at all).[11]

I think that some such faculty or disposition is responsible for the strength of belief that many of us feel when confronted with scientific facts about the alleged fine-tuning of the cosmos or even with mundane wierdness like owls and insects. Just as we "see" that we're not hooked up to the Matrix or that other people have minds like ours, we "see" that the natural world around us must result from a divine intellect of astounding power and creativity. No inference necessary. So then, whereas there may be decent arguments for God's existence from apparent design (and I think there are, but that's not my point here), what really compels many of us to "see" that God designed "all this" is a strong instinct to do so. Of course, the unbeliever can agree that humans indeed have a habit of seeing God in nature but attributes this habit to a kind of evolutionary trick played on us by our mischievous genes.

Why Would God Allow Us to Get It Wrong?

Now, according to many believers, the ultimate explanation for why we're able to understand the universe is that God has graciously designed the world—and our cognitive faculties—to more or less hook up,

---

[11] See Aquinas's comments, for example, in Mitch Stokes, *A Shot of Faith to the Head: Be a Confident Believer in an Age of Cranky Atheists* (Nashville: Thomas Nelson, 2012), 53.

epistemically speaking. That is, believers often attribute the success of science to God. But if our science gets it wrong about some pretty important things, doesn't that cast some doubt on such an explanation, or worse, a sinister shadow on God's character? If God has designed us and the cosmos, why make it so hard for creatures like us to get to the truth?

This is somewhat analogous to the problem of evil—why would God allow X, where X is something evil, atrocious, or bothersome? But perhaps to see our current scientific limitations in such a negative light is to see a glass half empty. Another way to look at it is this: we should be extremely grateful for how far we've come in science, even if we're far from the journey's end. We look at science as something extremely difficult, but it could have easily been much more so, even impossible. There's absolutely no doubt that current science works better than the science of a few centuries ago. We've learned a great many *true* things about the universe.

Suppose, for example, that our ability to control and predict physical phenomena was an all-or-nothing affair. That is, imagine that there are only two options: no science at all or else an entirely complete and perfect science. We would then have to go from absolutely no science immediately to the ultimate theory of everything, with no rest in between. There would be no room for error, no horseshoes or hand-grenades "close enough." There would be a kind of "irreducible complexity" to scientific theories. It seems plausible to think that we'd never be able to develop *any* science—since the only possible science would be a perfect science. And to err is human.

Perhaps, then, we have something like an "evolutionary" account of scientific theories, without the pesky Darwinian problem of there being no underlying mind or purpose. That is, our scientific theories "evolve" because they are designed to (by us).

In any case, patience is a virtue. But so is skepticism. And I think all of us should be skeptical about the claim that science has shown that God doesn't exist. Even if there were a scientific argument against God, we would do well to be skeptical of it, since there are good reasons to doubt the truth of the scientific premises themselves. In the next chapter—and the last before we turn to the topic of morality—I want to look again at the arguments from Hawking and Krauss. Suppose our scientific theories *were* true; should we believe their infomercials for the universe's all-natural origins?

10

God: The Failed Hypothesis?

So then, we've seen that it may be too soon to base substantial metaphysical claims on premises from contemporary physics. But let us suppose that everything that science says about the *physical* part of reality—even the part we can't observe—is entirely true. That is, suppose that not only are there fermions, bosons, and curved spacetime, but there are also strings, *p*-branes, and multiverses spawned from quantum fluctuations. Would this show that there is no God, or that even if there is, he isn't responsible for the cosmos's existence and behavior?

Not obviously.

Is M-Theory Inconsistent with Belief That God Created the Universe?

As you'll recall, Hawking argued that contemporary physics (in the form of M-theory) makes God superfluous—at least in that God isn't needed to explain the universe's existence and its astounding complexity and order. This is because M-theory's mathematics tells us, we are assured, that universes can be created spontaneously out of nothing by quantum fluctuations. Moreover, said Hawking, our universe is only one of many (perhaps 10^{500}). This is the multiverse view (and it isn't peculiar to Hawking or M-theory). In any case, the multiverse is a convenient tool (maybe too convenient) for taming all those pesky coincidences that resulted in you and me. That is, we shouldn't be in the least surprised—given the enormous number of universes—that one of them produced life. The prosecution rests.

Unfortunately, things aren't quite as easy for Hawking as he suggests. One problem stems from his instrumentalism or nonrealism (his view, remember, that physical theories need not get at the reality underlying the appearances; they need only get at the observable part of the world). If he's an instrumentalist, why should we take his argument seriously? He himself says that we shouldn't believe what science says about unobservables. So if we're to take his scientific authority seriously, shouldn't we take his instrumentalism seriously too? And more importantly, shouldn't *he* take his instrumentalism seriously?

But let's ignore that problem and suppose that Hawking is wrong about instrumentalism, and that M-theory isn't merely a useful tool for predicting and describing phenomena (despite its lack of empirical confirmation—ignore that too). That is, let us grant that it gives us the unvarnished truth about unobservable reality—that it's complete and has as much observational confirmation as Hawking could hope for. Let us also agree with Hawking that quantum fluctuations really are the immediate cause of the multiverse. Would there be anything about M-theory—even with this gaggle of concessions—that is inconsistent with God's existence or with his ultimate role in our universe's creation?

It's hard to see how. After all, it seems possible that these quantum fluctuations (if such there be) are simply God's means of creating all these universes (*ex nihilo*), intending that one of them produce humanity. At least Hawking doesn't give us any reason to think otherwise. And given the gravity of his claims, he should at least make an effort to shed some doubt on this possibility.

Furthermore, consider all the universes that M-theory posits, each one with different physical laws. This vast number of these different legal systems is further legislated by the more fundamental meta-laws of M-theory (maybe *M* should stand for "meta"). But, then, why *these* meta-laws? Where did *they* come from?

Hawking comes close to saying that the meta-laws of M-theory are logically necessary, that they couldn't have been otherwise: "Perhaps," he says, "the true miracle is that abstract considerations of logic lead to a unique theory that predicts and describes a vast universe full of the amazing variety that we see."[1] It isn't clear just what Hawking means by this. Is it logic alone that determines M-theory? Or is it logic plus something else—plus mathematics, plus observation? He doesn't say. But even if he thinks that pure logic dictates M-theory, he hasn't given us any reason to agree with him. And so he's given us no reason to think that God himself isn't the cause of the laws that M-theory says there are.

Could Science Ever Account for the Universe?

Lawrence Krauss, as you'll recall, said something similar to Hawking: the universe arose from nothing and therefore we don't need God to explain the universe's existence. Contrary to Hawking, however, Krauss didn't use M-theory. In fact, we saw that Krauss is not keen on any form of string theory.[2] Rather he uses (mostly) good-old-fashioned quantum field theory.

Unfortunately, by "nothing"—at least when he seems to stick to established quantum field theory—Krauss doesn't really mean *nothing* nothing. Instead, by "nothing" he means empty space: "I want to be clear about what kind of 'nothing' I am discussing at the moment. This is the simplest version of nothing, namely empty space."[3]

But empty space isn't nothing. For one thing, it's space. Yet, Krauss complains, to think that empty space isn't nothing is just philosophical nitpicking.

> Once again, I realize that . . . those who wish to continually redefine the word so that no scientific definition is practical, this version of nothing [empty space] doesn't cut the mustard. However, I suspect that, at the times of Plato and Aquinas, when they pondered why there was something rather than nothing, empty space with nothing in it was probably a good approximation of what they were thinking about.[4]

---

[1] Stephen Hawking and Leonard Mlodinow, *The Grand Design* (New York: Bantam, 2010), 181.
[2] Krauss doesn't think that string theory (and so presumably M-theory) has yet "demonstrated its ability to successfully resolve a single experimental mystery about nature" (Lawrence M. Krauss, *A Universe from Nothing: Why There Is Something Rather Than Nothing* [New York: Free Press, 2012], 130). He chides string theorists for telling us that there could be up to 10^{500} universes as being a bit permissive: "'A Theory of Everything' had suddenly become a 'Theory of Anything'!" (ibid., 134). This chiding is surprising, given that he also says, "Almost every logical possibility we can imagine regarding extending laws of physics as we know them, on small scales, into a more complete theory, suggests that, on large scales, our universe is not unique" (ibid., 126).
[3] Ibid., 149.
[4] Ibid.

Philosophers and theologians keep moving the goal posts, according to Krauss. Yet no one who understands the problem of "why there's something rather than nothing" thinks that empty space is nothing. Even according to contemporary science, empty space is something. Empty space can curve and contain energy; *it* has properties. Even Plato (contrary to Krauss's guess) knew that space was *something*—indeed something really strange. In the *Timaeus*, his creation account, Plato struggles with the very concept of space. He says that it seems to be a substance, something distinct from form and matter. He calls it the "receptacle" and the "wet nurse of becoming." This makes almost no sense, but one thing's clear: empty space doesn't even *approximate* nothing.

But later Krauss does go on to argue that the universe might have come from *nothing* nothing, not from merely empty space. "The lesson is clear: quantum gravity not only appears to allow the universe to be created from nothing—meaning, in this case, I emphasize, the absence of space and time—it may require them. 'Nothing'—in this case no space, no time, no anything!—*is* unstable."[5] Notice, however, that he's now gone beyond any existing quantum field theory to a theory of *quantum gravity*, something that quantum field theory cannot yet provide. There are quantum field theories that account for the other three forces, but not for the gravitational force, which is why superstring theories are needed in the first place.

But suppose I'm wrong about this, and suppose that Krauss has successfully argued that the laws of quantum field theory can explain how the universe came from nothing. We're still left with the question *whence these laws?* As philosopher of physics, David Z. Albert (who also has a PhD in physics) asks of Krauss:

> What if he were in a position to announce, for instance, that the truth of the quantum-mechanical laws can be traced back to the fact that the world has some other, deeper property X? Wouldn't we still be in a position to ask why X rather than Y? And is there a *last* such question? Is there some point at which the possibility of asking any further such questions somehow definitively comes to an end? How would that work? What would that be like?[6]

---

[5] Ibid., 170.
[6] David Albert, "On the Origin of Everything," review of *A Universe from Nothing*, by Lawrence M. Krauss, *New York Times*, March 23, 2012, http://www.nytimes.com/2012/03/25/books/review/a-universe-from-nothing-by-krauss-m-krauss.html?pagewanted=all&_r=0.

Krauss doesn't seem to even understand the problem he's set out to solve, much less answer it accurately. And that's more than a little disappointing, given the title of his book and the fact that he plumped for it on *The Colbert Report*.

Moreover, even if Krauss could account for the *laws'* origins, Albert says that the laws of physics just aren't the kind of things that could account for the *universe's* origins. Laws tell us how the elementary stuff of the universe is arranged, not how it got here.[7] That is, the laws of physics simply tell us how the universe behaves, not how it was born.

By the way, what if the universe has always been here? After all, it may be that the universe—though it seems to be expanding from a much smaller state—could merely be ever oscillating through all eternity. Would we then have an explanation for why there's something rather than nothing? Unfortunately, no: we'd still have the problem of why there is this eternal, bouncing universe rather than nothing at all.[8]

So then, despite all the scientific pyrotechnics, neither Krauss nor Hawking has given us much reason to think that physics has accounted for the universe. But the odds of success may have been stacked against them from the start. It's entirely plausible to think that science—no matter how advanced the theory—simply isn't equipped to handle such a task. To put this more provocatively, the question of why there's something rather than nothing simply isn't a scientific question all. Maybe it's a philosophical one, whatever that might mean.

Our Resistance Is Low

Why then are we so susceptible to such unwarranted claims by scientists? A big part of the problem is a lack of studied skepticism. We've become all too willing to believe metaphysical pronouncements based on scientific results. "Scientifically proven" is our new "Thus saith the Lord." And to be sure, science has gotten weirder and weirder, and this is largely because the world is even more so. The success-to-strangeness ratio seems to remain constant: as the successes pile up, so does the strangeness. But tracking the world's weirdness isn't the problem; the

---

[7] Ibid.

[8] You might think that we have the same problem with respect to God: why is there a God rather than no God? This is a legitimate question. The traditional answer is that God is a necessary being and could not possibly have *not* existed. This is obviously not an argument that God is a necessary being, but rather an explanation for why explanations bottom-out at God. The thought is that God and the universe (and any universe at all) have different skill sets.

problem occurs when we *invent* weirdness. The mere fact that scientists can propose quantum fluctuations of nothing—and do so with such straight faces—is pretty alarming. Such proposals wouldn't have seen the light of day in previous centuries, but after general relativity and quantum mechanics, we'll accept pretty much anything. Science tells us that we might be subjects of an alien computer simulation?[9] Well, why not? An eleven-dimensional world? Cool. Something from nothing? Sure, whatever.

Over the years—like frogs gradually boiled—we've been slowly conditioned to believe that *anything* is possible. We'll even accept logical contradictions and then change the laws of logic to accommodate our accommodation. We'll follow the mathematics almost anywhere. (As someone said somewhere, "I can do *all things* through mathematics, literally.") But once we're *this* epistemically promiscuous, it's really hard to say no to any belief. Our resistance is gone; we have no intellectual antibodies.

Again, I have no doubt that reality is beyond bizarre. The problem is discerning legitimate strangeness from literal nonsense. And this isn't always easy. I should also mention that we can't simply dismiss ideas because they're strange or uncomfortable. This is why any skepticism we adopt should be *studied*, as I put it. We should avoid the reactionary "it's false because science says it" silliness.

God the Hypothesis

But I want to look at Hawking and Krauss's overall strategy here. Could science ever show that God doesn't exist? Could it show that naturalism is true? To be sure, scientific evidence can potentially tell against certain specific religious doctrines, where those doctrines make claims about the physical world that we (potentially) have access to, say, a worldwide flood or the contemporaneous existence of humans and dinosaurs. And to find out that a religion gets things wrong could be a serious public-relations setback for it. So it's not as if science can say *nothing* about religion. Science and religion can "dialogue," as they say.

Moreover, beliefs about God can certainly affect the epistemic plausibility of a scientific hypothesis. For example, a trenchant belief in

---

[9] Ray Villard, "Are We Living inside a Computer Simulation?," *Discovery Newsletter*, December 16, 2012, http://news.discovery.com/space/are-we-living-in-a-computer-simulation-2-121216.htm.

naturalism will make certain theories more attractive, epistemically speaking. Take, for example, blind and unguided evolution. It's the only game in town for unbelievers, so no matter what the evidence, it has got to bear a lot of explanatory weight.

To take a more extreme example, if you begin by assuming that naturalism is true, making this a principle or axiom, then it is no wonder that one of your conclusions would be that God doesn't exist or that he didn't create the cosmos. But, you might object, no one would actually do this. Yet, consider what Smolin says in the first chapter of *Three Roads to Quantum Gravity* (a chapter titled "There Is Nothing outside the Universe"):

> We humans are the species that makes things. So when we find something that appears to be beautifully and intricately structured, our almost instinctive response is to ask, "Who made that?" The most important lesson to be learned if we are to prepare ourselves to approach the universe scientifically is that this is not the right question to ask. It is true that the universe is as beautiful as it is intricately structured. But it cannot have been made by anything that exists outside it, for by definition the universe is all there is, and there can be nothing outside it. And, by definition, neither can there have been anything before the universe that caused it, for if anything existed it must have been part of the universe. So the first principle of cosmology must be "There is nothing outside the universe."[10]

We should all admit that our beliefs about God—either way—can influence our attitude toward scientific evidence. But aside from this, how might science show that there's no God? Perhaps the thought is this: "The main reason you religious folk believe in God is that you think he's the best explanation for the universe's existence and workings. That is, your reason for believing in God in the first place is—at least largely—that he's the best way to account for the way things are. But if science can show that there's a perfectly natural explanation for the universe, then this would remove your main reason for believing in God."

That seems like a perfectly good line of reasoning. If you showed me that those crop circles were created by humans or high winds, I would

---

[10] Lee Smolin, *Three Roads to Quantum Gravity* (New York: Basic Books, 2001), 17.

immediately drop my belief in aliens. But how many people believe in God mainly *because* they think God's action is the best explanation for the world and all its furniture? Not many. As Plantinga puts it, "Maybe a few people accept religious beliefs strictly on the basis of what they take the evidence to be; perhaps, for example, this was true of [Antony] Flew."[11] In fact, it probably goes the other way: since many people already believe in God, he's going to be their first-round draft pick for an explanation of the universe. Of course, I can only speak for myself (and for the people with whom I've discussed this), and *my* belief in God is not built upon the belief that he created everything. That's not to say that I don't derive additional support for my antecedent belief in God from my belief that he's the explanation for the universe. But weakening, or even defeating my belief that God is the universe's cause wouldn't take away my ground for believing that God exists. It might cause me consternation, but my belief in God is not primarily based on an inference to the best explanation. God is not a scientific hypothesis in my case. And this is probably true for most believers.

And even if Hawking and Krauss's arguments were entirely success-ful, the most they may have shown is that it's not impossible that God didn't create the universe. Here's Krauss on the matter: "Without sci-ence, everything is a miracle. With science, there remains the possibility that nothing is."[12] But how strong is that? Plantinga gives us a possible analogy (Plantinga was discussing evolution at the time): "You've al-ways thought Mother Teresa was a moral hero; someone wanders by and tells you that we don't know that it's not astronomically improbable that she was a complete hypocrite. Would you be impressed?"[13] Even if Hawking and Krauss have shown that it's not impossible that the laws of physics alone can account for the existence of the universe—which I don't think they've come close to showing—we shouldn't be impressed.

Seers and Craftspeople

Lately, quite a number of famous scientists have criticized philosophy, particularly when philosophers butt into their scientific business. Hawk-ing, we saw, thinks that philosophy is dead. But others are also disdain-

---

[11] Alvin Plantinga, *Where the Conflict Really Lies: Science, Religion, and Naturalism* (Oxford: Oxford University Press, 2012), 124.
[12] Krauss, *A Universe from Nothing*, 183.
[13] Plantinga, *Where the Conflict Really Lies*, 41.

ful of philosophy: scientific players no less than Neil deGrasse Tyson,[14] Krauss,[15] and Freeman Dyson[16] have registered their strong disapproval.

This disapproval is ironic given the amount of philosophy that many of the same scientists (try to) engage in. We've seen that Hawking and Krauss have devoted entire books to philosophy. Of course, it is dismal philosophy, but it is philosophy nonetheless. To be sure, it might be difficult to pin down just what philosophy *is*, but this is true of science also. The point in any case is that these physicists have, at important junctures, reasoned very poorly, despite their obvious intellectual horsepower. They've tried to do what philosophers do—whatever you want to call it—and have failed (all the while, pointing the finger at philosophers).

But this sorry situation—the lack of philosophical acumen—might in fact be why physics has been stymied for decades. Lee Smolin says that physics is in a situation similar to that of the early 1900s, when the very foundations of the discipline were being questioned. And, Smolin points out, the scientists of that tumultuous age were natural philosophers in the original sense. They were *philosophers* as well as scientists and appreciated the depth of the philosophy needed to put science on a proper course. After the foundations of relativity and quantum theory were laid, the next generation—physicists like Dyson and Richard Feynman—built on that foundation. Smolin says that instead of masters of philosophical creativity, these scientists were technical virtuosos, capable of astounding mathematical feats, but not as adept at fundamental conceptual issues. Now is the time, says Smolin, for "seers" like Einstein, Heisenberg, and Schrödinger, not the "craftspeople" of the 1940s on.[17] Smolin adds, "We are indeed in a revolutionary period, but we are trying to get out of it using the inadequate tools and organization of normal science."[18]

---

[14] See Massimo Pigliucci, "Neil deGrasse Tyson and the Value of Philosophy," *Huffington Post* science blog, May 16, 2014, http://www.huffingtonpost.com/massimo-pigliucci/neil-degrasse-tyson-and-the-value-of-philosophy_b_5330216.html.

[15] See Ross Andersen, "Has Physics Made Philosophy and Religion Obsolete?," *The Atlantic*, April, 23, 2012, http://m.theatlantic.com/technology/print/2012/04/has-physics-made-philosophy-and-religion-obsolete/256203/

[16] See Freeman Dyson, "What Can You Really Know?," review of *Why Does the World Exist? An Existential Detective Story*, by Jim Holt, *New York Review of Books*, November 8, 2012, http://www.nybooks.com/articles/archives/2012/nov/08/what-can-you-really-know/?page=2.

[17] Lee Smolin, *The Trouble with Physics: The Rise of String Theory, the Fall of a Science, and What Comes Next* (Boston: Houghton Mifflin, 2006), 308.

[18] Ibid., 311.

From Fact to Value

Here's where we stand. Remember that I began the book as Captain Obvious, pointing out that unbelievers take reason and science very seriously. In parts 1 and 2, however, we've seen that many unbelievers aren't nearly as skeptical as they let on. It seems to me that they should— given their avowed eagerness to follow reason—be rather more skeptical about important matters like sense perception, reason, and science, and much less about the claim that science shows that God doesn't exist.

But suppose I've been entirely off base the whole time, and that there are good arguments for trusting reason and sense perception (or at least that a naturalistic story can underwrite such trust). Suppose further that science gives us the genuine goods on physical reality and that, furthermore, it tells us important things about nonphysical reality, namely, that there isn't one. Or at least that there's no being such as God. Suppose all this is true. What follows?

Something pretty unsettling.

Part 3

MORALITY

11

If God Is Dead,
Is Everything Permissible?

In part 2 I argued that although science is a wildly impressive human achievement, we should be cautious of what it seems to say about the ultimate furniture of the universe. Moreover, I gave what I thought are some pretty good reasons for thinking that science *doesn't* show that naturalism is true, that God doesn't exist. But what if I'm just plain wrong about this? What if science indeed tells us the truth about the ultimate constituents and character of the cosmos and, furthermore, that such truth implies there's no God? Of course, these would be enormous concessions, but they are entirely in line with what many atheists currently believe. Let us suppose they're right.

Here in part 3 I'll argue that if atheism or naturalism *were* true, and if the realm of science *were* "*all* that is or ever was or *ever will be*," then our common-sense morality is completely undone. I'll argue that if naturalism is true, then so is *moral nihilism*, the view that there are no objective moral standards and that anything goes, ethically speaking. I'll also call this view *moral relativism, moral subjectivism*, and *moral skepticism*. It is moral *relativism* because morality is relative only to human desires or preferences (I'll argue). It is moral *subjectivism* because morality, it seems to me, requires a personal subject, someone to do the valuing. The view is also (or leads to) moral *skepticism* because we can have no knowledge of objective moral standards—the reason being that there aren't any such standards to know.

So then, let's begin our discussion by returning—not coincidentally—to the Enlightenment, where many of the relevant problems began.

Science and Morality (1): Freedom

Recall that Immanuel Kant greatly admired Newtonian science and eagerly believed what it said about the "starry heavens above." But he also believed that science threatened something just as precious as those starry heavens, namely, the "moral law within."

Kant's overall philosophical project, then, was to reconcile the new scientific picture of the world with the apparently obvious fact that humans were autonomous moral creatures. If the universe is a vast cosmic machine made entirely out of lifeless, inert matter—as it seemed to be if Newtonian physics was right—then this raises questions about humans themselves. If we are, after all, composed of the same stuff as everything else, then it seems reasonable to suppose that we're governed by the same laws as that stuff. But these laws are deterministic. That is, the laws of physics entirely determine or dictate the behavior of every bit of matter in the universe. To put it differently, as Laplace did, if there were an immense intelligence that could know the position, velocity, location, etc. of every particle in the cosmos at an instant, then this intelligence, simply in virtue of following the laws of (a complete, if only future) physics, could calculate the exact state of the cosmos at any future instant. Imagine taking a "snapshot" of the cosmos at 3:45 tomorrow, a snapshot that contained all the pertinent physical information (and nothing more). In such a case, Laplace's imagined intelligence—called "Laplace's demon"—could, by simply following the math, know the exact whereabouts and behavior of every particle in the universe at 3:46, including all the particles that comprise you.

But if our physical bodies are determined in this way then how are we free? Rocks are not free to choose whether they fall. If humans are not free—and here's the real worry—how can we make sense of our moral lives: our moral obligations, our moral blameworthiness, and our moral praiseworthiness? You would neither praise nor blame a falling rock; it has no say in the matter. The problem, as I have just described it, is really a problem about how we might reconcile our apparently free will with the apparently undeniable facts of deterministic science.

Science and Morality (2): The "Experimental Method"

This wasn't the only problem that science seemed to cause for morality. Science also suggested that there was something wrong with the very concept. Hume, you'll remember, applied the "experimental method" of science to the human subject, inaugurating the "science of man." This science of man included ethics, perhaps the most important of all subjects. As Hume said, "Morality is a subject that interests us above all others: We fancy the peace of society to be at stake in every decision concerning it."[1] And all science, for Hume, must be ultimately grounded in experience, since science deals primarily with "matters of fact" (rather than with "relations of ideas"). For any matter of fact, if you can't see it (or taste it, touch it, smell it, or hear it), then you really should hold your horses when it comes to believing it. And even if you don't have a choice in the matter—perhaps nature is too strong—you can attenuate your enthusiasm if you know that your inevitable belief lacks the proper evidential support.

So then, Hume applied what he saw as the scientific method to moral psychology/epistemology, asking, for example, why do we believe that lying is wrong? According to Hume, the proposition *Lying is wrong* must be either a matter of fact or purely a relation of ideas. But it isn't simply about the relationship between concepts; nor is it true by mere definition. So, said Hume, "vice and virtue are not discoverable merely by reason, or the comparison of ideas."[2] But neither are moral judgments concerning vice and virtue grounded in something we can see. Although you can see that a certain action is an instance of lying, you never observe that lying is *wrong*. And if seeing is believing, perhaps we ought to doubt whether lying *is* wrong, or at least suspend judgment.

We'll look at Hume's moral skepticism in a bit more detail later, but for now, notice that science's success forced Hume to seriously reconsider a common-sense view of the "subject that interests us above all others." Then again, science seems to be in the business of surprising us.

---

[1] David Hume, *A Treatise of Human Nature* (Oxford: Clarendon, 1978), 455.
[2] Ibid., 470.

Science and Morality (3): Atheism

What's more, as the Enlightenment world followed a path from science to deism to atheism, the very idea of a moral law—the concept of morality itself—required new underpinnings. After all, Judeo-Christian (and Islamic) morality is founded on a moral law, and therefore, on a moral Lawgiver. This is often called the *divine command theory* of ethics. (By the way, I'll use the terms *moral* and *ethical* and their cognates as synonyms.) But without such a legislator—if the divine command theory is false—the concept of a moral law doesn't even seem coherent. Can there be laws without a Lawgiver?

The task of grounding morality in something other than God—a task that Alisdair MacIntyre calls "the Enlightenment Project"—has occupied nearly all of Western ethical philosophy ever since.[3] As we proceed, I'll point out some of this history's highlights, but I'm mostly concerned with the current state of the project. I don't think it has been at all successful; all the main moves have been tried and found wanting. Not that these attempts aren't valiant and often brilliant. But they're unsuccessful nonetheless.

I'll argue, then, that given the very nature of morality, if God does not exist—that is, if naturalism is true—there can be no morality in the robust sense that we understand it. Morality, whatever else it turned out to be, would be grounded in nothing more than human preference. And I think the implications of this failure are so dramatic that they've been the primary obstacles between atheists and moral nihilism. It's not a matter of reason but of revulsion.

Dostoyevsky's Nagging Doubt

So, my own position on the Enlightenment Project—that of justifying morality without God—is pretty pessimistic. Such pessimism isn't new; it goes all the way back to the project's beginning. There are always naysayers when it comes to heroic tasks. But perhaps the pessimistic view is most eloquently and memorably stated by Dostoyevsky in *The Brothers Karamazov*. Ivan's view is that if God is dead and the grave our final destination, "nothing would be immoral any longer, everything would be permitted, even anthropophagy [i.e., cannibalism]."[4]

[3] Linda Zagzebski, "Morality and Religion," in *The Oxford Handbook of Philosophy of Religion*, ed. William J. Wainwright (Oxford: Oxford University Press, 2005), 345.

[4] Fyodor Dostoevsky, *The Brothers Karamazov*, trans. Richard Pevear and Larissa Volokhonsky (New York: Farrar, Straus and Giroux, 2002), 69.

Dostoyevsky's message has been taken very seriously by some, including, famously, the French philosopher Jean-Paul Sartre. In "Existentialism Is a Humanism," Sartre says, "Existentialists find it extremely disturbing that God no longer exists, for along with his disappearance goes the possibility of finding values in an intelligible heaven. . . . Dostoyevsky once wrote: 'If God does not exist, everything is permissible.'"[5] Sartre shares Dostoyevsky's doubt about the possibility of morality without God: "Indeed, everything is permissible if God does not exist, and man is consequently abandoned."[6]

Calvin and Hobbes © 1989 Watterson. Reprinted with permission of Universal Uclick. All rights reserved.

But it's not *all* bad news, at least for those having an Enlightenment-style distaste for authority. In fact, such folks get their wish. Our abandonment by God means there isn't any divine legislator who demands our obedience. We're free to imagine there's no heaven (I've heard that this is easy if you try, imagining there's no hell below us, above us only sky).[7] In other words we're *entirely* free.

Of course, genuine moral autonomy means no ethical constraints in either direction. Christopher Hitchens expressed the concern:

> They [i.e., atheists] are now free, if they so choose, to become nihilists or sadists or solipsists on their own account. Some theories of the Superman derive from atheism, and a person who thought that heaven and hell were empty could conclude that he was free to do

---

[5] Robert K. Garcia and Nathan L. King, introduction to *Is Goodness without God Good Enough? A Debate on Faith, Secularism, and Ethics*, ed. Robert K. Garcia and Nathan L. King (Lanham, MD: Rowman & Littlefield, 2009), 3.

[6] Ibid.

[7] But contrary to what Lennon thought, imagining these things is not very easy at all, at least not consistently, hence this book.

exactly as he wished. The fear that this might be the outcome—well-expressed by Fyodor Dostoyevsky—underlies many people's reluctance to abandon religious dogma.[8]

This has been the worry ever since the Enlightenment, but has become particularly pressing since the appearance of evolution. As atheist Jerry Coyne (author of *Why Evolution Is True*) asks, "If, after all, we are simply beasts, then why not *behave* like beasts?"[9] He explains:

> The message of evolution, and all of science is one of naturalistic materialism. Darwinism tells us that, like all species, human beings arose from the working of blind, purposeless forces over eons of time. As far as we can determine, the same forces that gave rise to ferns, mushrooms, lizards, and squirrels also produced us.[10]

Sartre's own response to this was to conclude that intellectual honesty requires that we admit the incoherence of the Enlightenment Project and live "authentically," realizing the absurdity in attempts to justify morality.[11]

As we'll see, I disagree that naturalism requires that atheists muster their resolve to live authentically. Nor does naturalism require that atheists "behave like beasts." But this is only because a purely naturalistic world would require nothing of us whatsoever. Naturalism does not tell us how we *ought* to live or how we *ought* to behave. That is, if naturalism were true, there simply *are no* "oughts" or "shoulds." Neither are there "ought nots" or "should nots." And the fact that naturalism doesn't imply that atheists should behave badly (at least I will argue that this is a fact) has been largely ignored, not only by atheists but by theists as well. Even Dostoyevsky's Ivan makes the mistake:

> And even that is not all: . . . the moral law of nature ought to change immediately into the exact opposite of the former religious law, and that egoism, even to the point of evildoing, should not only be permitted to man but should be acknowledged as the necessary, the most reasonable, and all but the noblest result of his situation.[12]

---

[8] Christopher Hitchens, ed., *The Portable Atheist: Essential Readings for the Nonbeliever* (Philadelphia: Da Capo, 2007), xxi.
[9] Jerry A. Coyne, *Why Evolution Is True* (New York: Penguin, 2009), xvii.
[10] Ibid., 224.
[11] John Hare, "Is Moral Goodness without Belief in God Rationally Stable?," in Garcia and King, *Is Goodness without God Good Enough?*, 87–88.
[12] Dostoevsky, *The Brothers Karamazov*, 69.

So not only does Ivan claim that everything would be permissible without God, but he goes further and claims that evil would be good. This, I think, is a mistake, and an underappreciated one.

What's the Big Deal?

But why all this fuss about moral realism, about objective morality? Why is this even an issue? Why not simply accept the death of moral realism? We'll look at this more later, but for now let's just notice that were we to concede that morality is entirely subjective (that is, dependent on *human* values), we'd, at the very least, have to give up the extremely strong intuition that horrific acts like rape, torture, and murder are wrong regardless of what we think. As Princeton University ethicist Peter Singer says,

> Without the notion of an independent moral reality to back them up, however, claims made on behalf of these moral rules or principles can be no more than expressions of personal preferences which, from the collective point of view, should receive no more weight than other preferences.[13]

Perhaps we could change our way of thinking, but this would almost be like learning to believe we're hooked up to the Matrix—difficult at best.

And even if we could do this, as we look at more of the ramifications of moral subjectivism, I think we'll see that it's unlikely. If we truly believed that moral realism is false, it's tempting to think that all hell will break loose, rather than just some of it. Consider what the serial killer Ted Bundy once said (warning: what follows is disturbing):

> Then I learned that all moral judgments are "value judgments," that all value judgments are subjective, and that none can be proved to be either "right" or "wrong." . . . [There is no] "reason" to obey the law for anyone, like myself who has the boldness and daring—the strength of character—to throw off its shackles. . . . I discovered that to become truly free, truly unfettered, I had to become truly uninhibited. . . . Why is it more wrong to kill a human animal than any other animal, a pig or a sheep or a steer? . . . Why should I be willing

---

[13] Peter Singer, *The Expanding Circle: Ethics, Evolution, and Moral Progress* (Princeton, NJ: Princeton University Press, 2011), 110.

to sacrifice my pleasure more for the one than for the other? Surely, you would not, in this age of scientific enlightenment, declare that God or nature has marked some pleasures as "moral" or "good" and others as "immoral" or "bad"? In any case, let me assure you, my dear young lady, that there is absolutely no comparison between the pleasure I might take in eating ham and the pleasure I anticipate raping and murdering you. That is the honest conclusion to which my education has led me—after the most conscientious examination of my spontaneous and uninhibited self.[14]

Dostoyevsky's fear was that if naturalism is true, we can't rationally condemn this kind of behavior as morally wrong.

The moral stakes then are very high. This is why Dostoyevsky's doubt is such a big deal to us all. Unbelievers want to show that taking atheism seriously wouldn't be nearly the public-relations challenge that some claim, while believers want hell's gates to at least remain on their hinges where they can potentially be closed.

The Big Claim

So, the conclusion for which I'll be arguing is this: *If naturalism is true, then there is no morality.* Notice that this is a conditional statement. I'm only arguing that naturalism *implies* that there are no moral standards—no moral obligations, no right, no wrong, no evil, no good. Notice that the converse of this conclusion is that *if there is such a thing as morality, then naturalism is false.* And of course, if naturalism is false, then theism is true. So I'm also thereby arguing that *if there is such a thing as morality, then theism is true.* That is, theism is necessary for morality. But I won't be explicitly *arguing* that there is in fact such a thing as morality (although I very strongly believe there is). Nor will I be arguing for the thesis that naturalism is false, and therefore I won't be arguing for the conclusion that God exists. These will be left as exercises for the reader.

If it's true that God's existence is required for morality, then there are two paths for a naturalist to take. One is to concede that there *is* such a thing as morality and that therefore naturalism is false (and that theism is true). Not many atheists will take this route, nor do I much

---

[14] James Fieser and Louis P. Pojman, *Ethics: Discovering Right and Wrong*, 6th ed. (Belmont, CA: Wadsworth, 2009), 17.

expect them to. Such arguments aren't justified by reason alone. Much else besides is needed, as we saw when discussing scientific reasoning.

But the other path will, I think, prove to be just as untrodden as the first. This second option is to maintain that atheism is true and concede that there is no such thing as morality. Few atheists have ever accepted this. But some have tried their best. If we're to take Nietzsche and Sartre seriously—or at least common readings of their positions—such thinkers have offered *some* version of moral skepticism, subjectivism, or nihilism. (Again, I'll use these terms interchangeably, all of them meaning that there is no such thing as morality *apart from human preference*— more on this important italicized qualifier in a moment.) In any case, in the spirit of sober skepticism, I believe that the atheist should be—at the very least—highly suspicious of our traditional views on ethics.

Anyway, by far the most common (and straightforward) way for atheists to avoid either path—denying either atheism or traditional morality—is to deny that God's existence really is required for morality. In other words, they'll likely deny the truth of the proposition *If naturalism is true, then there is no morality*.

"... Apart from Human Preference."

When I say "there is no morality," I mean that there is no *objective* morality, no morality that is independent of human beliefs and desires. At least if naturalism is true. And if I'm right about this, then morality wouldn't have the kind of authority we need. As the great atheist J. L. Mackie says:

> We need morality to regulate interpersonal relations, to control some of the ways in which people behave towards one another, often in opposition to contrary inclinations. We therefore want our moral judgements to be authoritative for other agents as well as for ourselves: objective validity would give them the authority required.[15]

The philosophical view that there are human-*in*dependent moral standards is called *moral realism*. So we can say that the view I'll be arguing for here is this: *If naturalism is true, then moral realism is false.*

It has traditionally been much easier to accommodate moral realism on the divine command theory than on naturalism. After all, on this view

---

[15] J. L. Mackie, *Ethics: Inventing Right and Wrong* (1977; repr., London: Penguin, 1990), 43.

God himself is the ground of morality, and if anything is independent of human desires and beliefs, God is. In fact, according to Christian tradition, one of God's attributes is his *aseity*, the property of being entirely "of himself," being absolutely sovereign. In other words, God depends on nothing, while everything depends on him.[16] Including morality.

Yet very few atheists think that all moral bets are off. In fact, there are those who say that it is so obvious that naturalism can support objective morality that the topic is a nonissue, a pseudo-problem. The atheist philosopher Walter Sinnott-Armstrong—who has written extensively on morality and is, moreover, a leading expert on moral skepticism—describes the situation this way: "There really is no question about morality without God. There is just plain morality. This point should not be controversial, but it is. Many theists are theists mainly because they believe, for whatever reason, that morality depends on religion."[17] And, says Sinnott-Armstrong, citing the venerable philosopher Richard Taylor, even atheists and agnostics can mistakenly encourage the view that morality requires religion. Taylor says that "the concept of moral obligation [is] unintelligible apart from the idea of God. The words remain, but their meaning is gone."[18]

I think Sinnott-Armstrong has wildly overstated his case: the claim that naturalism can underwrite morality *should* be controversial. But before we get to the really substantive arguments, I want to dispense with a few common but largely irrelevant ones. And even though these arguments turn out to be beside the point, they're not obviously so at first glance.

---

[16] You might reasonably think that a view like Plato's is a way to support moral realism on the assumption of naturalism. On the Platonic view, moral reality is ultimately dependent on eternal forms that exist independently not only of humans but also of the cosmos itself. Although the issues surrounding Platonism are deep and perplexing, the fact that this independent moral reality—if such there be—is outside the natural world immediately renders naturalism false. Platonic forms, strictly speaking, would be *super*natural. For a fuller account of this kind of "Platonic" supernaturalism and the problems it raises for naturalists of a scientific bent, see chap. 18 of Mitch Stokes, *A Shot of Faith to the Head: Be a Confident Believer in an Age of Cranky Atheists* (Nashville: Thomas Nelson, 2012).

[17] Walter Sinnott-Armstrong, *Morality without God?* (Oxford: Oxford University Press, 2009), xi.

[18] Richard Taylor, *Ethics, Faith, and Reason* (Englewood Cliffs, NJ: Prentice-Hall, 1985), 84. By the way, there are decent reasons for thinking that Taylor was neither an atheist nor an agnostic, For example, in a debate with William Lane Craig over whether morality requires God, he says the following:

> Somewhere in his comments I think he attributed to me a thesis of atheism, and this is—I must set the record straight—not true. I am not an atheist; I believe in God. Once when I was giving a public lecture, one of the members of the audience said, "Do you believe in God?" It had nothing to do with what I was talking about, but he wanted to know the answer, and I replied quite truthfully, "It's the only thing I believe in."

"Is the Basis of Morality Natural or Supernatural?," *Reasonable Faith*, October 8, 1993, http://www.reasonablefaith.org/is-the-basis-of-morality-natural-or-supernatural-the-craig-taylor-debate#ixzz3g64EJsDU.

12

Some Brush Clearing

Taking Offense

We tend to be a little sensitive when it comes to subjects we care deeply about, so it's only natural that we take debates about morality to heart. But our feelings can get in the way of serious and sober discussion. In fact, merely broaching the topic of morality can cause offense. Listen to Sinnott-Armstrong:

> My previous book on religion was a debate with William Lane Craig, a prominent evangelical, who also abuses atheists. In his opening statement, Craig wrote, "On the atheistic view, there is nothing really *wrong* with your raping someone." I will show later why this claim is false. The point for now is that it is insulting. It also strongly suggests an unwillingness to try to see the world from the other point of view.[1]

Atheist philosopher Paul Kurz—to whom Victor Stenger dedicates his book *The New Atheism*, saying that Kurz "has contributed more to the advance of science and reason than any other of his generation"[2]—similarly attacks Craig (on a different occasion): "For Dr. Craig to imply that those who do not accept his particular dogma of religious theism are immoral nihilists, is patently false, libelous, and immoral."[3]

---

[1] Walter Sinnott-Armstrong, *Morality without God?* (Oxford: Oxford University Press, 2009), 7.
[2] Victor J. Stenger, *The New Atheism: Taking a Stand for Science and Reason* (Ahmherst, NY: Prometheus, 2009).
[3] Paul Kurtz and William Lane Craig, "The Kurtz/Craig Debate: Is Goodness without God Good Enough?," in *Is Goodness without God Good Enough? A Debate on Faith, Secularism, and Ethics*, ed. Robert K. Garcia and Nathan L. King (Lanham, MD: Rowman & Littlefield, 2009), 36.

The confusion here is to think that questioning a person's ethical grounds is *ipso facto* questioning that person's moral character. The good news, however, is that the mistake helps us diagnose the real problem, namely, that anyone making it misunderstands the real issue. Saying that it's immoral to question another person's ethical foundation is reasoning in a tiny circle. At least in this context. The mistake assumes that *there are* moral standards by which we can judge something immoral.

But that's the question.

Why Be Good?

Here's a related confusion, this one less obvious. Consider the question *If there is no God, why be good?* To ask this, says Richard Dawkins, reveals a deep and tragic fault in the questioner.

> Posed like that, the question sounds positively ignoble. When a religious person puts it to me in this way (and many of them do), my immediate temptation is to issue the following challenge: "Do you really mean to tell me the only reason you try to be good is to gain God's approval and reward, or to avoid his disapproval and punishment?"[4]

Michael Shermer calls the *why be good?* question a debate stopper. "If you agree that, in the absence of God, you would 'commit robbery, rape, and murder,' you reveal yourself as an immoral person, 'and we would be well advised to steer a wide course around you.'"[5] Part of the problem is the question itself. The believer looks like she's questioning the atheist's *motivation* for behaving, asking why the unbeliever would even *want* to act morally. And I suppose there's real truth to this. It does indeed sound like the believer could be asking this, suggesting that she only obeys God because she's afraid of getting punished. But the more fundamental question, strictly speaking, isn't *why be moral?* but, rather, *are there any objective moral standards at all?* Of course, once we answer this deeper question, we'll be in a better position to ask what reasons we have for behaving. And we'll consider possible reasons in due time.

---

[4] Richard Dawkins, *The God Delusion* (Boston: Houghton Mifflin, 2006), 259.
[5] Quoted in ibid.

So the most pressing question isn't *why* atheists should be moral (though it's not entirely irrelevant). Less pressing still is whether atheists *can* behave. Christopher Hitchens, rather pleased with his cleverness, said, "My own response [to the claim that morality requires God] has been to issue a challenge: name me an ethical statement made or an action performed by a believer that could not have been made or performed by a non-believer."[6] We'll leave aside, say, genuine acts of worship or the (sincere) proclamation "I believe in the Lord Jesus Christ," which many Christians believe to be ethical *in excelsis*; presumably the atheist couldn't sincerely perform these. But suppose Hitchens is right and that there's nothing a believer can do that an atheist can't. His comment is still beside the point. No one—or no one *I* know—thinks that atheists can't behave. Atheists can love their spouses, care for the poor, desire world peace, and enjoy long walks on the beach. Atheists can behave in accord with traditional moral standards, regardless of whether naturalism can ground these standards. We've all seen it done. The real question is whether naturalism can support or account for the moral standards themselves.

More Question Begging

So then, we can be easily sidetracked, and largely because our moral beliefs are so deeply ingrained. We have such a powerful sense of objective right and wrong that we often can't imagine alternatives. Added to this is the fact that most people share our beliefs about morality. Our core moral beliefs are nearly universal.[7] These two characteristics of our moral beliefs can make moral laws seem like logical laws—necessarily true.

And therefore many people—philosophers included—mistake the strength and universality of our moral beliefs for an argument that these beliefs are *true*. Atheist philosopher Kai Nielsen claims that morality need not be justified by religion. Why does he think this? He explains:

> Torturing human beings is vile; exploiting and degrading human beings is through-and-through evil; cruelty to human beings and animals is, morally speaking, unacceptable; and treating one's promises

---

[6] Christopher Hitchens, ed., *The Portable Atheist: Essential Readings for the Nonbeliever* (Philadelphia: Da Capo, 2007), xiv.
[7] I think this uniformity is sometimes overstated.

lightly or being careless about the truth is wrong. If we know anything to be wrong we know these things to be wrong and they would
be wrong and just as wrong in a Godless world and in a world in
which personal annihilation is inevitable as in a world with God and
in which there is eternal life.[8]

Of course, this is no argument at all. To say that we all know these
things are wrong, and that they would be wrong even if there were no
God, is to beg the question. After all, this is what we're questioning.[9]
At this point—and where Nielsen was at in the article quoted—this is a
conclusion that must be argued for, not merely restated.

Apparently this is an easy mistake to make. No less than Sinnott-
Armstrong is susceptible. He raises the question of whether it would be
wrong for you to hit someone in the face for no reason. He concludes,
as is natural (but not necessarily correct), that it is indeed wrong. He
goes on to explain:

> The only way around this conclusion [i.e., that it is morally wrong
> for you to hit someone for no reason] is either: (a) to admit that
> everyone in the world is allowed to hit you on the nose whenever he
> or she feels like it or (b) to claim that you are allowed to hit others
> when they are not allowed to hit you.[10]

Well, what's wrong with either (a) or (b)? Here's his reply: "Response
(a) is abhorrent. Response (b) is arbitrary. Some people might not care
about being hit or about being arbitrary. Nonetheless, their lack of concern need not stop us from criticizing them. Anyone who denies this
conclusion is, thus, subject to criticism."[11]

Suppose Sinnott-Armstrong is right and (a) is abhorrent and (b) is
arbitrary. What follows? Certainly nothing substantive about the foundation of morality. Look at it this way: we could find option (a) disagree-

---

[8] Kai Nielsen, "Death and the Meaning of Life," in *The Meaning of Life*, ed. E. D. Klemke (Oxford:
Oxford University Press, 2000), 155.
[9] By the way, to "beg the question" does not mean to "raise the question." Begging the question is a logical
crime in which the culprit uses the conclusion (usually implicitly) to prove that very same conclusion. It
is, surprisingly, an entirely valid form of logical argument, but it has little epistemological value—that is,
it's not very convincing, and rightly so.
[10] Sinnott-Armstrong, *Morality without God?*, 63–64. Here's the argument he's just offered: "It is morally
wrong for [someone] to hit you for no reason. If that is morally wrong, then it is also morally wrong for
you to hit him for no reason. Therefore, it is morally wrong for you to hit him for no reason" (ibid., 63).
Option (a) is a denial of the first premise; option (b) is a denial of the second.
[11] Sinnott-Armstrong, *Morality without God?*, 64.

able or repugnant while still *consistently* believing that moral nihilism is true. Our disagreeable feelings don't count much, in themselves, toward the truth of moral realism one way or the other. Similarly, the arbitrariness of option (b) is entirely consistent with nihilism (i.e., the denial of moral realism). Nihilism is completely compatible with—and perhaps even implies—that all our moral choices are ultimately arbitrary, ultimately grounded in mere preference.

In both cases, these philosophers appeal to the fact that we all *just know* that these acts are wrong. But again, that's the very thing we're questioning: are these things really wrong? And to answer this we must say *what makes them wrong*. And so that's our goal.

Hume's Sentimentalism

It's easy, then, to mistake our moral sentiments—our strong feelings about morality—for an argument in favor of the truth of our moral beliefs. But we saw that expression of these sentiments is often little more than a disguised way of stating our preference for moral realism, the view that there are objective moral standards. Whatever the case may be, this tendency reveals that it's easy to get carried away by our emotions.

Hume realized the importance of emotions for morality. I mentioned earlier that when he applied the "experimental method" to ethics, the only moral "matters of fact" he could find were facts about our moral feelings, or sentiments. Let's look more closely at what he says.

He asks us to consider a specific act we believe to be wrong. That is, in accord with empiricism and the experimental method, he asks us to *look and see*.

> Take any action allow'd to be vicious: Wilful murder, for instance. Examine it in all lights, and see if you can find that matter of fact, or real existence, which you call *vice*. In which-ever way you take it, you find only certain passions, motives, volitions and thoughts. There is no other matter of fact in the case. The vice entirely escapes you, as long as you consider the object.[12]

We can't observe that the action is wrong (that it's a vice); only that it's a deliberate killing.

---

[12] David Hume, *A Treatise of Human Nature* (Oxford: Clarendon, 1978), 468.

But that's not to say that we cannot observe *some* matter of fact. This fact, however, turns out to be merely a fact about our feelings.

> You never can find it [i.e., the matter of fact], till you turn your reflection into your own breast, and find a sentiment of disapprobation, which arises in you, towards this action. Here is a matter of fact; but 'tis the object of feeling, not of reason. It lies in yourself, not in the object. So that when you pronounce any action or character to be vicious, you mean nothing, but that from the constitution of your nature you have a feeling or sentiment of blame from the contemplation of it.[13]

That is, in some sense we "perceive" that lying is wrong, but what we perceive, says Hume, is our *feeling* of wrongness. The only thing you can point to—the only evidence you have that lying is wrong—is your feeling that it's wrong.

So then, Hume believed that if we take science seriously and apply it to ethics, we discover that morality is founded on nothing more than feelings or "sentiments." "All morality depends upon our sentiments; and when any action, or quality of the mind, pleases us *after a certain manner*, we say it is virtuous; and when the neglect, or non-performance of it, displeases us *after a like manner*, we say that we lie under an obligation to perform it."[14] It's not always clear whether Hume was outright denying moral realism or merely pointing out that the only aspect of morality we can perceive is our feelings. But given his empiricism, the latter implies the former. And in any case, he certainly believed that the methods of science cannot support the *truth* of our moral beliefs.[15]

But Hume believed that science has *something* to contribute to morality, indeed something surprising. He believed that his discovery was similar to that of *secondary qualities*. "Vice and virtue, therefore, may be compar'd to sounds, colours, heat and cold, which, according to modern philosophy, are not qualities in objects, but perceptions in the mind."[16] The astonishing fact is that the color of an apple isn't in the

---

[13] Ibid., 468–69.

[14] Ibid., 517.

[15] Nor can *reason* support their truth. We'll look at this more closely later, but Hume is famous for arguing that logic cannot bridge the gap between facts about the world and our moral values. We can't, he said, derive an "ought" from an "is." Moreover, because Hume is also skeptical about God's existence, he rejects the view that there are moral laws promulgated by a divine lawgiver.

[16] Hume, *A Treatise of Human Nature*, 469.

apple but in the person perceiving the apple. To be sure, the apple is composed of molecules of a specific structure, and the light that reflects off of the surface molecules has a specific wavelength, but the *color* is only psychological (or psychophysical). The color is *caused* by external factors, but *exists* only beneath the person's skin. The color is subjective (the person is the perceiving subject). Similarly, there are external factors that cause in us our moral sentiments, but we are the source of those sentiments, and so—on Hume's view—we're the source of moral value; morality is *subjective*.

Yet this shouldn't be disconcerting, Hume continues; after all, it won't change our actual behavior. And, again, this is due to the power that our moral beliefs hold over us.

> And this discovery in morals, like that other in physics, is to be regarded as a considerable advancement of the speculative sciences; tho', like that too, it has little or no influence on practice. Nothing can be more real, or concern us more, than our own sentiments of pleasure and uneasiness; and if these be favourable to virtue, and unfavourable to vice, no more can be requisite to the regulation of our conduct and behaviour.[17]

What more could we want or expect? In our everyday life, we still respond to sounds, colors, and smells the way we did prior to learning that they're not objective or out there in the world. So too after learning something similar about morality. We couldn't help ourselves anyway; nature is too strong.

We'll visit Hume again when we discuss the celebrated *is/ought* distinction. The point for now, however, is that moral feelings—our intuitions about right and wrong—are powerful players in ethical theory, as Hume recognized. And the strength of our moral beliefs can cause us to make some pretty serious errors when it comes to reasoning about ethics.

Few unbelievers have ever followed Hume to the conclusion that there's nothing more to our moral foundations than the strength of our convictions. So there must be good naturalistic reasons for thinking there's more to morality than sentiments. What then is the common naturalist story of our moral lives? This story must be convincing

---

[17] Ibid.

enough to overcome the Enlightenment's discovery that science presents serious puzzles for our common-sense ethical views.

Perhaps Darwin is the key. After all, Darwin allegedly allowed atheists to lead intellectually fulfilled lives. So then, what does Darwinist orthodoxy say about the origin of our moral beliefs? And does this story support moral realism? If so, how? If not, how does naturalism explain our recalcitrant belief in objective moral standards and obligations?

13

Moral Mammals:
The Evolution of Ethics

As I said, I'm concerned here with the foundation of morality: what *makes* actions right, wrong, and obligatory. Traditionally, at least in the West, God has been this foundation. But with the rise of modern science, and especially Darwinism, there's some doubt about whether God is still up to the task, in large part because science is thought to have shown that he doesn't exist. And even if we leave open the question of whether science has shown that there's no God, we're still left with a popular belief—popular at least among scientists and philosophers—that morality evolved, along with our heads, shoulders, knees, and toes. And given this biological account of morality, it seems reasonable to ask whether or not biology is all there is to morality. And if it is, what does this imply about the authority of our moral beliefs, if anything?

An Evolved Sense of Decency

In 1975, American biologist E. O. Wilson introduced the field of sociobiology, the attempt to explain social—including moral—behavior in purely evolutionary terms. Singer describes Wilson's seminal book *Sociobiology: The New Synthesis* as

> a pioneering multi-disciplinary study that aroused a storm of controversy because Wilson applied theories about the evolution of social

behavior—in organisms as different as bees and chimpanzees—to humans, thus challenging our cherished idea that we are entirely distinct from nonhuman animals. . . . Those parts of sociobiology that relate to human beings are now referred to as "evolutionary psychology."[1]

Although the book was controversial at the time, it's now common to take for granted the evolutionary origin of our moral beliefs. Hitchens, for example, states without fanfare that "our morality evolved. Just as we have."[2]

As far as evidence for the evolution of morality, Singer and former Harvard evolutionary biologist Marc Hauser point to studies that, to their minds,

provide empirical support for the idea that like other psychological faculties of the mind, including language and mathematics, we are endowed with a moral faculty that guides our intuitive judgments of right and wrong, interacting in interesting ways with the local culture. These intuitions reflect the outcome of millions of years in which our ancestors have lived as social mammals, and are part of our common inheritance, as much as our opposable thumbs are.[3]

The general picture is this: our moral beliefs have been fashioned over time to help us survive. "Ethical" behavior tends to keep us alive long enough to produce the next generation.

The Problem of Altruism

But can evolution really explain our moral sense, particularly something like altruism? After all, one of the paradigmatic characteristics of morality is that it is *others*-oriented; yet evolution allegedly winnows out traits that aren't in the interests of self-preservation. As Dawkins puts the question, "Where does the Good Samaritan in us come from? Isn't goodness incompatible with the theory of the 'selfish gene'?"[4]

Not if the path to self-preservation runs through the well-being of

---

[1] Peter Singer, *The Expanding Circle: Ethics, Evolution, and Moral Progress* (Princeton, NJ: Princeton University Press, 2011), xii.
[2] Christopher Hitchens and Douglas Wilson, *Is Christianity Good for the World?* (Moscow, ID: Canon, 2008), 59–60.
[3] Marc Hauser and Peter Singer, "Morality without Religion," *Free Inquiry* 26, no. 1 (2005): 19.
[4] Richard Dawkins, *The God Delusion* (Boston: Houghton Mifflin, 2006), 246.

others, others who will improve your chances of living to fight another day. The shark and remora need one another; the bee and flower provide mutual benefits that would otherwise go unmet. We see symbiosis all over the biological world, and so this you-scratch-my-back reciprocation makes evolutionary sense. So too for human animals. Societies and their necessary moral norms are far more conducive to preserving our genes than a life lived in total isolation. Thomas Hobbes remarked that our lives, lived entirely apart from other humans, would be brutish, nasty, and short.

Another pervasive form of altruism occurs among family members, among those who share exceptionally close genetic ties. As Dawkins says, "Animals tend to care for, defend, share resources with, warn of danger, or otherwise show altruism towards close kin because of the statistical likelihood that kin will share copies of the same genes."[5]

So then, in kinship- and reciprocation-altruism, an organism temporarily sacrifices its own well-being for that of another. This is, according to sociobiology, simply an adaptation that allows us more adeptly to survive in societies of organisms. It's merely one more survival tool—like potable water and trail mix—one ultimately used to benefit the individual wielding it. And so altruism, on this story, is a form of selfishness. Even at our best, we are, in the end, acting out of selfish ambition and vain conceit.

This explanation of altruism is certainly out of step with our standard view of traditional ethics. But Sam Harris puts a happy face on it: "There is a circle here that links us to one another: we each want to be happy; the social feeling of love is one of our greatest sources of happiness; and love entails that we be concerned for the happiness of others. We discover that we can be selfish together."[6] This is touching, but still not what we had in mind.

Puppets of Our Emotions

In any case, some of our moral sentiments—feelings of compassion, kindness, and sympathy—are allegedly natural instincts that we can hardly help. As Dawkins explains, "We can no more help ourselves feeling pity when we see a weeping unfortunate (who is unrelated and

---

[5] Ibid., 247.
[6] Sam Harris, *The End of Faith: Religion, Terror, and the Future of Reason* (New York: W. W. Norton, 2004), 187.

unable to reciprocate) than we can help ourselves feeling lust for a member of the opposite sex (who may be infertile or otherwise unable to reproduce)."[7]

So, on the purely evolutionary story, our moral judgments may merely be the result of biological processes, like sex drive, hunger, and our urge to visit Hawaii in January. Here we stand; we can do no other. Or as Hume would say, nature is too strong for us (although there's plenty of evidence that this is not at all true: we're pretty good at over-powering our altruistic urges).

Calvin and Hobbes © 1993 Watterson. Reprinted with permission of Universal Uclick. All rights reserved.

Being the puppets of our emotions is troubling enough. But there's something else: our moral judgments were selected for long ago, and for situations far removed. And today these judgments often put us in situations that aren't at all beneficial for our survival. Take the example of adopting a child or having sex with someone who is on the pill.[8] When we sacrifice our well-being for those who can't return the favor or who don't share our blood, we're really being tricked by our biology. Dawkins calls these erroneous urges *misfirings*, but doesn't want the term to sound pejorative.[9] They are, he says, misfirings only insofar as evolution is concerned: they're "Darwinian mistakes" but "blessed, precious mistakes" nonetheless.[10]

It's easy then to see how a naturalist might be pessimistic about the prospect of finding an objective foundation for traditional morality—or any objective morality at all. It seems plausible that evolution has

---

[7] Dawkins, *The God Delusion*, 253.
[8] Ibid., 252–53.
[9] Ibid., 252.
[10] Ibid., 253.

simply programmed us to mistakenly believe in moral realism just so we can live long enough to add our DNA to the gene pool. As Harvard psychologist Joshua Greene says:

> We are, in fact, so well adapted to making moral judgments that our making them is, from our point of view, rather easy, a part of "common sense." And like many of our common sense abilities, our ability to make moral judgments feels to us like a perceptual ability, an ability, in this case, to discern immediately and reliably mind-independent moral facts. As a result, we are naturally inclined toward a mistaken belief in moral realism. The psychological tendencies that encourage this false belief serve an important biological purpose, and that explains why we should find moral realism so attractive even though it is false. Moral realism is, once again, a mistake we were born to make.[11]

The moral implications of what atheist philosopher Daniel Dennett calls "Darwin's dangerous idea" seem bleak indeed, at least compared to the familiar idea of a divinely given moral law. Indeed, as Dennett says, "today, more than a century after Darwin's death, we still have not come to terms with its mind-boggling implications."[12]

Not that we haven't tried. As Mackie points out, the possibility of objective morality "was discussed vigorously in the nineteen thirties and forties, but since then has received much less attention. This is not because it has been solved or because agreement has been reached: instead it seems to have been politely shelved."[13] Nor is it that people no longer argue over what sorts of actions are right and wrong; this too seems to be something we can't help. But the question *says who?* or *by what standard?* must again come back into the limelight. All other ethical questions are secondary.

It's time, then, for naturalists to take their neo-Darwinian worldview seriously, including whatever it says about morality. It's time for them to embrace their story. What if Dawkins, for example, is right and "absolutist [i.e., objective] moral discrimination is devastatingly undermined

---

[11] Quoted in Sam Harris, *The Moral Landscape: How Science Can Determine Human Values* (New York: Free Press, 2010), 65.
[12] Daniel C. Dennett, *Darwin's Dangerous Idea: Evolution and the Meanings of Life* (New York: Simon & Schuster, 1995), 19.
[13] J. L. Mackie, *Ethics: Inventing Right and Wrong* (1977; repr., London: Penguin, 1990), 20–21.

by the fact of evolution"?[14] Does the current Darwinian story of human origins—including the origins of our beliefs about right and wrong—indicate what Humeans have always believed? Are our moral beliefs nothing more than sentiments or feelings? When we say that Hitler was wrong to kill six million Jews, are we (truthfully) saying nothing more than that we dislike what he did?

How the Leopard Got Its Spots

In all of this, I haven't considered the possibility that sociobiologists have their facts wrong. This is a legitimate possibility, however, the worry being that, in the words of atheist philosopher Philip Kitcher, "evolutionary explanations . . . run the risk of becoming exercises in storytelling—just-so stories without Kipling's wit."[15] After all, Kitcher says, "reconstructing the *actual* history of the ethical project, from its beginnings to the present, is plainly beyond the evidence available—and probably beyond the evidence anyone could ever hope to obtain."[16] And this, we saw, is true of evolution in general. Though some hypotheses can perhaps be defended,[17] an evolutionary story of our ethical development "cannot be advertised as a 'how actually' explanation; instead it is a 'how possibly' explanation."[18]

I myself am fairly skeptical about the evolutionary explanations as a whole. I have no doubt that our moral code(s) provide survival advantage over many of the alternatives. But this biological benefit does not in itself imply that our ethics developed naturalistically. It may be, for example, that a divine Lawgiver hardwired us with knowledge of moral laws, and one of the benefits of following them is that things will generally go better for us, as well as for others.

In much of what follows, however, I'll take the evolutionary story for granted and see where it leads. I'll argue that naturalism implies moral nihilism, since this is what I think the evolutionary story of ethics implies. But there have been some serious naturalistic attempts to ground morality in something more objective than our evolved sentiments. We'll consider these in the next chapter. But before we do, I want

---

[14] Dawkins, *The God Delusion*, 340.
[15] Philip Kitcher, *The Ethical Project* (Cambridge, MA: Harvard University Press, 2011), 10.
[16] Ibid., 11.
[17] Ibid.
[18] Ibid., 12.

to raise two general concerns I have about the evolutionary picture of our moral origins.

Could Our Sentiments Be Correct?

Is it possible that our biologically conditioned moral feelings are accurate? Might they identify or align with genuine moral standards "out there" in the world. After all, we believe that other mental states correctly portray the mind-independent world. For example, the perceptual image you have of a traffic-free street correctly represents an objective state of affairs outside your mind. Or so we're assuming. Similarly, your moral intuitions just may in fact glom on to an objective morality.

This is certainly possible, but there's really no evolutionary explanation for such accuracy. That is, an evolutionary account doesn't *require* an external moral standard to make sense. In fact, such a standard wouldn't *make sense* according to evolution. This is in total contrast to the evolutionary account of our perceptual states of material objects. As Thomas Nagel says, "From a Darwinian perspective, the hypothesis of value realism is superfluous—a wheel that spins without being attached to anything. From a Darwinian perspective our impressions of value, if construed realistically, are completely groundless."[19] That is, moral *beliefs* (which are grounded in feelings) are all that we need to account for the survival benefits that morality provides, whereas a perceptual belief that there's no oncoming traffic requires that there also *be* no oncoming traffic out there in the world.[20] Citing philosopher Sharon Street, Nagel explains:

> Street points out that if the responses and faculties that generate our value judgments are in significant part the result of natural selection, there is no reason to expect that they would lead us to be able to detect any mind-independent moral or evaluative truth, if there is such a thing. That is because the ability to detect such truth, unlike the ability to detect mind-independent truth about the physical world, would make no contribution to reproductive fitness. . . . [It] is completely irrelevant whether those faculties enable us to de-

[19] Thomas Nagel, *Mind and Cosmos: Why the Materialist Neo-Darwinian Conception of Nature Is Almost Certainly False* (Oxford: Oxford University Press), 109.
[20] We're ignoring the possibility that we're BIVs.

tect mind-independent moral truth, should there be such a thing, or whether they lead us radically astray.[21]

That's not to say that moral realism is false, but merely that it's not needed to explain the usefulness of our moral beliefs. Ockham's razor shaves off the superfluous objective moral standards.

Notice that it's much more plausible to think that our moral beliefs glom on to some objective moral reality if theism is true. You'll remember that St. Paul says that humans have the law written on their hearts. This is taken by some—including me—to suggest that God has designed us with a cognitive faculty—a belief-forming mechanism—that reliably recognizes his moral values. At least it was reliable prior to humanity's fall into sin. And despite the resulting damage to all our cognitive faculties, our moral faculty functions properly enough to give a decent gauge of God's moral law. (More on this when we discuss how God provides us with binding and human-independent moral standards.)

Still Evolving after All These Years?

The first problem with the evolutionary picture of morality, then, is that objective moral standards would perform no explanatory work when it comes to our moral beliefs. And this is because there's simply no work for them to do.

The second problem with the evolutionary account is that our moral beliefs *evolved*. If these beliefs have evolved, might not they continue doing so as humans adapt to different environments? It seems the height of arrogance—or at least an impressive lack of imagination—to think that we've "arrived" at a final, internal ethical code. As Hauser and Singer argue, "What was good for our ancestors may not be good for human beings as a whole today, let alone for our planet and all the other beings living on it."[22] And Hauser and Singer go on to say that not only does morality evolve, but we need not wait for generations of biological adaptation; we can go ahead and choose a morality that fits our current needs.

Insights into the changing moral landscape (e.g., animal rights, abortion, euthanasia, international aid) have not come from religion,

---

[21] Nagel, *Mind and Cosmos*, 107.
[22] Hauser and Singer, "Morality without Religion," 19.

but from careful reflection on humanity and what we consider a life well lived. In this respect, it is important for us to be aware of the universal set of moral intuitions so that we can reflect on them and, if we choose, act contrary to them. We can do this without blasphemy, because it is our own nature, not God, that is the source of our species morality.[23]

After all, we're aware of how we've changed our tune on important ethical issues, as we look back sheepishly on previously held moral beliefs. Dawkins gives examples of Thomas Huxley and Abraham Lincoln both asserting the superiority of white people. And Dawkins rightly says, "Had Huxley and Lincoln been born and educated in our time, they would have been the first to cringe with the rest of us at their own Victorian sentiments and unctuous tone. I quote them only to illustrate how the *Zeitgeist* moves on."[24] Times change, and so do our moral beliefs. Why think they'll stop?

And as they change, why think that they're getting closer to the moral truth? Can we say that our current moral beliefs are an improvement over our previous ones? Kitcher asks, "Is the evolution of ethics a matter of *mere change*? Is it analogous to a Darwinian picture of the history of life, revealing only local adaptations without any overall upward trend? . . . Is it just one damn thing after another?"[25] Well, we can certainly say that we *like* our current set of ethical standards better than our previous ones; but can we say that they're *objectively* better? By what standard would we measure this? Or does "best" mean "what we now believe."

Although the possibility of modifying our moral beliefs might be unsettling, there's at least one consolation. According to the evolutionary story, our moral beliefs are merely survival tools, not the apprehending of eternal truths. But it's plausible that certain currently untoward behaviors aid our survival: rape, aggression, xenophobia, and male promiscuity.[26] These are not only natural but arguably advantageous. Yet they now offend us. Since morality is up to us, however, we can choose to put rape and aggression on the immoral list. This is the good news.

[23] Ibid.
[24] Dawkins, *The God Delusion*, 303.
[25] Kitcher, *The Ethical Project*, 138.
[26] Samir Okasha, *Philosophy of Science: A Very Short Introduction* (Oxford: Oxford University Press, 2002), 131.

But the bad news would be that morality seems to be merely a matter of preference. We can *choose* our standards.

What Should a Poor Primate Do?

A common charge leveled at naturalism is that, since behavior like rape and aggression aid in our survival, evolution implies that we *ought* to behave in these ways. In other words, we ought to do whatever is natural. This has been a common inference from Darwinism since the nineteenth century. According to Dennett, people like Herbert Spencer believed that we should adopt a "survival of the fittest" approach to life. That is, the survival of the fittest, "Spencer proclaimed, is not just Mother Nature's way, but *ought* to be *our* way. According to the Social Darwinists, it is 'natural' for the strong to vanquish the weak, and for the rich to exploit the poor."[27] Of course, this has been picked up on by those who oppose naturalism. William Lane Craig, for example, says:

> If life ends at the grave, then it makes no difference whether one has lived as a Stalin or as a saint. Since one's destiny is ultimately unrelated to one's savior, you may as well live as you please. . . . On this basis, a writer like Ayn Rand is absolutely correct to praise the virtues of selfishness. Live totally for self; no one holds you accountable! Indeed, it would be foolish to do anything else, for life is too short to jeopardize it by acting out of anything but pure self-interest. Sacrifice for another person would be stupid.[28]

Although I agree with much of what Craig says here (and elsewhere), even if naturalism is true and selfishness is the most reliable way to ensure an organism's survival, does it follow that we *should* behave selfishly?

I don't see why, at least not simply by virtue of the fact that selfish acts give us reproductive advantage. *Natural* means neither "good" nor "ought." Many natural things are quite bad. As Dennett points out, "It is equally 'natural' to die young and illiterate, without benefit of eyeglasses for myopia, or medicine for illness."[29] Naturalness alone isn't an indicator of what we ought to value.

---

[27] Dennett, *Darwin's Dangerous Idea*, 510.
[28] William Lane Craig, "The Absurdity of Life without God," in *The Meaning of Life*, ed. E. D. Klemke (Oxford: Oxford University Press, 2000), 43.
[29] Dennett, *Darwin's Dangerous Idea*, 461.

Of course, if your overarching goal is to survive at any cost, then perhaps—given our assumption that selfish behavior is always selected for—it would be "foolish to do anything else," as Craig says. Nothing, however, in evolution says that you *ought* to value your own survival above all else. It is simply silent on the matter. Here I agree with atheist Jerry Coyne: "How can you derive meaning, purpose, or ethics from evolution? You can't. Evolution is simply a theory about the process and patterns of life's diversification, not a grand philosophical scheme about the meaning of life. It can't tell us what to do, or how we should behave."[30]

But even if evolution proper cannot dictate what we should or shouldn't do, most atheists believe that naturalism in general can support objective morality. They believe, for example, that there are naturalistic accounts of objective morality—and perhaps of objective value in general. In the next chapter we'll look at the most common and plausible ways that a naturalist might successfully account for human-independent moral standards.

---

[30] Jerry A. Coyne, *Why Evolution Is True* (New York: Penguin, 2009), 225.

An All-Natural Morality?

The "Well-Being" Theory of Morality

As we've seen, there are *prima facie* reasons to doubt that the standard naturalistic story can support objective morality. Maybe Dostoyevsky was right: maybe everything would be permissible if there were no God.

Or maybe not. There's actually a pretty obvious way to naturalistically ground morality in facts that don't depend on simply what we *believe* about morality. In this chapter I'll do two things. The first will be to present this naturalistic version of morality, focusing on Sam Harris's view. After that I'll look at what I consider to be substantial problems with Harris's account.

So then, consider that there's an objective fact about whether a human being is suffering. Suppose the pain in your lower back is excruciating. You're suffering, regardless of anyone's beliefs. Suppose that, a few days later, the pain is gone. All things being equal, you're better off than you were. In fact, your well-being seems traceable to facts about your physiology—to physical facts. And these physical facts—facts about your brain states for example—are objective. Moreover, they can be studied by science.

This is Harris's line of reasoning in *The Moral Landscape: How Science Can Determine Human Values*. For example, he says:

> Questions about values—about meaning, morality, and life's larger
> purpose—are really questions about the well-being of conscious

creatures. Values, therefore, translate into facts that can be scientifically understood: regarding positive and negative social emotions, retributive impulses, the effects of special laws and social institutions on human relationships, the neurophysiology of happiness and suffering, etc. The most important of these facts are bound to transcend culture—just as facts about physical and mental health do. Cancer in the highlands of New Guinea is still cancer; cholera is still cholera; schizophrenia is still schizophrenia; and so, too, I will argue, compassion is still compassion, and well-being is still well-being.[1]

If, as Harris explains, "human well-being depends entirely on events in the world and on states of the human brain,"[2] then well-being is something that science can speak to directly. And therefore if morality is ultimately a matter of the well-being of conscious creatures, then science can speak directly to *morality*. Or as Harris puts it, science can determine human values.

This would be a big step forward for naturalists. Imagine a culture that practices infanticide (as the ancient Greeks did). Are their moral values worse than ours? "Most people," says Harris, "imagine that science cannot pose, much less answer, questions of this sort."[3] Dawkins confesses that he was one such person. In his praise of Harris's book, Dawkins admits:

> I was one of those who had unthinkingly bought into the hectoring myth that science can say nothing about morals. *The Moral Landscape* has changed all that for me. Moral philosophers, too, will find their world exhilaratingly turned upside down, as they discover a need to learn some neuroscience.[4]

No doubt neuroscience is in its infancy, but as Harris says,

> If there are objective truths to be known about human well-being—if kindness, for instance, is generally more conducive to happiness than cruelty is—then science should one day be able to make very precise

---

[1] Sam Harris, *The Moral Landscape: How Science Can Determine Human Values* (New York: Free Press, 2010), 1–2.
[2] Ibid., 2.
[3] Ibid., 1.
[4] Ibid.

claims about which of our behaviors and uses of attention are morally good, which are neutral, and which are worth abandoning.[5]

Notice, then, that Harris—who himself has a PhD in neuroscience—is in his own way applying the "experimental method" to the human subject. Hume would be proud.

And Harris's Humean project depends on morality being reduced to matters of well-being—that is, to matters of happiness and suffering manifested in brain states. What reason does Harris offer for making ethics a matter of well-being? It's pretty simple, he says:

> We need only admit that the experiences of conscious creatures are lawfully dependent upon states of the universe—and, therefore, that actions can cause more harm than good, more good than harm or be morally neutral. Good and evil need only consist in this, and it makes no sense whatsoever to claim that an action that harms everyone affected by it (even its perpetrator) might still be "good."
> . . . The main criterion, therefore, is that misery and well-being not be completely random.[6]

Harris defines *good* as anything that "supports well-being"[7] and *bad* as that which causes harm: "It seems uncontroversial to say that a change that leaves everyone worse off, by any rational standard, can be reasonably called 'bad,' if this word is to have any meaning at all."[8] As he puts it elsewhere, "A rational approach to ethics becomes possible once we realize that questions of right and wrong are really questions about the happiness and suffering of sentient creatures."[9]

In one sense, Harris's view isn't at all new. It's a version of *utilitarianism*, made famous by the nineteenth-century philosopher John Stuart Mill, who said:

> The creed which accepts as the foundations of morals "utility" or the "greatest happiness principle" holds that actions are right in proportion as they tend to promote happiness; wrong as they tend to produce the reverse of happiness. By happiness is intended pleasure

---

[5] Ibid., 8.
[6] Ibid., 198n4.
[7] Ibid., 12.
[8] Ibid., 39.
[9] Sam Harris, *The End of Faith: Religion, Terror, and the Future of Reason* (New York: W. W. Norton, 2004), 171.

and the absence of pain; by unhappiness, pain and the privation of pleasure.[10]

Mill's view of good is often summarized as "the greatest happiness for the greatest number of people." Views such as Mill's and Harris's are known as *consequentialist* views because the rightness or wrongness of an action depends on the act's *results* or *consequences* (as opposed to the intention of the agent or laws set down by a divine being). According to consequentialist views, the end justifies the means. Mill's and Harris's accounts are also called *hedonistic* theories because they identify goodness with (or reduce it to) pleasure or happiness, although this pleasure need not be simply physical pleasure but includes "higher" pleasures like love, friendship, and education. (For Harris, though, even these higher pleasures can, presumably, be reduced to physical properties, like brain states.)

In *Morality without God?*, Sinnott-Armstrong argues for a similar view, what he calls a "harm-based morality." According to this view, "What really makes certain acts immoral is . . . that such acts cause harm to other people for no good reason."[11] The benefit of this view, according to Sinnott-Armstrong, is that it is "completely secular." "Those harms occur and those acts cause them regardless of whether the agent or the victim believes in God, and also regardless of whether there is a God."[12] Even though there may be disagreements about "what counts as a harm and about what counts as causing harm as well as about which harms are worse,"[13] "there is no reason to doubt that death, pain, and disability are bad."[14] This is no doubt true. But is it enough to account for morality?

What Is Well-Being?

We've seen the most (ahem) natural way for an unbeliever to account for objective morality without having to rely on God: to define a moral act as one that contributes to well-being, and an immoral act as one that reduces it. In what follows I'll look at a number of reasons for being suspicious about Harris's account.

---

[10] John Stuart Mill, *Utilitarianism*, 2nd ed., ed. George Sher (Indianapolis: Hackett, 2001), 7.
[11] Walter Sinnott-Armstrong, *Morality without God?* (Oxford: Oxford University Press, 2009), 65.
[12] Ibid., 68.
[13] Ibid., 59.
[14] Ibid.

Perhaps the first question we might ask of Harris is this: what exactly *is* well-being? Is there a way to define it so that we'll have something precise to guide us? That might be asking a bit too much, but Harris says, reasonably enough: "It seems to me . . . that the concept of well-being is like the concept of physical health: it resists precise definition, and yet it is indispensable. In fact, the meanings of both terms seem likely to remain perpetually open to revision as we make progress in science."[15] This is probably right: the concept of well-being or happiness is vague, and we shouldn't ask for more precision than is reasonable for the subject. Maybe the most we can do is point to uncontroversial examples and hope for the best. A stubbed toe decreases my well-being, all things considered. A knee replacement will likely increase it, despite the obvious downsides. Getting married could go either way. And what about going to church?

When it comes to the details, our definition of well-being will depend on our worldview. That is, whatever we count as "well-being" will be influenced by what sorts of things we value and what we think reality is like. In other words, the concept of well-being is *theory-laden*. For example, it will depend on what you believe about the *origins* and purposes of sentient creatures. Your view of human beings might imply that brain states aren't the only things to consider when it comes to our well-being. And when it comes to issues like these, believers and unbelievers may see things differently.

Identical Brain States

And here's a reason to think that brain states aren't the only things that matter for well-being (and therefore for morality). Notice that two identical brain states (regardless of their causes) would result in identical "levels" of well-being. Imagine a scenario in which there are two identically happy brain states. The first is that of a BIV hooked to a vast computer that can, by stimulating the proper neurons, produce the requisite amount of happiness. From its point of view the BIV is leading a life of bliss such as (insert your idea of bliss here), but in reality it's nothing more than a brain in a vat. The second and identical brain state belongs to a person who is actually living the blissful life you imagined. Which would you rather be? The one seems far better off than the other.

---

[15] Harris, *The Moral Landscape*, 11–12.

Yet, if brain states are all there are to well-being, then according to Harris's account, both states are flourishing equally. But this seems to be the wrong answer. So even if morality is only a matter of well-being, it seems doubtful that well-being is simply a matter of brain states.

Individuals versus the Collective

Well-being is usually cashed out in terms of the greatest good for the greatest number of people. But no one ever experiences this *collective* happiness. That is, Harris's brain-state view trucks in the happiness or well-being that is experienced by humans (and perhaps other sentient beings). But no one experiences more than a single brain's state—namely, his or her own. Of course, other people's well-being may contribute to yours, but that is a different issue—one of what *causes* an individual's brain states. The maximum pleasure ever experienced by anyone is still that of a sole individual's brain state. A collective or additive happiness or well-being is something that no one experiences. It doesn't exist.

Who Is My Neighbor?

Let us suppose, however, that we *can* countenance a kind of collective well-being. According to Harris's account, we'll need to include the entire human species *and then some*. That is, morality might need to take into account additional species, not just humans. Harris's theory is that morality can be reduced to the brain states of conscious or sentient creatures. By this he means any organism that can experience pain and pleasure to any degree whatsoever. And since morality is a matter of pleasure and pain only—as it is for utilitarian views generally—it seems that our moral community increases significantly. This is the conclusion Singer takes for his own utilitarian view. In *The Expanding Circle*, he says:

> In my earlier book, *Animal Liberation*, I showed that it is as arbitrary to restrict the principle of equal consideration of interests to our own species as it would be to restrict it to our own race. . . . The expansion of the moral circle should therefore be pushed out until it includes most animals. (I say "most" rather than "all" because there comes a point as we move down the evolutionary scale—oysters, perhaps, or even more rudimentary organisms—when it becomes

doubtful if the creature we are dealing with is capable of feeling anything.)[16]

But that's not to say that all animals are morally *equal*. It's not the case, according to Singer,

> that a human being and a mouse must always be treated equally, or that their lives are of equal value. Humans have interests—in ideas, in education, in their future plans—that mice are not capable of having. It is only when we are comparing similar interests—of which the interest in avoiding pain is the most important example—that the principle of equal consideration of interests demand that we give equal weight to the interests of the human and the mouse.[17]

Nevertheless, allowing every sentient creature into our "moral circle" will require a significant change in our moral outlook. Singer concedes that "the idea of equal consideration for animals strikes many as bizarre, but perhaps no more bizarre than the idea of equal consideration for blacks seemed three hundred years ago. We are witnessing the first stirrings of a momentous new stage in our moral thinking."[18] And to be sure, if pleasure and pain are the only criteria, Singer is being entirely consistent.

I agree with Singer that it seems "bizarre," if for no other reason than that we seem to be forced to acknowledge all manner of animal wickedness. It would, for example, be immoral and evil—and not merely repulsive—for a male lion to rape a female lion or eat a lion cub.[19]

But this certainly goes against our ordinary conception of morality. That is, it's tempting to think that Richard Taylor is right when he says, "A hawk that seizes a fish from the sea *kills* it, but does not *murder* it; and another hawk that seizes that fish from the talons of the first *takes* it, but does not *steal* it—for none of these things is forbidden."[20] The well-being of these animals is certainly impacted; things are going well for the one and badly for the other. The results are *good for* the one, and *bad for* the other. Even so, it doesn't *seem* that there is anything relevant

---

[16] Peter Singer, *The Expanding Circle: Ethics, Evolution, and Moral Progress* (Princeton, NJ: Princeton University Press, 2011), 121.

[17] Ibid.

[18] Ibid.

[19] You don't even want to know what naked mole rats are capable of. See (if you dare) Daniel C. Dennett, *Darwin's Dangerous Idea: Evolution and the Meanings of Life* (New York: Simon & Schuster, 1995), 484.

[20] Richard Taylor, *Ethics, Faith, and Reason* (Englewood Cliffs, NJ: Prentice-Hall, 1985), 14.

to morality going on here. And therefore well-being doesn't *seem*, in itself, to imply anything about morality.

Again, if Harris and Singer are right, we may just have to change our minds about including animals within our moral circle. But it would be nice to have a reason for doing so that is independent of Harris's theory, since including animals in this way seems to be one of the theory's downsides.

Reason Is on Our Side

By expanding our moral circle to include animals that are red in tooth and claw, we would increase the global crime rate to unheard-of levels (at least insofar as immorality is outlawed). But maybe we don't have to. Maybe there's something special about humans that makes *their* well-being different from the well-being of other conscious creatures. This would be worth knowing because then we wouldn't be saddled with the idea that animals are morally blameworthy. Although Harris and Singer do not limit their theories to humans, we should consider this option. It might make their utilitarianism seem more plausible.

Although each of us is special—a unique and beautiful snowflake—there's something common to us all that makes the human species stand out. Or so we're told. The standard claim is that *reason* elevates us above the other animals. Mark Murphy, for example, says:

> [The natural] kind *human* is obviously a distinct sort of organism, and distinct in ways that are obviously ethically significant. To take one example: human beings possess *reflective* and *objectivizing* intelligence, which enables them to call their inclinations into question and to see themselves as one person among others.[21]

Let us assume that—contrary to fact, it seems to me—humans are the only beings on earth endowed with reason. Ignore evidence that monkeys, dogs, and even pigs and crows have such a faculty. William Lane Craig asks us to perform a thought experiment:

> Imagine that an extraterrestrial race came from another planet, who was as superior to us in intelligence as we are to pigs and cows, and

---

[21] Mark C. Murphy, "Theism, Atheism, and the Explanation of Moral Value," in *Is Goodness without God Good Enough? A Debate on Faith, Secularism, and Ethics*, ed. Robert K. Garcia and Nathan L. King (Lanham, MD: Rowman & Littlefield, 2009), 125.

that they began to farm the earth and began using us as food and laboring animals. What could the atheist say to show them that human beings have intrinsic moral value? That they ought not do this to *human beings*?[22]

It seems to me that the answer is *nothing*, meaning not even reason. Moreover, even if the aliens were no more rational than we are, it seems that the answer would still be the same. I don't think we could point to our rationality alone as something that *ought* to prevent them from harvesting or harnessing us. It is entirely conceivable that our reason would simply make us more useful to them.

This isn't a full-blown argument against thinking that reason makes a moral difference and thereby excluding rats from our moral circle, but it does put a speed bump in the road to that conclusion.

Is Well-Being a Prudential or Moral Good?

So, there are reasons to think that merely taking well-being into account isn't enough to make Harris's theory a theory of *morality*. And there are additional and more general reasons for thinking this. But such reasons become much more abstract, and we'll have to wade carefully into such foreboding waters. I warn you that the going may be rough and uncomfortable. But it's necessary nonetheless. After all, ignoring such considerations makes Harris's view plausible—not only to Harris but to others as well (remember Dawkins's glowing endorsement). And we can't have that.

Let's back up. Remember that we're looking for a naturalistic theory of *morality*. And Harris has offered a popular version of such a theory, one to which he adds the word *neuroscience*. His view is that morality is a matter of well-being, and that if science can determine what constitutes well-being, then it can determine morality. If he's right, we need not engage in endless debates over whether abortion is wrong: we need only read the answer directly off of science. Does abortion increase or decrease well-being (i.e., happiness or pleasure)? Yes or no?

But we've seen a few problems with Harris's view. For one thing it seems highly questionable that morality can be reduced to well-being alone. And even if it could, there are reasons to doubt that brain states

---

[22] Paul Kurtz and William Lane Craig, "The Kurtz/Craig Debate: Is Goodness without God Good Enough?," in Garcia and King, *Is Goodness without God Good Enough?*, 41.

are all there are to well-being. Furthermore, we've seen that Harris's theory places cats and naked mole rats within our "moral circle," and there seems to be no way to prevent this. Just because humans alone are capable of reason, this isn't enough to prevent these unseemly creatures' inclusion, even if it were true that only humans have a rational faculty.[23]

So Harris's theory isn't faring so well, it seems to me. But there may be further problems with it. To see these, as I've said, we'll need to take at least one step up in abstraction. We need to look at the difference between prudential value and moral value. It may be that Harris's theory is really about the former and not about the latter.

To be prudentially valuable is to be good *for a subject*, not simply good.[24] As Murphy says, "To be prudentially valuable is to be what makes a subject well-off, what makes his or her life go well, what constitutes his or her well-being."[25] But even nonhuman creatures can have goods or values in this sense. To see this, consider Thomas Nagel's naturalistic story of how value—in the sense of well-being—arose in the cosmos. (Nagel offers it only as a possibility, not as the sober truth.) "First," he says, "with the appearance of life even in its earliest forms, there come into existence entities that *have* a good, and for which things can go well or badly. Even a bacterium has a good in this sense, in virtue of its proper functioning, whereas a rock does not."[26] Again, this kind of good—prudential good—is merely *good for* a subject. It is good *for you* to avoid being hit by that bus or ingesting salmonella. But these are not, generally speaking, moral goods.

Moral goods are (allegedly) good, *period*.[27] Telling the truth, for instance, isn't merely good for you; it's just plain good—morally good. Telling the truth is good "from the point of the view of the universe."[28] (Of course, there are times when it isn't—say, when the Nazis or soldiers of Jericho are at your door asking whether you are harboring any Jews.) Telling the truth isn't good merely because it increases your well-being or even the well-being of others. It can also be good even when it harms you; you should tell the truth even if it hurts.

23 Dear cat lovers: I'm totally kidding.
24 Murphy, "Theism, Atheism, and the Explanation of Moral Value," 122.
25 Ibid.
26 Thomas Nagel, *Mind and Cosmos: Why the Materialist Neo-Darwinian Conception of Nature Is Almost Certainly False* (Oxford: Oxford University Press, 2012), 117.
27 Murphy, "Theism, Atheism, and the Explanation of Moral Value," 123.
28 Ibid.

To be sure, prudential value has some of the earmarks of moral value, which is why the two types are easily conflated. For one thing, as Murphy points out, prudential value is *objective* in that it is not "determined by the subject's own judgments of well-being."[29] (It is *good for* you to brush your teeth.) Moreover, prudential value is *universal* in that "we can give a general account of what makes all humans well-off," an account that applies to everyone.[30] (Brushing your teeth is good for us all.) Not only that, but prudential value is *normative*: there are *reasons* to pursue health, for example; there are reasons you *ought* to seek it. (Brushing your teeth can give you a winning smile.)

Despite the similarities between prudential and moral value, there are important differences. For one thing, even though prudential and moral values are *objective*, *universal*, and *normative*, prudential values appear to be conditional rather than absolute. That is, the *ought* in the prudential case—for example, you ought to brush your teeth—depends on your desires (as well as what the world is like). That is, *if* you wish to avoid unneeded trips to the dentist, and want a winning smile that will someday attract a mate, and want to avoid debilitating pain and even death, then you ought to brush your teeth.

But moral oughts don't seem to be conditional in this way; they seem to lack an "if" part. You ought to love your neighbor *no matter what*: regardless of what you or anyone else thinks; regardless of your goals, desires, or needs. There don't seem to be any ifs, ands, or buts about it.[31]

Prudential goods also seem to differ from moral goods in that moral value is *others-directed*. That is, when we say that you ought to brush your teeth, the reasons we typically give are those that benefit *you*. On the other hand, suppose we said that brushing your teeth is a form of loving your neighbor (for obvious reasons). This seems to elevate the prudential good of brushing your teeth into a moral one in that it is directed toward others and not merely yourself.

So then, all of this is to say, as Murphy says, "It does seem clear that we can distinguish conceptually between what is good for a person and what is just morally good," even if these often coincide in practice.[32] But this is a distinction that Harris's view doesn't make. In other words, he

---

[29] Ibid.
[30] Ibid.
[31] I will question this appearance later.
[32] Murphy, "Theism, Atheism, and the Explanation of Moral Value," 123.

seems to be in danger of changing the subject and not giving us a theory of morality at all. Well-being *alone* seems to be a prudential good, something that is merely good *for the subject experiencing it*. Another way of stating the problem with Harris's view is that the concepts of morality and well-being can come apart.

Harris would probably say that he has in mind the well-being of others as well as that of the subject performing the relevant act. And perhaps he does. But what reason do we have to extend the theory beyond the subject's own mental states? Is it a moral reason or a prudential one? In either case, Harris's view doesn't seem to say.

Would Perfect Correlation Be Enough?

Remember, the problem we're addressing is how a naturalist might account for moral realism, for the human-independent existence of moral laws. More specifically, we're looking for an explanation of morality that doesn't refer to entities that would make a naturalist uncomfortable. And it's clear that, for any unbeliever worth his or her salt, a divine Lawgiver is going to make things uncomfortable. The natural alternative we've been considering is that an action is right insofar as it promotes the well-being of conscious creatures (while an action is wrong insofar as it does the opposite).

And as we saw, there's something to this naturalistic view. Harris makes a plausible case for connecting well-being to morality. After all, it can be difficult to find examples in which a morally wrong action doesn't harm someone without reason. Harm does seem to track moral wrongness. Let's suppose it does. That is, we'll assume that all (and only) morally wrong actions harm someone for no good reason. Moreover, let's assume that all (and only) morally *right* actions are those that don't harm someone for no good reason. Now, if this were right, and morality and well-being track together *perfectly*, would it be enough to secure Harris's view, to show that morality is only a matter of the well-being of sentient creatures?[33] Or to put the question more precisely, would Harris be correct in saying that well-being is what *makes* an action right?

---

[33] Some readers might recognize that we're in the neighborhood of supervenience and logically equivalent properties. See Alvin Plantinga's helpful discussion about the supervenience of moral properties on naturalistic ones in Plantinga, "Naturalism, Theism, Obligation and Supervenience," *Faith and Philosophy* 27, no. 3 (2010).

Well, certainly not merely in virtue of the fact—supposing it's a fact—that morally wrong actions always decrease the well-being of the relevant individuals for no good reason (and that morally right actions don't). After all, there's a difference, we are often reminded, between cause and correlation. Here's a simple example: the reading on the thermometer outside your kitchen window tracks the outside temperature—whenever the thermometer reading increases/decreases, the temperature outside also increases/decreases proportionally. But obviously the thermometer reading has no effect on the temperature outside your window; the causal chain runs in the other direction. Here's a second and admittedly extreme example of correlation without causation, one in which there appears to be no causal chain in either direction: one study shows (let us imagine) that every mortal is under nine feet tall. Not only that, but results cited in that same study indicate that every person under nine feet tall is mortal. That is, a person is mortal (can die) if and only if that person is under nine feet tall. That's a pretty tight correlation. It seems tolerably clear, though, that being under nine feet tall is not itself the *cause* of death (and vice versa). Correlation and causation are obviously different.

xkcd.com

Of course, in many important cases it's not always easy to distinguish correlation and cause. But I think there are reasons to doubt the calm that well-being is what *causes* or *makes* an act moral or immoral. Indeed, there may be a perfect correlation between morality and well-being (pleasure/pain), but this wouldn't, in itself, imply that well-being is what makes an act right or wrong. This allegedly perfect correlation is, after all, consistent with God being the cause of what makes an act right or wrong.[34] If the divine command theory of morality is true (more

---

[34] For a much more thorough and technical description of this disconnect between logical equivalence and causation, see ibid.

on this theory in a later chapter) then what makes an act wrong, say, is that God commands us not to perform it. And this is entirely consistent with every forbidden action being one that results in unnecessary harm.

Think of it another way. Taking the thermometer example further, notice that the thermometer's reading can be an accurate indicator of temperature, but the temperature itself—the heat or energy contained in the air surrounding the thermometer—is caused by the motion of the air molecules. Similarly, it may be that unnecessary harm is a good indicator or detector of a wrong act, but it need not be what makes the act wrong.

Of course, none of this *shows* that God's command makes the act wrong, that his decree is the ground, explanation, or cause of an act's wrongness (although I think it is). But it does seem to show that this religious explanation is consistent with well-being and morality correlating perfectly.

Furthermore, I haven't shown that well-being *isn't* what makes an action moral or immoral; I've merely said that the (alleged) perfect correlation doesn't connect the two causally. To argue that moral rightness *isn't* causally dependent upon well-being (that well-being doesn't determine morality), I'll need to do some more work. I'll need to offer my own, positive account of morality.

But before I do that, I want to look at some general considerations about science and morality, considerations that might prove to be the death knell for *any* attempt to underwrite morality with science (and not simply Harris's account). To put it differently, I think that any Humean project of applying the experimental method to "moral philosophy" will show little more than Hume's did. So then, can science, as Harris claims, "determine human values"?

15

Can Science Determine
Human Values?

The *Is/Ought* Distinction

In the last chapter we saw Harris's attempt to analyze morality in terms of all-natural ingredients. But there's another way to think about what he and other atheists are doing: they're attempting to bridge the gap between *fact* and *value*. In Harris's specific case, he's trying to move from *descriptive physical facts* about the well-being of sentient creatures to *value judgments* about such facts. That is, what Harris would really like is for science to be able to determine value.

We met the fact/value dichotomy early on, in the introduction, a dichotomy that's also called the *is/ought* distinction.[1] Harris says that science can bridge this fact/value (*is/ought*) gap. But there are decent reasons for thinking that bridging this gap is impossible—not only for Harris's view, but for any view whatsoever.

So then, we have the following situation. Harris says that there are clear facts about the well-being of conscious creatures, facts about brain states. Let us suppose he's right. And let's also suppose that science can study these facts, perhaps through neuroscience or whatever. Notice that now Harris needs to be able to infer or otherwise move from these

---

[1] There may actually be two distinctions hiding here: between fact and value, and between value and obligation. I'll ignore this distinction-within-a-distinction since it won't change my argument (and it would only make things harder for the naturalist).

purely physical facts about brain states to statements about what we ought to do.

Students of philosophy might immediately reply that this is all moot. Didn't Hume show—centuries ago—that the gap between *is* and *ought* cannot be bridged, that we can't "derive an *ought* from an *is*"?

Perhaps. Let's see.

When Hume applied science to ethics, he found only two things, you'll remember. For one thing, he found facts about the physical world. In the case of, say, "willful murder" we might observe one person with his hands around the neck of another person, this second person losing consciousness, etc. (we need not get into the sordid details). And perhaps if we add the tools of neuroscience, we might add to these facts further ones about the brain states of the victim and murderer. These are all facts about what *is* the case. Hume also found sentiments or feelings *toward* these facts: for example, that they are repulsive and wrong, but again, feelings are paltry things to base something as important as morality upon.

But, said Hume, we never *observe* that murder is wrong; we only *feel* that it is. And just as important is Hume's claim that we cannot use *reason* to get from physical facts to value judgments. To put it differently, there is no *logical inference* from beliefs about *the facts* to beliefs about the *wrongness* of the act. So then, neither sense perception nor reason can support morality, if Hume is right. (Notice that we're back to the observation/theory distinction, with neither source capable of arriving at morality.)

Hume famously marveled at other philosophers' effortless leaps over the is/ought gap. *Oughts* would arise from nowhere, out of nothing, like magic (although today, quantum fluctuations are now suspected): "I am surpriz'd to find, that instead of the usual copulations of propositions, *is*, and *is not*, I meet with no proposition that is not connected with an *ought* or an *ought not*."[2] But there was no sign of the source of the mysterious *oughts*, neither observations nor inferences. And this is because, said Hume, *oughts* cannot appear from physical facts or by way of inferences from those facts. And so morality cannot be grounded in sense perception or reason, no matter how tempting it proves.

So then, we neither *observe* nor *infer* that murder is wrong. If so,

---

[2] David Hume, *A Treatise of Human Nature* (Oxford: Clarendon, 1978), 469.

then that's a real drawback to Harris's view: science seems incapable of telling us what we ought to value. But notice that this unfortunate result is independent of whether morality is a matter of well-being or anything else. It depends only on the concepts of *is* and *ought*. There's an irreconcilable difference between them, and so if there is the yawning *is/ought* gap that Hume thought there is, this will put a damper on scientific attempts to dictate human values.

But before we look further at the ability of science to determine what we should value, let's see how Harris defends his own view from Hume.

Harris contra Hume

You'll not be surprised, but Harris is less than enthusiastic about the *is/ought* gap. He complains:

> Many moral skeptics piously cite Hume's is/ought distinction as though it were well known to be the last word on the subject of morality until the end of the world. They insist that notions of what we ought to do or value can be justified only in terms of other "oughts," never in terms of facts about the way the world is. After all, in a world of physics and chemistry, how could things like moral obligations or values really exist? How could it be objectively true, for instance, that we *ought* to be kind to children?[3]

Of course, if Harris's complaint is that modern-day moral skeptics merely defer to Hume's authority without presenting actual arguments (either Hume's or their own), then more power to him. Merely summoning Hume's ghost isn't an argument, no matter how scary.

But Harris himself offers no argument against Hume. He merely warns us that proponents of the *is/ought* gap are playing a dangerous game: "Fanciers of Hume's is/ought distinction never seem to realize what the stakes are, and they do not see how abject failures of compassion are enabled by this intellectual 'tolerance' of moral difference."[4] Apparently tolerance of moral differences is going *too* far. We can tolerate only so much tolerance. In any case, Harris seems to say that we should disagree with Hume merely because an *is/ought* gap would have

---

[3] Sam Harris, *The Moral Landscape: How Science Can Determine Human Values* (New York: Free Press, 2010), 38.
[4] Ibid., 42.

unwelcome consequences, namely, that we can't get authoritative *oughts* from scientific facts. And on Harris's naturalistic worldview, this would result in there being no objective moral laws. But this is something for which he'd need an argument.

Because Harris doesn't give us an argument against Hume, neither has he given us a reason to think that science could underwrite morality by deriving *oughts* from physical facts about brain states.

What Ought We to Value?

Notice something else. Science can't tell us to value the well-being of sentient creatures in the first place; we've come to science already valuing *that*. Even if science can tell us which things will result in an increase of well-being, it can't tell us we *ought* to value well-being—even our own, much less someone else's. As Singer notes,

> Since information about the consequences of our actions does not tell us which consequences to value, but only which action will or will not bring about the consequences we do value, most ethical theories simply incorporate new information about the consequences of our actions into our ethical decisions in a way which does not affect the fundamental theory of value itself.[5]

So then, science can't determine our antecedent valuing of well-being. Much less the well-being of *others*. Nor could it. Again, science gives us facts only about the physical world. And though, says Singer, "I need facts to make a sensible decision, . . . no amount of facts can make up my mind for me. Hence no amount of facts can compel me to accept any value, or any conclusion about what I ought to do."[6] I need antecedent values, and science simply cannot determine these, despite all its facts.

Moreover, science alone cannot tell us that well-being is a *moral* property or that well-being is simply a matter of brain states. Remember, we saw that these depend on larger issues like worldviews, which would include our antecedent views on morality. And since these will further depend on things we can't observe, they're probably beyond the reach of science—even if science were part of the picture.

---

[5] Peter Singer, *The Expanding Circle: Ethics, Evolution, and Moral Progress* (Princeton, NJ: Princeton University Press, 2011), 64.
[6] Ibid., 75.

What then is the source of our morality? Well, as I'll argue in the next chapter, in an important sense *we* are. What we value morally is up to us, not science. Or as Singer puts things, "No science is ever going to discover ethical premises inherent in our biological nature, because ethical premises are not the kind of thing discovered by scientific investigation. We do not find our ethical premises in our biological nature, or under cabbages either. We choose them."[7] And we choose these ethical principles based on what we value.[8] At their most fundamental, they are *our* values and no one else can value them for us.

Again, it's possible for science to influence our moral actions by telling us that certain actions will result in certain consequences. That is, given that we value the well-being of others (for example), science might tell us that certain behaviors or medical treatments or government policies harm people. Science might also tell *against* fundamental moral principles. Suppose I think that science shows that naturalism is true. A commitment to consistency or rationality might force me to further conclude that there are no human-independent moral standards. (And notice, significantly, that the fact that we value rationality is itself not something that science can dictate.)[9]

In any case, in the next chapter I'll (finally) argue for what I think is morality's foundation, namely, *persons*. That is, moral value is nothing more than personal value, since *all* value is personal. If I'm right about this, then we'll have more reason to think that science could never determine human values, as well as even more reason to doubt Harris's account of morality.

---

[7] Ibid., 77.

[8] So how *do* we choose our values? The answer is probably something like "we often don't" but, as with our beliefs, we can influence which values we'll have. Also, it is plausible to suppose that we always do what we want, *all things considered*. Unfortunately, this includes only the options open to us, which are limited. Even in *Sophie's Choice*, the main character did what she wanted, all things considered. But tragically, her options were limited to horrific ones.

[9] Although to value something is to say that we want or desire it, we may, of course, have conflicting values. That is, there are relative values, and we might *prefer* one value over another. Philosopher Stephen Wykstra says that to *prefer* something is not exactly the same thing as *valuing* it. He gives an example of someone who smokes despite knowing its harmful consequences. Should we say, asks Wykstra, that this person *values* smoking? Wykstra thinks not (Stephen Wykstra, "Of Cats, Values, and Cognition," *Logoi* [Spring 2014], 10). Suppose this is correct. Would this substantially affect anything we've said here? No. There are all manner of complications associated with values, desires, and wants (if these are different). But this doesn't change the fundamental claim that science cannot dictate or determine what to value.

16

Morality Is Personal

Value: It's All in Your Head

Harris and I agree on at least one thing: we both believe that all value—including moral value—requires a valuing subject. He says: "Let us begin with the fact of consciousness: I think we can know, through reason alone, that consciousness is the only intelligible domain of value."[1] If I understand him correctly, I think he's right to say that value always requires a mind to do the valuing. But his view is going to cause him problems.

His most pressing problem will be that this close link between morality and consciousness proves too much and eliminates the possibility of moral realism—of objective morality—at least if naturalism is true. That is, if all value depends on a conscious valu*er*, on a valuing subject, *and if naturalism is true*, then all value is entirely dependent on *human* preference, and therefore, fails to be authoritative in the way morality requires. To put it differently, it would be perfectly permissible, morally speaking, if everyone did what was right in his own eyes. At least this is what I'll argue are consequences of his view.

To illustrate, consider what makes gold valuable. *We* make gold valuable. There's no intrinsic value to gold; gold is valuable only because we value it. That is, the "value-maker" of gold is the human mind, particularly wants and desires. Imagine you're stranded on an island,

---

[1] Sam Harris, *The Moral Landscape: How Science Can Determine Human Values* (New York: Free Press, 2010), 32.

starving to death and being chased by all manner of beasts; nature is trying its best to kill you. Right now, the thing you desire most is to survive with as little pain as possible (let's assume you don't merely wish to be put out of your misery). You need food, shelter, defense, and the like. Suppose you stumbled upon a cave where pirates, centuries earlier, had stored huge amounts of gold bullion, but nothing else. The gold, in this scenario, would be a big disappointment; it wouldn't be valuable at all—because you wouldn't value it

This is similar to how everything becomes valuable: through valu*ers*. Or so *I* say. Something is valuable because some conscious mind or intelligence values it. And this will go for moral value as well as goods like food, water, and medicine. If we—we humans, that is—valued different things than we do now, then *those* things would actually *be* valuable—that is, no less valuable that our previous values. And, I will argue, further, that a way out of this subjective picture—perhaps the only way—is through theism. For the near future, however, I'll merely argue that naturalism implies moral subjectivism, moral relativism, moral nihilism, and moral skepticism, all of which will mean or imply the same thing: there are no objective (human-independent) moral values.

The first thing to do is look at the nature of morality. What is it?

Obligation Is Relative to Persons

Let's begin with the Christian philosopher Elizabeth Anscombe. In her groundbreaking 1958 article "Modern Moral Philosophy," she famously argued that now that most philosophers are atheists, we should eliminate the notion of moral obligation from philosophy. (Fun fact for philosophy nerds: in the article she also coined the term *consequentialism*). Anscombe says:

> The concepts of obligation, and duty—*moral* obligation and *moral* duty, that is to say—and of what is *morally* right and wrong, and of the *moral* sense of "ought," ought to be jettisoned if this is psychologically possible; because they are survivals, or derivatives of survivals, from an earlier conception of ethics which no longer generally survives, and are only harmful without it.[2]

---

[2] G. E. M. Anscombe, "Modern Moral Philosophy," in *Twentieth Century Ethical Theory*, ed. Steven M. Cahn and Joram G. Haber (Upper Saddle River, NJ: Prentice-Hall, 1995), 351.

Notice that Anscombe is targeting the *moral* sense of duty or obligation, not the *prudential* (or what she calls the "ordinary") sense.

> The terms "should" or "ought" or "needs" relate to good and bad: e.g. machinery needs oil, or should or ought to be oiled, in that running without oil is bad for it, or it runs badly without oil. According to this conception, of course, "should" and "ought" are not used in a special "moral" sense.[3]

There's no problem with retaining their "ordinary" prudential sense. Rather, the problem arises when we conflate the prudential sense with the moral sense. Anscombe goes on to say that the rise of Christianity made this conflation natural:

> The ordinary (and quite indispensable) terms "should," "needs," "ought," "must"—acquired this special sense by being equated in the relevant contexts with "is obliged," or "is bound," or "is required to," in the sense in which one can be obliged or bound by law, or something can be required by law. How did this come about? The answer is in history: between Aristotle and us came Christianity, with its *law* conception of ethics. For Christianity derived its ethical notions from the Torah. In consequence of the dominance of Christianity for many centuries, the concepts of being bound, permitted, or excused became deeply embedded in our language and thought.[4]

But it seems to Anscombe that this moral sense of obligation can't coherently survive outside a religious context, outside a context that countenances a divine moral law. And so, as she explains, "The situation, if I am right, was the interesting one of the survival of a concept outside the framework of thought that made it a really intelligible one."[5] This situation led to the "Enlightenment Project," the attempt to justify moral laws apart from a divine Lawgiver.

Richard Taylor, in his book *Ethics, Faith, and Reason*, echoes Anscombe's view that law makes no sense without a lawgiver. He begins by saying that the concepts of right and wrong (and the corresponding concept of law) were once recognized as being grounded purely in human

---

[3] Ibid., 354.
[4] Ibid.
[5] Ibid., 355.

custom.[6] He says, "Prior to the rise of Christianity, virtually everyone, including philosophers, had thought of right and wrong as corresponding to what is permitted and what is forbidden by tradition, custom, and law—in short, by rules that are of human origin whether written or unwritten."[7] He says that, with the rise of Christianity, the lawgiver became divine: "Morality now went beyond obedience to merely human laws, customs, and traditions, and came to be thought of instead as obedience to divine law. Thus, what had hitherto been merely political and social obligation became distinguished, with the idea of a higher lawgiver, as moral obligation."[8] Whether in human or divine law, to say that someone is obligated is to say that something is *required* of that person, whereas right and wrong refer, respectively, to *that which is permitted* and *that which is forbidden*.

Of course, the question that immediately comes to mind, says Taylor, is "Who is it that thus permits, forbids, or requires that certain things be done or not done?"[9] And as we saw, prior to Christianity it was merely *we* who did these things.

> The answer to this was taken for granted by the ancient moralists and, indeed, by virtually all the Greeks; up to a point it is just as obvious to us. The answer is *human beings*, meaning *people in general* or, more precisely, the people of a given culture if we are referring to the customs transmitted from one generation to another within such a culture. At another level the answer is *rulers and legislators*, when we are speaking of the actual laws of a political society.[10]

Again, in the Christian West, God usurped mankind as Lawgiver, and over the centuries we've become accustomed to thinking that questions of right, wrong, and obligation are independent of us, that it would, for example, be wrong to torture someone in order to gain some mild pleasure *regardless of what humans believed*. But this is a theistic view.

There are now two ways to try to make sense of our deeply ingrained belief that morality is human independent. One is to maintain the person-

---

[6] As an aside, when customs become laws, then their violation is a *crime*. The notion of *justice* in such cases means, Taylor says, a respect for these laws, with a disregard for them being *injustice*. We typically think of there being a distinction between the concept of what is moral and what is legal, despite there being some overlap. But there are cases—in a theocracy let's say—where they coincide.

[7] Richard Taylor, *Ethics, Faith, and Reason* (Englewood Cliffs, NJ: Prentice-Hall, 1985), 7.

[8] Ibid.

[9] Ibid., 9.

[10] Ibid.

relative aspect of laws and (continue to) ground them in a supernatural person. The other is to reject a personal ground altogether and ground them in nature. That is, says Taylor, "since there appear to be no law-makers superior to those that are human, then . . . we must suppose that moral right and wrong are just part of the fabric of nature itself, however inherently implausible this bizarre supposition may seem."[11]

That is, we ground morality either in God or in the cosmos. And so, with the decline of Christianity's influence—but while retaining the idea of an objective, absolute, or human-independent moral standard—modern philosophers took up the search for a way to ground morality *objectively* without God.

Obligations Are Relational

In any case, if Anscombe and Taylor are right—and I think they are—the moral concepts of right, wrong, and obligation require a mind, some-one to do the permitting, the forbidding, or the requiring. And this is something that the cosmos cannot do. So if naturalism is true, the role of permitting, forbidding, and requiring falls to humans to play.

Moral concepts also require at least one additional person, obvi-ously enough: someone who is being permitted, forbidden, or obligated. Morality, in other words, requires a society or community, however small. Right, wrong, and obligation are concepts related to the actions that people perform in relation to some standard set by another person or persons. These ethical concepts express, in Taylor's words, "certain relationships of a person or persons to others."

> Nothing, for example, is simply "permitted," "forbidden," or "re-quired." . . . A given action is permitted, forbidden, or required *of* certain persons *by* other persons. . . .
>
> Similar observations can be made concerning the ideas of *duty* and *obligation*. A duty is something that is owed, something *due*, and to be obligated is, literally, to be *bound*. But something can be owed only *to* some person or persons. . . . Similarly, one can have no obligations just as such; it must, again, be an obligation to some person or persons.[12]

---

11 Ibid., 26.
12 Ibid., 74–75.

To put it more provocatively, right, wrong, and obligation are *person relative*.

And so this raises another problem for Harris's view. The concepts of well-being—of suffering and happiness—are not grounded in personal relationships in the way the concepts of right, wrong, and obligation are. I can be injured or harmed by a shark, without attributing any moral wrongdoing to the shark. As Taylor points out: "No rules, customs, nor even social life are needed in order for someone to suffer injury. Rules are needed only for describing such injury as wrongful; they are no precondition of injury itself."[13] It seems we need more than mere well-being for morality, and one of the additional things we need is a community of persons.

Taking Stock

Before moving on, let's pause to regroup. We've been looking at a cluster of moral concepts related primarily to *actions*. Given what we've learned, we should probably summarize their meanings. An *obligation* or *duty* is something we're *required* to perform (or abstain from, if it pertains to something *forbidden*). That is, an obligation or duty is something you *ought* to do (or not do).

A *right* action is something we're permitted to do (which could even be something we're obligated to do, since we're obviously permitted to do something we *must*); a *wrong* action, on the other hand, is something we're forbidden to do. And again, all of these are standards for measuring actions.

The terms *good* and *bad* are also related to actions, as in *It is good for you to care for your children and bad for you to neglect them*. But often we say that an action is right/wrong, rather than good/bad. On the other hand, we usually apply good/bad to *people*, as in *It's hard to find a good man*. It's good and right for you to keep all this in mind. But you're not obligated to do so.

For the next few sections I'll mostly discuss the concepts of obligation, right, and wrong, and later the concepts of good and bad. All of this helps toward the goal of understanding the fundamental nature of morality. Trust me.

---

[13] Ibid., 14.

Obligations Are Never Absolute

If naturalism is true, what then dictates or determines which actions are required, forbidden, and permitted? The specific answer(s) will depend on which humans we're talking about, on the individuals, groups, or cultures in question. But if what I've said is true, then we can say one thing with reasonable certainty: the determination *will depend on what humans value.*

Another way to put this is that obligations (or moral imperatives) are not, as Kant believed, *categorical*, but are instead *hypothetical* or *conditional*. That is, all obligations or duties depend upon—are conditional upon—what we value, and therefore take the following form: *If you value X, then you ought to do Y.* To put it differently, there's an "if" part (usually implicit). When a parent says, "You ought to clean your room," there's a tacit "If you know what's good for you." Or less cynically, it's probably more like this: "Because you know that I love you, you love me, you take delight in pleasing me, you don't want to lose dessert for a week . . ." (We'll look at a more morally substantial example in a moment. I merely want to get the general point across first.)

If, on the other hand, moral imperatives were categorical—*a la* Kant—there would be nothing conditional about them; they'd be of the form we generally expect: "You ought to clean your room," with no qualifying conditions. Categorical imperatives do not depend on what we value—or on anything else. As philosopher Philippa Foot explains, categorical imperatives allegedly "tell us what we have to do [regardless of] our interests or desires, and by their inescapability they are distinguished from hypothetical imperatives."[14] J. L. Mackie elaborates:

> There are commonly believed to be intrinsic requirements, the situation itself or the nature of things is seen as demanding some action (or refraining from action); an agent is felt to be half bound to do something, and yet not by his own desires or by any specifiable institution or by the speaker's attitude, or at any rate not only by these; some intrinsic requirement backs up, say, an institutional one. When "ought" refers to reasons or semi-bindings of this supposed sort, it is thought to be a peculiarly moral "ought."[15]

---

[14] Philippa Foot, "Morality as a System of Hypothetical Imperatives," in *Ethics: The Big Questions*, ed. James P. Sterba, Philosophy: The Big Questions (Oxford: Blackwell, 1998), 100.
[15] J. L. Mackie, *Ethics: Inventing Right and Wrong* (1977; repr., London: Penguin, 1990), 76.

Intrinsic requirements in this case are those that exist *in* the world, apart from any human-dependent considerations. So if moral imperatives are categorical, as Kant argued, they contain only stone cold *shoulds*, *oughts*, and *musts*.

But again, I think we've seen some decent reasons to deny Kant's view. If what I've said so far about morality is anywhere near correct, then morality is conditional upon subjective value (and therefore hypothetical rather than categorical). That is, it's conditional upon the valuing subject, the person doing the valuing. Moreover, I think this is true of *any* kind of value, not merely of the moral kind: that is, all value is dependent on a valu*er*. After all, values are things *we* value. If I'm right about this, then the *ought* in moral statements is used conditionally just as in prudential statements (e.g., *If you want to be healthy, you ought to stop smoking*.) They are conditional upon our desires, wants, or values.

Of course, this makes morality sound pretty subjective. But that's because it *is*. Let's look a bit closer at this conditional or subjective aspect.

Value: It's Complicated

Now, the antecedent of *If you value X, then you ought to do Y*—the "If you value X" part—is often shorthand for an entire host of values (and facts). Consider a prudential *ought*, such as *you should quit smoking*. Is it true that you should quit smoking? Well, that depends, as Mackie puts it:

> If smoking has the effects it is alleged to have, [and] if a heavy smoker wants to live long and be healthy, and doesn't get much enjoyment from smoking, and, if he gave it up, would not feel it much of a loss and would not switch to other indulgences, such as overeating, which were likely to be even worse for his prospects of long life and health, then he ought to give up smoking. When we put in enough factual conditions about the agent's desires and about causal, including psychologically causal, relations, the "ought" conclusion follows. . . . "Ought," as we shall see, says that the agent has a reason for doing something, but his desires along with the causal relations constitute the reason.[16]

Of course, that's for *prudential* imperatives. Are *moral* imperatives or *oughts* really conditional in this way? What about causing someone

---

[16] Ibid., 66.

extreme physical or emotional pain just to feel a mild sense of satisfaction? Isn't that something I just *should not do*?

Well, no, not *just*. But if I feel sympathy toward others, and value their well-being, and don't want to be thought of as cruel, and am afraid of what might happen if others knew of my behavior, and so on, well, *then* I shouldn't cause someone unnecessary harm. Of course, different people will have different values, but they'll have *some* values that guide their moral behavior.

Consider it from another angle. Imagine you tell me that I ought to pay back my loan, and I respond, "Why should I?" Suppose you reply, "Because paying back your loan is the right thing to do." Suppose I respond, "Why should I do the right thing?"[17] How would you reply? It seems that I could always—at least according to reason alone—resist the imperative. As Foot explains, "People may indeed follow either morality or etiquette without asking why they should do so, but equally well they may not. They may ask for reasons and may reasonably refuse to follow either if reasons are not to be found."[18]

The correct answer to "Why should I pay back my loan?" seems to be something like, "Because you *want* to pay back your loan, *all things considered*." Now, I might not have initially considered all the relevant things—such as the demise of my pristine credit rating or a possible stay in prison—so perhaps the real answer is "Because you want to pay back your loan, all things considered. And here are some of the relevant things to consider . . ." Morality isn't simply a matter of logic; nor is it a brute impersonal fact about the cosmos. It's a matter of personal value, this latter phrase being utterly redundant.

Nature or Nurture?

So neither moral nor prudential *oughts* are categorical. No doubt, moral *oughts feel* different from prudential *oughts*—and, for that matter, different from the *oughts* of social etiquette. But it isn't obvious at all that there's anything objective beyond the feelings themselves. At least if naturalism is true.

This is a hard teaching; who can accept it? Have our feelings tricked

---

[17] Let us assume here that "right" does not carry with it a hidden *ought*. Otherwise we're back where we started. That is, the question becomes *Why should I do the thing I should?*, which is little more than *Why should I?*

[18] Foot, "Morality as a System of Hypothetical Imperatives," 102.

us into thinking that moral imperatives are categorical and therefore more objective than prudential oughts? As Foot asks, "Are we then to say that there is nothing behind the idea that moral judgments are categorical imperatives but the relative stringency of our moral teaching?"[19] It would seem so, according to her: there seems to be little beyond the sentiments conditioned by our ethical upbringing. The "binding force" of morality, Foot says, "is supposed to be inescapable in some special way [but] this may turn out to be merely the reflection of the way morality is taught."[20]

I think Foot is right: moral upbringing and societal pressure are crucial to forming our moral sentiments. And when done correctly, this is an excellent thing; in any case, it's unavoidable. But morality is more than nurture—nature too plays a role. Many theists will think that God has designed us with a moral faculty that produces strong moral sentiments; other people will think that evolution is responsible (I considered this in an earlier chapter, and I'll say more about it later). The point here is simply that, on my view of obligation, moral imperatives are hypothetical: they depend on (are conditional upon) what we value, desire, prefer. Our natural tendency to miss this can be chalked up to the fact that the values spelled out in the "if" part of the conditional are so familiar that they become transparent.

My view that moral imperatives are conditional is in essential agreement with Mackie's, which is that a "moral 'ought' does not have an essentially different meaning or sense from other 'oughts.'"[21] "So far as ethics is concerned," says Mackie, "my thesis that there are no objective values is specifically the denial that any such categorically imperative element is objectively valid."[22] I mention Mackie because he's famous for being one of the few atheists who is also a moral skeptic or nihilist. John Burgess says—in an issue of *Ethical Theory and Moral Practice* devoted to Mackie's book *Ethics: Inventing Right and Wrong*—that "until the recent appearance of J. Mackie's *Ethics*, it has been hard to find even one expression of the [nihilist] position in print."[23] This is

---

[19] Ibid., 101.

[20] Ibid., 102.

[21] Mackie, *Ethics*, 76.

[22] Ibid., 29.

[23] John P. Burgess, "Against Ethics," *Ethical Theory and Moral Practice* 10, no. 5, Moral Skepticism: 30 Years of Inventing Right and Wrong (2007): 427. Instead of *nihilism* Burgess uses the terms *anethicism* and *moral skepticism*, by which he means the view "there *are* no such objective values, so moral thinking involves a fundamental mistake and illusion. Anethicism is to ethics as atheism is to theology" (ibid.).

because the ramifications of this position are extreme and severe. They are *so* extreme and severe that they would be a public-relations disaster for atheism, as well as just plain difficult to live out consistently. At least given our current values. But perhaps we might evolve to love it. And none of these difficulties shows in itself that moral nihilism is wrong.

The Objectivity of Meeting Standards

Even if the standards of morality are based on what we value, this doesn't mean that there isn't *anything* objective about morality. There can be an objective fact of the matter about whether something meets a moral standard, even if the standard itself is subjective.

This is pretty obvious with some things, like the taste of food. Once we decide that vanilla ice cream is good (a subjective standard), the question of objective fact is whether this ice cream *is* vanilla. But this point applies to standards generally. A knife is a good one if it is sharp. That is, a knife *ought* to be sharp. Moreover, the sharpness or dullness is an objective fact, independent of whether I believe it's sharp. That is, we're realists with respect to a knife's sharpness: we believe that there is objective sharpness, even if *valuing* sharpness is subjective. Says Mackie: "Given any sufficiently determinate standards, it will be an objective issue, a matter of truth and falsehood, how well any particular specimen measures up to those standards. Comparative judgements in particular will be capable of truth and falsehood."[24]

So then, it seems that there is indeed evaluative objectivity despite the subjectivity of the value itself. That is, there are normative facts— facts about whether something meets a standard—that are independent of whether humans believe them or not. Not only is a knife's sharpness human independent; that is, *whether* a knife is sharp is an objective fact. But we can go further: we can say that there's an objective fact about whether a knife is *good*. That is, whether the knife *meets the standards* of a good knife is objective.

Again, the standard itself is not objective. We dub the sharp knife *good*. That is, humans declare that a knife *ought* to be sharp because we value sharp knives in most contexts. And our choice of the standard for a good knife depends on a knife's intended function, what the knife is *for*.

Remember that we're ultimately looking for the source of the moral

---

[24] Mackie, *Ethics*, 26.

standards themselves, and if I'm right, that source is our values, desires, and preferences. To put it differently, *we're* the source. *At least if naturalism is true.* If, on the other hand, theism is true, then the standards depend on God's values, as we'll see.

In any event, once the standards of morality are in place, it's an objective fact whether a particular action measures up to this standard. That is, once we deem reneging on a promise to be wrong, it's an objective fact that your reneging is wrong. These values might be entirely pragmatic, like a group's desire for survival or its desire for order in a pluralistic society. And how the specific standards are established in a culture may be complicated and lost in the sands of time. But the point is the same: moral standards are a matter of preference, of what persons value.

What Makes a *Person* Good?

We're now in a position to consider what makes a person good. Whether something is good or bad, we saw, often depends on the function or purpose of the thing in question. This goes for *people* too. A good doctor is someone who can help a person gain health; a good accountant is someone who can keep track of money, among other things.

But what makes someone good as a *person*? A good person would be, it seems, someone who adequately performs the function of a person, who successfully fulfills the role of "human being." A good person is what a person ought to be.[25] But what's the function of a person in general? Whereas we know what a *doctor* is for and what an *accountant* is for, it's not clear what a *human* is for.

Of course, this assumes that humans *have* a function, that they're *for* something, that they have an end or *telos*. And this was a reasonable assumption prior to the scientific revolution, when most things were thought to have ends or goals or *teloi*. But with the rise of modern science, teleological (and theological) explanations were banished in favor of mathematical descriptions of mechanical, purposeless processes. Of course, according to theists, humans still had a purpose, but as Christianity declined and naturalism became more prevalent, it became commonplace for humans to be viewed as simply collections of inert matter, with no *telos* or function.

---

[25] Taylor, *Ethics, Faith, and Reason*, 6.

Now, if naturalism is true, what is a human *for*? Well, says who? It would appear that humans don't have an objective (human-independent) function. That is, it's reasonable to think that a function or purpose requires a mind, a consciousness that has intentions. A telos or end or goal seems to require a mind that can have that goal *in mind*. For example, we can determine what a watch is for by appealing to the intentions, goals, and purposes of the watch's designer. If naturalism is true, there's *no* purpose outside of the subjective purposes that humans choose for themselves. These purposes or goals will vary from one person to the other; and even if they were uniform, they would still be entirely human dependent.[26]

But Thomas Nagel—an atheist, you'll recall—suggests a return to the Aristotelian-like notion of a *natural*, nonintentional teleology. This natural telos of the cosmos would, in general, have *value* as its explanatory end.[27] That is, it would be the universe's *goal* to produce value, not merely fact. Nagel concedes, however, that he's not sure this notion of person-independent teleology makes sense; but neither does he see why it wouldn't.[28] Fair enough. My own initial response to a nonintentional telos would be that I don't see how it's coherent: again, an end, goal, or purpose seems to require, perhaps by definition, an intentional mind, something that can have a goal in mind. Perhaps Nagel can make this concept work, but we'd have to hear more.

So then, it seems that moral value ultimately requires a person who does the valuing. But ultimately, if naturalism is true, the only persons are human, and therefore *good* is defined by our desires and preference. As Mackie says, "'Good' . . . always imports some reference to something like interests or wants."[29] This applies to both moral and prudential goods. Again, morality is a matter of taste. What makes a person good is whatever we say makes a person good.

Kant's Concern: Can You Really Blame Us?

When we first began our discussion, we saw that the Scientific Revolution raised three problems for our traditional view of morality. One

---

[26] For a helpful discussion, see Alvin Plantinga, "Naturalism versus Proper Function," in Plantinga, *Warrant and Proper Function* (Oxford: Oxford University Press, 1993).
[27] Thomas Nagel, *Mind and Cosmos: Why the Materialist Neo-Darwinian Conception of Nature Is Almost Certainly False* (Oxford: Oxford University Press, 2012), 92.
[28] Ibid., 93.
[29] Mackie, *Ethics*, 58.

problem was that when Hume applied the "experimental method" to the study of ethics, all he could find, morally speaking, were our ethical intuitions or sentiments. A second problem was that science made it seem that the divine command theory of morality had little going for it, if for no other reason than theism seemed to have little going for it. We've discussed both of these problems extensively (the second one in part 2, where I argued that science in no way suggests that theism is false or improbable).

But we haven't discussed the third problem, namely, whether we're free to choose to do the right (or wrong) thing, much less choose our values that underwrite morality. The notion of a moral law implies that in some important sense we have the ability to choose which moral actions we perform. That is, we usually assume that "ought implies can." To perform some immoral act, for example, is to be blameworthy or culpable, and this idea of culpability depends on the notion of free will.

Now, if naturalism were true and it implied that we have no free will, then our notions of morality would certainly be drastically impacted. And indeed, it's not easy to see how to avoid the view that we *aren't* free if naturalism is true. Alexander Rosenberg describes the naturalist position this way:

> The mind is the brain, and the brain is a physical system, fantastically complex, but still operating according to all the laws of physics— quantum or otherwise. Every state of my brain is fixed by physical facts. In fact, it is a physical state. Previous states of my brain and the physical input from the world together brought about its current state. They were themselves the result of even earlier brain states and inputs from outside the brain. All these states were determined by the operation of the laws of physics and chemistry. These laws operated on previous states of my brain and on states of the world going back to before my brain was formed in embryogenesis. They go back through a chain of prior events not just to before anyone with a mind existed, but back to a time after life began on this planet.[30]

Rosenberg is simply stating scientific orthodoxy, and so most unbelievers should find it pretty uncontroversial. But many unbelievers

---

[30] Alexander Rosenberg, *The Atheist's Guide to Reality: Enjoying Life without Illusions* (New York: W. W. Norton, 2011), 236.

somehow avoid the conclusion from this that we aren't free. Maybe it's because science has not, *ex cathedra*, pronounced the death of free will; science hasn't just come right out and said that we're not free.[31] And perhaps the reason isn't hard to find. As Harris says, "If the scientific community were to declare free will an illusion, it would precipitate a culture war far more belligerent than the one that has been waged on the subject of evolution."[32] Maybe many unbelieving scientists realize this and so shy away from openly embracing determinism. And who could blame them (if determinism is true).

But Harris is one of the few unbelievers bold enough to openly admit that-which-we-do-not-admit (although, again, I don't suppose we ought to praise him if he's right: he can't help it): "Free will *is* an illusion. Our wills are simply not of our own making. Thoughts and intentions emerge from background causes of which we are unaware and over which we exert no conscious control. We do not have the freedom we think we have."[33] He's not the only brave soul. Rosenberg—that "mad dog naturalist"—is also willing to concede that science has killed free will. After his description of the physical situation above, he goes on to say, "Everything—including my choice and my feeling that I can choose freely—was fixed by earlier states of the universe plus the laws of physics."[34] On this view, our behavior isn't ultimately up to us. Here we stand. We can do no other.

I simply don't have the space or time (or spacetime) here to give free will anything like the attention it deserves, so I'm not going to say any more about it other than that I agree with Harris and Rosenberg that science plus naturalism gives us good reason to think we're not free. Oh—and I also agree that more naturalists should believe likewise. They should approach the topic of freedom with a sober skepticism.

---

[31] By the way, if we are governed ultimately by quantum events, then our actions aren't *determined* by physical laws, but that's only because they are random, or at least probabilistic.
[32] Sam Harris, *Free Will* (New York: Free Press, 2012), 1.
[33] Ibid., 5.
[34] Rosenberg, *The Atheist's Guide to Reality*, 236.

17

Can God Ground Morality?

Remember, It's Personal

My view on the foundations of morality is that all value—and moral value in particular—is subjective in that all value depends on a valu*er*, a valuing subject. All morality is ultimately personal. By definition, then, there is no impersonal value or value from the "point of view of the universe." And so, in a naturalistic universe, morality is relative to human desires, interests, and preferences. Your morality is up to you. This gave us further reason to think that science cannot determine human values, contrary to what Harris claims. Science can't tell me what to desire (although it can sometimes tell me how to obtain it).

But value is subjective even if something like traditional theism is true. That is, it's simply in virtue of value's nature that it requires a person or mind to do the valuing. On the face of it, this might not seem like a problem for theists. After all, God is a person and can therefore value things. It seems plausible, then, to say that morality depends on what he values. God values (or disvalues) certain states of affairs, which is what makes these states of affairs good (or bad); moreover, he commands us to behave in accordance with these values, and this is what—according to many theists—makes such behavior obligatory. This, as we've seen, is often called the *divine command theory* of ethics.

But there appears to be a serious problem for the divine command theory, one raised by the great Plato himself in his dialogue the *Euthyphro* (and therefore called the "Euthyphro objection" to the divine command theory). Many people believe that the Euthyphro objection shows that God cannot ground morality. In fact, this objection is often thought to be the Achilles' heel of religious ethics. And my subjective view of value appears to increase the power of the Euthyphro objection, as I'll explain. I should, therefore, briefly describe how a purely subjective view of ethics fits with the traditional divine command theory.

The Divine Command Theory

The divine command theory is really twofold and not simply about commands. First, it grounds moral values in God's nature. As Craig puts it:

> On the theistic view, objective moral values are rooted in God. He is the locus and source of moral value. God's own holy and loving nature supplies the absolute standard against which all actions are measured. He is by nature loving, generous, just, faithful, kind, and so forth. Thus if God exists, objective moral values exist.[1]

So then, telling the truth and aiding widows and orphans are good *simply because* God values these things. And a good person will behave accordingly because this is what a person is *supposed* to do. Moreover, God values these things because it's in his nature to value them. Evaluations of good and evil are identified with those things that God *likes* and *dislikes*, respectively.[2] To say that something is morally good is to say no more (or less) than that God likes it.

So that's *value*: moral goodness and moral badness. And these are determined by God's *nature*, by the way he is. This is the first part of the divine command theory.

The second part is specifically about which actions are permitted, forbidden, and obligatory. The rightness or wrongness of an act is again determined by God's nature, by what he likes or dislikes. But what makes these actions obligatory, forbidden, or permitted are God's *commands* to us. That is, his values are communicated and dictated to us through his commands. That's how we become bound to them. Our duties or obligations to behave in accord with God's values—our

---

[1] Walter Sinnott-Armstrong, "Why Traditional Theism Cannot Provide an Adequate Foundation for Morality," in *Is Goodness without God Good Enough? A Debate on Faith, Secularism, and Ethics*, ed. Robert K. Garcia and Nathan L. King (Lanham, MD: Rowman & Littlefield, 2009), 103.
[2] See Mark C. Murphy, "Theism, Atheism, and the Explanation of Moral Value," in Garcia and King, *Is Goodness without God?*, 127.

oughts—are *created by* God's commands. And again, these commands derive from God's values, which are the result of his nature, of what he is like. Again, says Craig: "God's moral nature is *expressed toward us* in the form of divine commands that constitute our moral duties. Far from being arbitrary, these commands flow necessarily from his moral nature."[3] Good and evil, right and wrong, then, are defined first by God's nature; our duties to conform to these values arise by God commanding us to behave in accord with them.

So, again, divine *commands* are really only part of the theory, and not even the most fundamental part. The foundation of the theory is what God wills, values, desires, or prefers. And according to traditional theism, his values are determined by his nature or essence. In other words, the reason he prefers some things over others is that this is just what he's like, the kind of being he is. It might, then, be better to call the theory the *divine nature theory* of ethics. But I'll stick with its standard name.

The Euthyphro Objection

As I said, probably the most powerful objection to the divine command theory comes from Plato's *Euthyphro*. In this dialogue, Euthyphro, in a conversation with Socrates, says that pious acts are those that are loved by the gods.[4] Socrates, in characteristic form, realizes that this definition is ambiguous: are the acts pious *because* the gods love them, or do the gods love these acts *because* these acts are pious?

Either option seems to put the believer in an awkward spot. On the first option, what *makes* an act pious is the gods' love of the act. The gods define which acts are pious. But what if the gods had happened to love rape? Then rape would be a pious act.

The second option isn't much better. According to this option, it's inherently the piety of the act that *makes*, or explains why, the gods love it.[5] That is, the piety of an act is independent of the gods. The gods don't get to determine or define which acts are pious; they must consult some standard outside themselves.

So then, the objection goes, either moral value depends on God and

---

[3] Paul Kurtz and William Lane Craig, "The Kurtz/Craig Debate: Is Goodness without God Good Enough?," in Garcia and King, *Is Goodness without God Good Enough?*, 30; emphasis added.
[4] Louise Antony, "Atheism as Perfect Piety," in Garcia and King, *Is Goodness without God Good Enough?*, 70.
[5] Ibid.

is therefore arbitrary (i.e., it depends simply on what he likes and dislikes); or else the source of moral value is independent of God entirely. Either way, the divine command theory results in bad news for the theist. It's quite the dilemma.

The Horn of Arbitrariness

Now, most divine command theorists have traditionally chosen the first horn of the dilemma. That is, what *makes* it right to care for the poor is that God likes it. And, moreover, his preference gets turned into one of our obligations by way of his commanding us to take care of the poor.[6] I think this is the right choice. (Divine command theorists everywhere— past and present—will be so relieved to know that I approve.)

We can see how this traditional choice is consistent with the view that all moral value is subjective, that is, how moral value is dependent on (grounded in, explained by) a valuing subject or mind. Of course, in this case, the mind is God's, and so value is not subjective in the sense that it depends on a *human* subject. Moral value is "objective" in that it is entirely independent of what *we* think is morally valuable. So it would still be wrong to torture a kitten just for the fun of it, even if everyone on the planet believed that this was a perfectly fine thing to do. Nevertheless, value is not something that exists (on this view) "in the world" so to speak. There are no impersonal laws of morality independent of what *anyone at all* values.

But what of arbitrariness? This was the problem with the dilemma's first horn. Here I think the theist should concede that if God had commanded us to torture cats, then torturing cats would be obligatory. Of course, according to traditional theism, God's nature is *necessary* and God is therefore "constrained" (by his nature, which isn't independent of him) to abhor the torture of kittens, and so this wouldn't really be much of a concession. Although I agree with this traditional view, I think there's something surprising here all the same, something that the divine command theory says—or at least confirms—about the nature of value itself.

To see this, suppose that God's nature were *not* necessary.[7] That is,

---

[6] Notice that I'm not addressing how we *know* what God's commands are, which is an epistemological issue, not an ontological one.
[7] Before you respond that we can't imagine this, I should point out that there is a sense in which we *can* reasonably do this. After all, we don't know whether Goldbach's conjecture (which says that every even

imagine that God values love, kindness, generosity, selflessness, and so on, just like we think he does, but that these characteristics, although part of his nature, aren't necessarily so. We might think of it this way: God is like a father who has all these qualities; he might not have, but we're glad he does. And just as we can imagine having a father who doesn't have these qualities, it also seems possible to imagine that a different kind of God had created the cosmos. If the universe had been under different management, things could be much worse off. We could, for example, have a God who valued cruelty and who, furthermore, commanded us to practice it. In such a case, we *would* be obligated to be cruel.

Does the divine command theory then imply that morality is ultimately arbitrary? That depends on what we mean by *arbitrary*. If we mean that morality is "based on or determined by individual preference or convenience rather than by necessity or the intrinsic nature of something [impersonal]," then perhaps it's technically arbitrary.[8] That is, morality is based on God's preference and not on the intrinsic nature of an impersonal cosmos. On the other hand, God's preferences can also be said to be the result of his intrinsic nature, which dictates his preferences. But if values depend on a subject who values, this kind of "arbitrariness" will be entirely expected.

"So You Admit It Then?"

Opponents of the divine command theory think that choosing the "arbitrariness" option is a *reductio ad absurdum* against the divine command theory. That is, if the divine command theory really does imply that we would be obligated to rape had God commanded it, then the divine command theory is obviously wrong. Here's Sinnott-Armstrong's complaint:

> If a divine command constitutes our moral duty not to rape, for example, then what makes it morally wrong to rape is just that God commanded us not to rape. Moreover, whenever God commands us to do (or not to do) any act, we have a moral duty to do (or not to do) that act.

---

number greater than two is the sum of two prime numbers) is true, and yet we can discuss the possibility that it's false. And we can do this even though if it is true, it's *necessarily* true (and if it's false, it's necessarily false). Anyway, it's controversial whether God's nature is necessary (or even whether he *has* a nature). Issues of necessity and natures are difficult enough, but the skinny branches are stretched to little more than threads when we transfer these topics to God himself.

[8] *Merriam-Webster's Collegiate Dictionary*, 11th ed. (Springfield, MA: Merriam-Webster, 2008), sense 3a.

I find this view incredible. If God commanded us to rape, that command would not create a moral requirement to rape. . . . Moreover, even if God in fact never would or could command us to rape, the divine command theory still implies the counterfactual that, if God did command us to rape, then we would have a moral obligation to rape. That is absurd.[9]

Of course, this isn't an actual *argument* against choosing the "arbitrariness" horn of the Euthyphro dilemma, but merely an expression of disagreement with anyone who makes that particular choice. Sinnott-Armstrong assumes this is a poor choice. But that is exactly what's in question.

Notice something else he says: "If morality depends on what God thinks, then it is not independent of whether anyone thinks so, and then morality is not objective."[10] And so he and I are in agreement here. Morality on my view *isn't* objective in the sense of *person independent*; it's person *dependent*.

"Why Do You Call God 'Good'?"

There's another common objection leveled at the divine command theory, one that can be encouraged by the way we theists describe God's nature. Sinnott-Armstrong objects that, according to traditional theism, "God is all-good," and that from this fact theists go on to conclude that "God must be loving, generous, just, faithful, and kind."[11] But, Sinnott-Armstrong objects, "This line of reasoning assumes that it is good to be loving, generous, just, faithful, and kind."[12]

The complaint seems to be that we can't identify God as *good* without falling into trivial tautology. Louise Antony objects that divine command theorists are using the term *good* merely as a synonym or placeholder for *commanded by God*. But we're not allowed to do this, she says: God is where we get our definition of *good* in the first place, so to say that "God is all-good" is merely to say that "God is like God," which should go without mentioning.[13]

[9] Sinnott-Armstrong, "Why Traditional Theism Cannot Provide an Adequate Foundation for Morality," 106.
[10] Ibid., 107.
[11] Ibid., 104.
[12] Ibid.
[13] Antony, "Atheism as Perfect Piety," 72.

Fair enough. Let's remedy this problem by refraining from phrases like "God is good" (at least while we're doing philosophy here—otherwise, go for it). Instead, we'll simply say that God's nature determines what is good.

The main thing we want to remember, in any case, is that *good* is defined as "what God values."

Why Should We Obey God?

But if this is true, Antony complains, how is morality any different from etiquette or fashion? She says that, according to the divine command theory, God is the "ultimate Miss Manners," and that *good* is similar to *cool*:

> In contemporary American culture, it's probably safe to say that the cool things are the things that popular people like. . . . that whatever the popular crowd happens to like *thereby* becomes cool. If that's the case, then there is nothing inherently true about cool things that gives them this status.[14]

I think that in one sense, Antony is right. But what makes morality different from coolness is that it's *God* who determines the standards of morality, not merely humans. If humans were the final word in morality, then her point would have more weight. In fact, it would be spot-on.

Of course, this appeal to a difference between God-ordained morality and human-ordained coolness isn't going to impress Antony. She'll doubt whether God could make enough of a difference. And so the real question is this: what is it about God that makes him (relevantly) different from humans? Why should we obey God? Is it because if we didn't, he would punish us? Is it because he created us and so has authority over us? These strike some people as less-than-admirable reasons for doing what God says. Hear again Antony:

> One does not owe allegiance to another being simply because that being is stronger. And it does not matter if the being in question is responsible for your very existence. No one thinks that an abused child is morally obliged to obey an abusive parent, simply because the parent gave the child life. Parents do not own their children,

---

14 Ibid., 73.

and their right to expect obedience is contingent upon their being benevolent and competent trustees of the child's own welfare.[15]

Again, there's something to Antony's point (even if rights, ownership, and obligations aren't simply things we "just have" but are moral and therefore person dependent on my account). Most theists—or at least the many that *I* know—aren't motivated primarily because God is stronger, nor even simply because he created them. They obey God because they *want* to (more on this in a moment).

On the other hand, God's authority and power are nothing to sneeze at. Because God is in charge of this cosmological establishment, he can be its Lawgiver. He can tell us what is permissible, that is, what *he* permits. It's entirely up to him. This isn't technically "might makes right," but God's infinite power is most certainly one of those things that sets him apart from human lawgivers.

This is one reason why atheists find God so distasteful: they see him as an overbearing authoritarian dictator. And as long as they interpret him this way, seeing only the "shall nots," it's perfectly understandable why they would resist the theistic picture of morality.

But most theists see it differently, viewing God as a loving Father who cares for them, and as someone they can trust, despite not fully understanding why he does the things he does. And it should be obvious that many children obey their parents not simply because they fear punishment or because they are their parents' offspring. Rather, they obey, often enough, because they love their parents, feel loved *by* them, and are grateful for the care and comfort their parents provide. There's a sense of loyalty and belonging. Their parents—and the rest of the family—are "their people." Anyone from a halfway decent family knows how precious this is. And so it is with believers' attitudes toward God.[16] Again, they want to obey God.

But the bottom line is this: we obey God because we want to; and we want to because we value certain things.

And, thankfully, God can influence our values. In fact, according to

---

[15] Ibid., 80.

[16] And it is interesting that even in the Old Testament—which some people think portrays an angry and harsh deity—God appeals to the Israelites' gratitude as the main reason for obeying him. Immediately prior to giving the Israelites the Ten Commandments, God says, "I am the LORD your God, who brought you out of the land of Egypt, out of the house of slavery" (Ex. 20:2). That's not to say that there is *no* fear of discipline or punishment for disobedience, but again it often isn't the primary reason for many believers' desire to obey God.

one main tradition in Christian theology, God absolutely *must* influence our values before we want to obey him, before we value the things he values. Through "regeneration" and "sanctification" God is said to change our hearts, to change what we value. In the case of Christianity, God's values are becoming our values.

Again, on the view I've presented, morality requires persons. Now we've seen that divine command theory takes this into account. Morality is bound up in relationships, particularly, in a "personal relationship" with God. Believers obey primarily out of love and gratitude. Or we should.

Important but Irrelevant Questions

I've really only given a thumbnail sketch of how God might ground morality. There are many more questions that we might reasonably ask about the divine command theory, many of them epistemological. For example, how do humans know which God, of all the many religions, we should obey, if any? Similarly, how do we know what God's commands are?

And what are the real origins of our moral intuitions or beliefs? Is God the source of these beliefs? Do sociobiological explanations of our moral beliefs—if true—count against the divine command theory? Can our moral beliefs have both a natural and supernatural origin? Is it coherent to think that we come hardwired with moral intuitions while also requiring that God reveal (some of his) moral commands to us?

Suppose, moreover, we have in mind the God of the Old and New Testaments; how do we reconcile some of the "embarrassing" passages—God's command to Abraham to kill Isaac, for example—with other parts of Scripture that seem to portray God as someone who wouldn't do such a thing?[17]

The answers to these questions are important, but little of substance turns on them for what I've argued here. Moreover, even if my account of how God grounds morality is wrong—indeed, even if there is no God at all—this wouldn't affect my main point about morality:

---

[17] I'll say something very briefly on this. Whatever God's commands turn out to be, on my view believers cannot coherently question these commands' rightness, only whether we like them. It makes no sense to question whether God is right to order the death of the Canaanites or to condemn people to hell. These are right and good by definition, on my view. Obviously there are things about God's commands that we neither understand nor particularly like. But this is our fault, not God's.

namely, that if there is no God, then morality depends ultimately on human tastes and desires. I've added the discussion of how God might ground morality in order to allay some pretty obvious concerns about my person-dependent theory of value (e.g., how could God adequately ground morality given such a theory?).

18

Living with Moral Nihilism

Why Aren't There More Nihilists?

I began my discussion of morality with Dostoyevsky's nagging question, if God is dead, is everything permissible? You've no doubt gleaned that my short answer is yes: without God there are no universally binding moral rules. Sure, there are all manner of "moral" rules that we impose on ourselves and others. But none of these are actually binding in the way we imagine moral laws to be. If naturalism is true, there's no morality apart from what humans value, want, or prefer. Morality is purely a matter of taste. In short, naturalism implies moral nihilism, the view that there are no human-independent moral rules.

The claim that atheism implies nihilism isn't new.[1] But it's most certainly a minority view among atheists. Perhaps this is because most atheists have carefully considered all the arguments that run from naturalism to nihilism, and have seen that none of them are any good. But I hope I've made enough of a case to set that possibility aside. Let's suppose I have.

Sam Harris suggests another possible reason for nihilism's limited appeal: nihilism isn't merely false; it's incoherent. In *The Moral Landscape*

---

[1] Nietzsche comes immediately to mind. Although it's a delicate business to interpret Nietzsche, there are passages that, on their face, endorse nihilism. He says, in *The Gay Science*, "Whatever has *value* in our world now does not have value in itself, according to its nature—nature is always value-less" (quoted in Brian Leiter, *The Routledge Philosophy Guidebook to Nietzsche on Morality* [London: Routledge, 2002], 147). There is also Jean-Paul Sartre, who (as we saw earlier) says, "Indeed, everything is permissible if God does not exist, and man is consequently abandoned, for he cannot find anything to rely on—neither within nor without" (quoted in Robert K. Garcia and Nathan L. King, introduction to *Is Goodness without God Good Enough? A Debate on Faith, Secularism, and Ethics*, ed. Robert K. Garcia and Nathan L. King [Lanham, MD: Rowman & Littlefield, 2009], 3).

he says that nihilism—what he calls "moral relativism"—undermines itself. "Moral relativism, however, tends to be self-contradictory. Relativists may say that moral truth exists only relative to a specific cultural framework—but *this* claim about the status of moral truth purports to be true across all possible frameworks."[2]

But this is a confusion on Harris's part. To be sure, some forms of relativism are about *truth* and therefore can be self-defeating. For example, one ham-fisted version says that "all truth is relative." This view is going to have serious problems staying afloat since we might plausibly ask whether *it* is true (absolutely and not relatively). But moral nihilism (or moral relativism) doesn't deny that there are absolute moral truths; it doesn't say that all *truths about morality* are relative. Rather, moral nihilism denies that there are absolute moral *standards*. To say that all moral standards are relative to humans doesn't at all compromise itself. To say that all moral truths are relative does.

So most atheists probably don't resist moral nihilism because there's a lack of evidence for it, or because it's incoherent. At least they shouldn't. My guess is that the main reason for their resistance is that nihilism is just plain hard to stomach. Philosopher James Rachels makes the point as follows:

> Consider what it would be like for someone actually to believe that nothing is right or wrong. Someone who said this would mean, presumably, that rape is neither right nor wrong; that torture is neither right nor wrong; that murder is neither right nor wrong; and so on for anything else that might be mentioned. If all this were said *seriously*, and not just as part of a philosophical discussion, it would be alarming in the extreme.[3]

The difficulty with nihilism, then, isn't that it's hard to see how it follows from naturalism; that much is fairly straightforward, it seems to me. Rather, it's that nihilism itself is disturbing. Ted Bundy? Jeffrey Dahmer? The Asmat people of New Guinea? Their behavior isn't *wrong*? Could it really be true that there's nothing wrong with skinning someone alive? Is it plausible that my revulsion toward this kind of horror differs only

[2] Sam Harris, *The Moral Landscape: How Science Can Determine Human Values* (New York: Free Press, 2010), 45.
[3] James Rachels, "Subjectivism," in *A Companion to Ethics*, ed. Peter Singer (Oxford: Blackwell, 1991), 434.

in degree from my revulsion toward cold, slimy asparagus? It's going to be hard to get naturalists to sign up for this; nihilism is not an easy position to rally around.

Rosenberg acknowledges this difficulty. Recall that he believes that the deliverances of science pretty obviously imply moral nihilism. But he worries that people will think nihilism means that we can't "condemn Hitler, Stalin, Mao, Pol Pot, or those who fomented the Armenian genocide or the Rwandan one."[4] Yet it's difficult to see how we might avoid this conclusion. After all, Rosenberg says:

> We have to acknowledge (to ourselves, at least) that many questions we want the "right" answers to just don't have any. . . . Many enlightened people, including many scientists, think that reasonable people can eventually find the right answers to such questions. Alas, it will turn out that all anyone can really find are the answers that they like. The same goes for those who disagree with them. Real moral disputes can be ended in lots of ways: by voting, by decree, by fatigue of the disputants, by the force of example that changes social mores. But they can never really be resolved by finding the correct answers. There are none.[5]

And this is just the way it is. We have to accept what science seems to tell us about the world and live the best we can. (Although, strictly speaking, if naturalism-plus-nihilism is true, we don't *have* to do anything.)

On the other hand, maybe we believe so strongly that rape is wrong that we should reject any argument that concludes otherwise. Suppose I'm correct and the premise *If naturalism is true then nihilism is true* is itself true. Perhaps then we should give up the belief that naturalism is true. That is, maybe whatever convinced us of naturalism is itself wrong. Say, for example, we believe that science shows that God doesn't exist. Well maybe, if we can't block the inference from naturalism to nihilism, this might give us enough reason to question whether science really shows that there's no God (in addition to the reasons we saw in part 2). In any case, if naturalism implies nihilism, then a consistent naturalist

---

[4] Alexander Rosenberg, *The Atheist's Guide to Reality: Enjoying Life without Illusions* (New York: W. W. Norton, 2011), 98.
[5] Ibid., 96.

must either accept moral nihilism or else give up naturalism. Of course, most do neither.

Nihilism to the Bitter End?

The bottom line is that nihilists cannot (rationally) condemn other people's morality *as wrong* or *incorrect*. Take the most horrendous act you can imagine (and whatever you imagine, there are even worse things, as some law enforcement officers could tell you). According to nihilism, the revulsion you feel is simply that: a feeling. Morality is ultimately a matter of taste or preference as I've said repeatedly.

But this position proves difficult to practice consistently, even for someone as daring as Rosenberg. Later on in his book, Rosenberg revisits the question of moral disagreement and condemnation. He admits that he and others *do* condemn the moral actions that most of us consider morally wrong.

> But wait. Where do we scientistic types get off condemning purda and suttee, female genital mutilation and honor killings, the Hindu caste system, the Samurai Code of Bushido, the stoning of women who have committed adultery, or the cutting off of thieves' right hands? Isn't the high dudgeon we want to effect in the face of this sort of barbarism flatly inconsistent with nihilism?[6]

Here's his answer: "Not only do we condemn the blinkered morality of intolerant religions and narrow-minded cultures, nowadays, we condemn some moral norms that we ourselves used to embrace. We think of this change as progress, improvement, and enlightenment in our moral conscience."[7] This is difficult to take seriously, given that Rosenberg believes that there are no correct answers to moral disagreements. My guess is that, if pushed, he would say that he's not interested in correct answers, after all. But then this is difficult to square with the rhetorical point of his question *Where do we get off condemning other people's moral codes?* Maybe his response is really just "It's a free country." As Albert Camus said, "It is always easy to be logical. It is almost impossible to be logical to the bitter end."[8]

---

[6] Ibid., 143.
[7] Ibid.
[8] Albert Camus, *The Myth of Sysyphus and Other Essays*, trans. Justin O'Brien (New York: Alfred A. Knopf, 1961), 9.

"Nice Nihilism"

But again, I'm not saying that nihilism implies that we *ought* to murder, rape, and pillage. Nor am I saying that nihilism implies that we shouldn't. Nihilism says nothing whatsoever about what we should do, morally speaking. I do think, however, that over time genuine belief in nihilism would seriously affect the way humans behave. Not necessarily this generation—since we've been raised on moral realism; but eventually things would probably get much uglier than they are now.

Rosenberg disagrees. He says that evolution will keep us in line.

> This nihilistic blow is cushioned by the realization that Darwinian processes operating on our forbearers [*sic*] in the main selected for niceness! The core morality of cooperation, reciprocity and even altruism that was selected for in the environment of hunter-gatherers and early agrarians, continues to dominate our lives and social institutions.[9]

This is what he calls *nice nihilism*. "The good news is that almost all of us, no matter what our scientific, scientistic, or theological beliefs, are committed to the same basic morality and values."[10] He goes on: "Adopting nihilism as it applies to morality is not going to have any impact on anyone's conduct. Including ours."[11] If Rosenberg is right, then the consequences of nihilism are not as dire as I think. Our biology often forces us to behave. Or as my mom used to tell us kids, "Biology constrains ideology."

Of course, Rosenberg concedes, our morals could continue to evolve and therefore we ought to "hope the environment of modern humans does not become different enough eventually to select against niceness."[12]

I think there's truth to the claim that our biology plays a role in constraining our values. But I also think that our biology is ultimately explained by divine design, not by unguided evolution. Moreover, to my mind, human nature isn't as rosy as Rosenberg paints it. I'm much more

---

[9] Alexander Rosenberg, "Disenchanted Naturalism," http://people.duke.edu/~alexrose/Disenchanted Naturalism.pdf, p. 8. Also published in *Contemporary Philosophical Naturalism and Its Implications*, ed. Bana Bashour and Hans D. Muller, *Routledge Studies in the Philosophy of Science* (New York: Routledge, 2014).
[10] Rosenberg, *The Atheist's Guide to Reality*, 95.
[11] Ibid., 96.
[12] Rosenberg, "Disenchanted Naturalism," 8.

pessimistic about humans than he is. As I said, it seems to me that, were everyone convinced of nihilism, we'd be in a world of hurt. But maybe this is just an example of "to the pure, all things are pure."

How Should Atheists Then Censure?

So then, nihilism doesn't recommend that its adherents live a life of moral turpitude. Neither does it suggest that they become the next Mother Teresa (Hitchens's criticisms notwithstanding[13]). Again, nihilism doesn't imply any *oughts*. It would be perfectly consistent with nihilism for you to force the entire human race into harsh and cruel slavery; so too would it be consistent with nihilism to always put others' needs and desires above our own.

If nihilism is true, we're not bound to *any* morality. Of course, we might be persuaded or coerced to behave in accord with other people's views of morality, for fear of untoward repercussions. But as for which morality we ourselves should endorse—in the deepest recesses of our hearts, where we live most authentically—it's up to us. We can "choose" which moral laws we prefer (even if our deterministic biology ultimately dictates our preference and it only seems like we're choosing). We are in that sense autonomous.

Autonomy, you'll recall is really the most important thing that humans can value, according to most Enlightenment thinkers. They wanted the freedom to think, say, and act as they wished, without any interference from "the Man," whether it be the church, traditional philosophy, the state, or whoever.

But remember that this emancipation may not be as welcome as expected. In fact, there are those who think it's pretty dismal news. Sartre, for example, laments that "man is condemned to be free: condemned, because he did not create himself, yet nonetheless free, because once cast into the world, he is responsible for everything he does."[14] We might plausibly wonder if nihilism would be more than the Enlightenment bargained for.

So then, if nihilism is implied by naturalism, this does seem to take some of the rhetorical wind out of the atheist's censorious sails. Can

---

[13] Hitchens denounced Mother Teresa in a number of places, but see his article "Mommie Dearest" in *Slate*, where he denounces her as "a fanatic, a fundamentalist, and a fraud," http://www.slate.com/articles /news_and_politics/fighting_words/2003/10/mommie_dearest.html.
[14] Jean-Paul Sartre, *Existentialism Is a Humanism* (New Haven, CT: Yale University Press, 2007), 29.

they rationally condemn *any* behavior as wrong, or are they merely disagreeing aloud with other people's tastes? If the latter, then the atheist movement would take an enormous hit. As I said at the beginning of this book, there are few things more salient than the righteous indignation of unbelieving authors.

Recall that these authors' favorite target is the great evils inflicted upon the world in the name of religion. These ills are often paraded out in grand fashion, as if everyone just knows that these are evil. Of course these ills *feel* evil; but the atheist is acting in bad faith by citing "moral wrongs" in arguments against religion. In response to any act of alleged wickedness that the atheist points to, we can reasonably ask, what's *wrong* with that?

Of course, if naturalism were true, we could say neither that acting in bad faith is objectively bad nor that atheists ought not do it. All we could say is that we don't like it.

Calvin and Hobbes © 1995 Watterson. Reprinted with permission of Universal Uclick. All rights reserved.

But there's an *ought* nearby. Nihilism—combined with other values commonly held by atheists—suggests that they *ought* to stop arguing against the immorality of religions. Imagine that Duane is an atheist who, in addition to being a nihilist, values rationality and logical consistency. I think we can see that, on his own terms, Duane's behavior *ought* to (prudentially speaking) reflect his nihilism.

And what might such belief/action consistency look like? Well, not like the following. Suppose Duane is arguing that religion is evil or morally wrong because he believes that it condones, and even encourages, oppression, hatred, and murder. Fair enough. His *feelings* about religion are neither true nor false (feelings aren't those kinds of things). The problem is with his attempt to provide moral *reasons* for his opposition to religion. It's odd that Duane would try to convince others of the *correctness* of his moral view. He might appeal to moral values that he shares with his audience—and preach to the choir—but it would be in some sense inconsistent for him to appeal to these values as something to which everyone is bound. He might as well argue that his preference for chocolate over vanilla provides reasons for us to change our own preferences.

I can tell you how *I* would respond to Duane: I wouldn't take him the least bit seriously. There's a scene in *The Big Lebowski* where three German nihilists confront "The Dude" and his friends in the parking lot of a bowling alley. The nihilists want a ransom for a hostage that they don't actually have. And so, naturally enough, The Dude and his friends aren't going to pay. When one of the friends (played by John Goodman) explains to the nihilists the rules governing ransoms (namely, that there must be a hostage), one of the disappointed nihilists loudly protests in a heavy Teutonic accent, "Iss not fair!" Goodman's character yells back, "Fair?! Who's the . . . nihilist around here?!"

When I hear an atheist complain about the immorality of anything at all, I only hear, "Iss not right!"

Right? Who's the nihilist around here!

19

What's the Point of It All?

Moral nihilism, we saw, is the view that there are no objective moral values. In arguing for moral nihilism I also argued that *all* value—not merely the moral kind—requires a valuing subject. And so I've not only argued that *moral* nihilism is true, but that nihilism *in general* is true, if naturalism is. That is, naturalism implies plain ol' nihilism—nihilism neat; *tout court*; straight, no chaser.

Nihilism would have serious ramifications for the meaning of one's life. If there's no value, then what's the point? What makes our lives valuable or worthwhile?[1] Nihilism would imply that there's nothing objectively valuable about our lives, nothing independent of us, anyway. Our lives have no objective worth or meaning.[2]

A Desert Landscape

It seems easier for naturalists to be nihilists when it comes to life's meaning than when it comes to *moral* nihilism. Perhaps it's easier to step "all the way back" and look at the cosmos as a whole than it is to look at morality per se. And maybe it's easier to do this because our feelings about moral value are much stronger than our feelings about life's value. Or maybe our desire to simply exist is so strong that it's almost entirely

---

[1] Whether something is worthwhile and whether it's intrinsically valuable are different questions. But for our purposes, this difference makes no difference. For a helpful discussion on the logic of value judgments, see Paul Edwards, "The Meaning and Value of Life," in *The Meaning of Life*, ed. E. D. Klemke (Oxford: Oxford University Press, 2000).
[2] Notice that, whereas we've been asking the question *says who?* we're now asking *so what?* Of course, the latter depends in part on the former.

transparent to us, even more so than our moral beliefs. I don't know. But whatever the reason, atheists seem to be more willing to admit nihilism with respect to life's meaning than to swallow moral nihilism.

Consider the following description of the human condition: "Brief and powerless is Man's life; on him and all his race the slow, sure doom falls pitiless and dark. Blind to good and evil, reckless of destruction, omnipotent matter rolls on its relentless way."[3] This gritty picture was painted by Bertrand Russell in 1903, in his famous essay "A Free Man's Worship." Russell tells us how we might find hope and meaning in life, given that man's "origin, his growth, his hopes and fears, his loves and his beliefs, are but the outcome of accidental collocations of atoms."[4] In light of this, says Russell, "only on the firm foundation of unyielding despair, can the soul's habitation henceforth be safely built."[5]

Kai Nielsen puts our situation this way:

> Even if you produce a great work of literature which continues to
> be read thousands of years from now, eventually the solar system
> will cool or the universe will wind down or collapse, and all trace
> of your efforts will vanish. . . . If there's any point at all to what we
> do, we have to find it within our own lives.[6]

And in the opinion of physicist Steven Weinberg, "The more the universe seems comprehensible, the more it also seems pointless."[7] The great Dawkins himself says, "The universe that we observe has precisely the properties we should expect if there is, at bottom, no design, no purpose, no evil, no good, nothing but pitiless indifference."[8]

Even according to unbelievers, then, naturalism pretty clearly implies that there's no purpose to the universe—or to any of its parts, including us. And so our lives have no ultimate meaning. There's no overarching point to anything. All our personal goals, purposes, and strivings amount to nothing in the end.

Albert Camus realized this. He opens his famous essay *The Myth of Sisyphus* with these chipper words: "There is but one truly serious

---

[3] Bertrand Russell, "A Free Man's Worship," in Klemke, *The Meaning of Life*, 77.
[4] Ibid., 72.
[5] Ibid.
[6] Thomas Nagel, "Prologue: The Meaning of Life," in Klemke, *The Meaning of Life*, 5.
[7] Steven Weinberg, *The First Three Minutes: A Modern View of the Origin of the Universe* (New York: Basic Books, 1993), 154.
[8] Quoted in Victor J. Stenger, *God: The Failed Hypothesis—How Science Shows That God Does Not Exist* (Amherst, NY: Prometheus, 2008), 71.

philosophical problem, and that is suicide."[9] Histrionics aside, he had a point. "Judging whether life is or is not worth living amounts to answering the fundamental question of philosophy. All the rest—whether or not the world has three dimensions, whether the mind has nine or twelve categories—comes afterwards."[10] In an important sense, it's true that we must first find life worth living before finding anything else.

Calvin and Hobbes © 1993 Watterson. Reprinted with permission of Universal Uclick. All rights reserved.

It's Kinda Up to You

But, Russell says, in the face of these potentially disheartening truths, we can still choose to live purposeful and meaningful lives. Even though in actuality we "must submit perpetually to the tyranny of outside forces," we can at least "in thought, in aspiration" consider ourselves "free from our fellow-men, free from the petty planet on which our bodies impotently crawl, free even, while we live, from the tyranny of death."[11]

Again, this will be a difficult philosophy to rally around. But if we're nothing but the "accidental collocations of atoms"—a result of physical processes with no end, goal, or purpose—what choice do we have?

Now, you might think that this worry over the lack of "ultimate purpose" in the universe is really just something that overly sensitive philosophers fret about. Nielsen recommends that we open a Can of Man and stop our whining. "We know we must die; we would rather

---

[9] Albert Camus, *The Myth of Sysyphus and Other Essays*, trans. Justin O'Brien (New York: Alfred A. Knopf, 1961), 3.
[10] Ibid.
[11] Russell, "A Free Man's Worship," 73. By the way, Russell thinks that his bleak views about our actual position come from the deliverances of science: "Whatever knowledge is attainable, must be attained by scientific methods; and what science cannot discover, mankind cannot know" (Bertrand Russell, *Religion and Science* [Oxford: Oxford University Press, 1997], 243). Thanks to Alice Stout for pointing me to Russell's quotation.

not, but why must we suffer *angst*, engage in theatrics and create myths for ourselves. Why not simply face it and get on with the living of our lives?"[12] And as Thomas Nagel asks, "Does it matter that it doesn't matter?" Why not, he says, adopt the following attitude? "It's enough that it matters whether I get to the station before my train leaves, or whether I've remembered to feed the cat. I don't need more than that to keep going."[13] And he concedes, "This is a perfectly good reply." But, he cautions, it "only works if you really can avoid setting your sights higher, and asking what the point of the whole thing is."[14]

And so you make your own meaning. That is, if a person values something, then it *is* valuable, since that's all there is to the concept of value. If you want your life to *have* meaning, you need only *find* it meaningful.

If meaning is really grounded in a valu*er*, then we'll never find meaning outside of persons. There is, then, no meaning from the universe's point of view; universes aren't the kinds of things that can have points of views. Or values. So, in one sense the bar is set very low: if you find something meaningful, then it *is* meaningful. If you value something, then it *is* valuable. To you. *Your* values are not *my* values, just as your feelings are not my feelings, nor are your beliefs my beliefs, strictly speaking. Of course, you and I can value the same kinds of things. That is, we might both find meaning in the same cause, for example. We might both value communism or education or world peace or gardening.

What Should an Atheist Do?

As in the case of moral value, so too for life's meaning: there's nothing atheists *should* do about it. The fact of nihilism—if it were a fact—wouldn't dictate how we ought to behave. If you can keep yourself from asking too many questions and ignore nihilism's implications, fine. And even if you *do* spread nihilism into the corners of your worldview, you *need not* feel bothered by it. Or you might. Whatever.

This is similar to how some philosophers respond to skepticism about the external world, for example. They can concede intellectually that they don't know they're not a brain in a vat and yet find it impos-

---

[12] Kai Nielsen, "Death and the Meaning of Life," in Klemke, *The Meaning of Life*, 155.
[13] Nagel, "Prologue: The Meaning of Life," 6.
[14] Ibid.

sible to take such a skeptical scenario seriously. As Hume said in this justly famous passage:

> It is true; so fatal an event is very little to be dreaded. Nature is always too strong for principle. And though a *Pyrrhonian* [i.e., a skeptic] may throw himself or others into a momentary amazement and confusion by his profound reasonings; the first and most trivial event in life will put to flight all his doubts and scruples. . . . When he awakes from his dream, he will be the first to join in the laugh against himself, and to confess, that all his objections are mere amusement, and can have no other tendency than to show the whimsical condition of mankind, who must act and reason and believe.[15]

It's perhaps the same with nihilism. Even those naturalists who are convinced by reason that nihilism is true will usually continue to *feel* that life has meaning enough to carry on. As Rosenberg says, "Fortunately for our genes, introspection by itself can't often overcome natural selection. Even when it comes to the conclusion that there is nothing that makes life worth living, the result is almost never suicide or even staying in bed in the morning. Just ask Jean-Paul Sartre."[16] Our will to live is unreasonably resolute. People in the worst conditions imaginable will struggle obsessively to survive. Even if we imagine ourselves in a Sisyphus-like position, rolling the stone up the hill only to watch it fall back down simply so we can repeat the struggle, humans will very often carry on.

But not always. There are people who don't *feel* like carrying on, and are willing to stop. The remedy for this feeling, says Rosenberg, is to "take two of whatever neuropharmacology prescribes."[17] And if that doesn't work, he says, "switch to another one. Three weeks is often how long it takes serotonin reuptake suppression drugs like Prozac, Wellbutrin, Paxil, Zoloft, Celexa, or Luvox to kick in. And if one doesn't work, another one probably will."[18] And to be sure, these drugs have helped many people. Better living through chemistry, we might say. In any case, despite our natural inclinations to carry on with life, taking nihilism seriously will be no picnic.

---

[15] David Hume, *An Enquiry concerning Human Understanding*, 2nd ed. (Indianapolis: Hackett, 1993), 110–11.
[16] Alexander Rosenberg, *The Atheist's Guide to Reality*, 281.
[17] Ibid.
[18] Ibid.

Calvin and Hobbes © 1992 Watterson. Reprinted with permission
of Universal Uclick. All rights reserved.

What Makes Theism Any Different?

Person-dependent value and meaning raises a number of important questions for Christians and other theists. For one thing, can *God* provide our lives with meaning? Yes, in the sense that we can value him and his values. Of course, many things can do that. As I alluded to, communism has captured the hearts of many. So have gardening, painting, and music—as have cocaine and pornography.

So, then, is God just one choice among many? Well, on the one hand, God is different, that is, literally *holy* or set apart. God, according to Christians, designed and created the universe and now continually keeps it in existence and running up to code. The universe and all its furniture—including us—are his. He is the ultimate authority regardless of what we think of it. Some of us interpret this authority as that of a loving father; others as that of a cruel dictator.

Moreover, God has designed us so that we function properly only when we love the things he loves and hate the things he hates. We are made to value the things he values; we flourish when our preferences align with his. This includes our goals, purposes, and meaning(s) in life; they should match his, at least insofar as we are able as creatures. We're happiest when things go right in this way. And because this is God's show, the things he finds meaningful are as objective as things get, in that they're human independent (but not person independent). They are, in a very real sense, eternal values.

On the other hand, we can in some sense choose God from among other things. This is pretty plain. After all, we often *don't* value what God values; we frequently find meaning where he finds little or none.[19] This is the case with us all, Christians too, insofar as believers are still sinners. And the paradigmatic case is Satan and his demons. So it's not a foregone conclusion that we'll value what God values, or find meaning where he does. We can apparently choose to align with or against God.

But the point is this. The cosmos is profoundly personal. It's a place where the highest value turns out to be placed on relationships. God calls us to a relationship of mutual love. In fact, God himself is a relationship among (divine) persons, according to the doctrine of the Trinity. It is only in the proper relation to these persons that *we* find value and meaning that are ultimately satisfying. Of course, I'm not presenting an *argument* for this here—merely an explanation of how Christians can make sense of the view that all value and meaning are subjective or person dependent. Of course, if what I say here is right, then there's also a sense in which there is objective value in the *human*-independent sense, namely, God's values.

And here we come to the point of why I've jumped up and down on the fact that value is ultimately personal. We (theists) typically argue that our view makes sense of objective moral and natural laws. But this is a mistake. To be sure, I think a theistic view of the cosmos makes better sense of our world—and the Christian view does this best of all. But as long as we continue to argue for objective values and laws—in the full-blooded *person*-independent and therefore *God*-independent sense of "objective"—we naturally give the impression that there *are* such things. We unintentionally perpetuate the lie that there's an impersonal view of the universe, a "view from nowhere" as Nagel famously put it. This lie has kept the Enlightenment project alive and is why atheists like Harris continue to search for an impersonal ground of moral value. But there can be no such thing. What we cherish most is personal—and indeed relational. As the old hymn puts it, "This is my Father's world."

---

[19] Of course, the term "find" is dangerous because it can be misleading in precisely the way I've been guarding against. There aren't meanings "out there" to be found. So maybe a better way to put it is to replace "we find meaning" with "we value." In that case, we would say instead that we sometimes value things that God doesn't value.

Bibliography

Anscombe, G. E. M. "Modern Moral Philosophy." In *Twentieth Century Ethical Theory*, edited by Steven M. Cahn and Joram G. Haber, 351–64. Upper Saddle River, NJ: Prentice-Hall, 1995.

Antony, Louise. "Atheism as Perfect Piety." In *Is Goodness without God Good Enough? A Debate on Faith, Secularism, and Ethics*, edited by Robert K. Garcia and Nathan L. King, 67–84. Lanham, MD: Rowman & Littlefield, 2009.

Brink, David. "Mill's Moral and Political Philosophy." In *Stanford Encyclopedia of Philosophy*, edited by Edward N. Zalta. Stanford, CA: Metaphysics Research Lab, CSLI, Stanford University, 2014.

Brown, J. R., and P. C. W. Davies, eds. *The Ghost in the Atom: A Discussion of the Mysteries of Quantum Physics*. Cambridge: Cambridge University Press, 1995.

Burgess, John P. "Against Ethics." *Ethical Theory and Moral Practice* 10, no. 5, Moral Skepticism: 30 Years of Inventing Right and Wrong (2007): 427–39.

Camus, Albert. *The Myth of Sysyphus and Other Essays*. Translated by Justin O'Brien. New York: Alfred A. Knopf, 1961.

Carroll, Sean. "Does the Universe Need God?" In *The Blackwell Companion to Science and Christianity*, edited by Alan G. Padgett and J. B. Stump, 185–97. Oxford: Blackwell, 2012.

Coyne, Jerry A. *Why Evolution Is True*. New York: Penguin, 2009.

Craig, William Lane. "The Absurdity of Life without God." In *The Meaning of Life*, edited by E. D. Klemke, 40–56. Oxford: Oxford University Press, 2000.

Curd, Martin, and J. A. Cover, eds. *Philosophy of Science: The Central Issues*. New York: W. W. Norton, 1998.

Dawkins, Richard. *The Blind Watchmaker*. New York: W. W. Norton, 1986.

———. *The God Delusion*. Boston: Houghton Mifflin, 2006.

Dennett, Daniel C. *Darwin's Dangerous Idea: Evolution and the Meanings of Life*. New York: Simon & Schuster, 1995.

DeWitt, Richard. *Worldviews: An Introduction to the History and Philosophy of Science*. 2nd ed. Oxford: Wiley-Blackwell, 2010.

Dostoevsky, Fyodor. *The Brothers Karamazov*. Translated by Richard Pevear and Larissa Volokhonsky. New York: Farrar, Straus and Giroux, 2002.

Duhem, Pierre. *To Save the Phenomena: An Essay on the Idea of Physical Theory from Plato to Galileo*. Chicago: University of Chicago Press, 1969.

Edwards, Paul. "The Meaning and Value of Life." In *The Meaning of Life*, edited by E. D. Klemke, 133–52. Oxford: Oxford University Press, 2000.

Faye, Jan. "Copenhagen Interpretation of Quantum Mechanics." In *Stanford Encyclopedia of Philosophy*, edited by Edward N. Zalta. Stanford, CA: Metaphysics Research Lab, CSLI, Stanford University, 2014.

Feynman, Richard Phillips. *QED: The Strange Theory of Light and Matter*. Princeton, NJ: Princeton University Press, 2006.

Fieser, James. "David Hume." *Internet Encyclopedia of Philosophy* (2011).

Fieser, James, and Louis P. Pojman. *Ethics: Discovering Right and Wrong*. 6th ed. Belmont, CA: Wadsworth, 2009.

Fine, Arthur. "The Natural Ontological Attitude." In *Philosophy of Science: The Central Issues*, edited by Martin Curd and J. A. Cover, 1186–208. New York: W. W. Norton, 1998.

———. *The Shaky Game: Einstein, Realism, and the Quantum Theory*. Edited by David L. Hull. 2nd ed. Science and Its Conceptual Foundations. Chicago: University of Chicago Press, 1996.

Foot, Philippa. "Morality as a System of Hypothetical Imperatives." In *Ethics: The Big Questions*, edited by James P. Sterba, 99–105. Philosophy: The Big Questions. Oxford: Blackwell, 1998.

Garcia, Robert K., and Nathan L. King. Introduction to *Is Goodness without God Good Enough? A Debate on Faith, Secularism, and Ethics*, edited by Robert K. Garcia and Nathan L. King, 1–21. Lanham, MD: Rowman & Littlefield, 2009.

Gould, Stephen Jay. *Dinosaur in a Haystack: Reflections in Natural History*. New York: Three Rivers, 1995.

———. *Wonderful Life: The Burgess Shale and the Nature of History*. New York: W. W. Norton, 1989.

Greene, Brian R. *The Elegant Universe: Superstrings, Hidden Dimensions, and the Quest for the Ultimate Theory*. New York: W. W. Norton, 2003.

———. *The Fabric of the Cosmos: Space, Time, and the Texture of Reality*. New York: Vintage, 2004.

Greig, J. Y. T., ed. *The Letters of David Hume*. Vol. 1, *1727–1765*. New York: Oxford University Press, 2011.

Gribbin, John. *In Search of Schrödinger's Cat: Quantum Physics and Reality*. New York: Bantam, 1984.

Hare, John. "Is Moral Goodness without Belief in God Rationally Stable?" In *Is Goodness without God Good Enough? A Debate on Faith, Secularism, and Ethics*, edited by Robert K. Garcia and Nathan L. King, 85–99. Lanham, MD: Rowman & Littlefield, 2009.

Harris, Sam. *The End of Faith: Religion, Terror, and the Future of Reason*. New York: W. W. Norton, 2004.

———. *Free Will*. New York: Free Press, 2012.

———. *The Moral Landscape: How Science Can Determine Human Values*. New York: Free Press, 2010.

Hauser, Marc, and Peter Singer. "Morality without Religion." *Free Inquiry* 26, no. 1 (2005): 18–19.

Hawking, Stephen, and Leonard Mlodinow. *The Grand Design*. New York: Bantam, 2010.

Heath, Thomas. *A History of Greek Mathematics*. Vol. 1, *From Thales to Euclid*. Mineola, NY: Dover, 1981.

Hesse, Mary B. *Forces and Fields: The Concept of Action at a Distance in the History of Physics*. Mineola, NY: Dover, 1962.

Hitchens, Christopher. *God Is Not Great: How Religion Poisons Everything*. New York: Twelve, 2007.

———, ed. *The Portable Atheist: Essential Readings for the Nonbeliever*. Philadelphia: Da Capo, 2007.

Hitchens, Christopher, and Douglas Wilson. *Is Christianity Good for the World?* Moscow, ID: Canon, 2008.

Holder, Rodney D. "Quantum Theory and Theology." In *The Blackwell Companion to Science and Christianity*, edited by Alan G. Padgett and J. B. Stump, 220–32. Oxford: Blackwell, 2012.

Hume, David. *An Enquiry concerning Human Understanding*. Edited by Eric Steinberg. 2nd ed. Indianapolis: Hackett, 1993.

———. *A Treatise of Human Nature*. Oxford: Clarendon, 1978.

Kaku, Michio. *Introduction to Superstrings and M-Theory*. 2nd ed. Graduate Texts in Contemporary Physics. New York: Springer, 1999.

Kant, Immanuel. *Critique of Practical Reason*. Translated by Werner S. Pluhar. Indianapolis: Hackett, 2002.

———. "What Is Enlightenment?" In *The Portable Enlightenment Reader*, edited by Isaac Kramnick, 1–7. New York: Penguin, 1995.

Kitcher, Philip. *The Ethical Project*. Cambridge, MA: Harvard University Press, 2011.

Kosso, Peter. *Appearance and Reality: An Introduction to the Philosophy of Physics*. Oxford: Oxford University Press, 1998.

Krauss, Lawrence M. *A Universe from Nothing: Why There Is Something Rather Than Nothing*. New York: Free Press, 2012.

Kuhn, Thomas S. *The Structure of Scientific Revolutions*. 3rd ed. Chicago: University of Chicago Press, 1996.

Kurtz, Paul, and William Lane Craig. "The Kurtz/Craig Debate: Is Goodness without God Good Enough?" In *Is Goodness without God Good Enough? A Debate on Faith, Secularism, and Ethics*, edited by Robert K. Garcia and Nathan L. King, 25–46. Lanham, MD: Rowman & Littlefield, 2009.

Kurtz, Paul, and Timothy J. Madigan, eds. *Challenges to the Enlightenment: In Defense of Reason and Science*. Buffalo, NY: Prometheus, 1994.

Ladyman, James. *Understanding Philosophy of Science*. New York: Routledge, 2002.

Laudan, Larry. "A Confutation of Convergent Realism." *Philosophy of Science* 48, no. 1 (1981): 19–49.

Leiter, Brian. *The Routledge Philosophy Guidebook to Nietzsche on Morality*. London: Routledge, 2002.

Mackie, J. L. *Ethics: Inventing Right and Wrong*. 1977. Reprint, London: Penguin, 1990.

Monton, Bradley. "Prolegomena to Any Future Physics-Based Metaphysics." In *Oxford Studies in Philosophy of Religion*. Vol. 3, edited by Jonathan L. Kvanvig, 142–65. Oxford: Oxford University Press, 2011.

———. *Seeking God in Science: An Atheist Defends Intelligent Design*. Peterborough, ON: Broadview, 2009.

Murphy, Mark C. "Theism, Atheism, and the Explanation of Moral Value." In *Is Goodness without God Good Enough? A Debate on Faith, Secularism, and Ethics*, edited by Robert K. Garcia and Nathan L. King, 117–31. Lanham, MD: Rowman & Littlefield, 2009.

Nagel, Thomas. *Mind and Cosmos: Why the Materialist Neo-Darwinian Conception of Nature Is Almost Certainly False*. Oxford: Oxford University Press, 2012.

———. "Prologue: The Meaning of Life." In *The Meaning of Life*, edited by E. D. Klemke, 5–7. Oxford: Oxford University Press, 2000.

———. *The View from Nowhere*. Oxford: Oxford University Press, 1986.

Newton, Isaac. *Mathematical Principles of Natural Philosophy*. Translated by I. Bernard Cohen and Anne Whitman. Berkeley: University of California Press, 1999.

Nielsen, Kai. "Death and the Meaning of Life." In *The Meaning of Life*, edited by E. D. Klemke, 153–59. Oxford: Oxford University Press, 2000.

Okasha, Samir. *Philosophy of Science: A Very Short Introduction.* Oxford: Oxford University Press, 2002.

Plantinga, Alvin. "Naturalism, Theism, Obligation and Supervenience." *Faith and Philosophy* 27, no. 3 (2010): 247–72.

———. *Where the Conflict Really Lies: Science, Religion, and Naturalism.* Oxford: Oxford University Press, 2012.

Popper, Karl. "Emancipation through Knowledge." In *Challenges to the Enlightenment: In Defense of Reason and Science*, edited by Paul Kurtz and Timothy J. Madigan, 58–72. Buffalo, NY: Prometheus, 1994.

Quine, W. V. "Two Dogmas of Empiricism." In *Philosophy of Science: The Central Issues*, edited by Martin Curd and J. A. Cover, 280–301. New York: W. W. Norton, 1998.

Rachels, James. "Subjectivism." In *A Companion to Ethics*, edited by Peter Singer, 432–41. Oxford: Blackwell, 1991.

Rosenberg, Alexander. *The Atheist's Guide to Reality: Enjoying Life without Illusions.* New York: W. W. Norton, 2011.

———. "Disenchanted Naturalism." In *Contemporary Philosophical Naturalism and Its Implications*, edited by Bana Bashour and Hans D. Muller, 17–36. Routledge Studies in the Philosophy of Science. New York: Routledge, 2014.

———. "Hume and the Philosophy of Science." In *The Cambridge Companion to Hume*, edited by David Fate Norton, 64–89. Cambridge: Cambridge University Press, 1993.

———. *The Philosophy of Science: A Contemporary Introduction.* 3rd ed. New York: Routledge, 2012.

Russell, Bertrand. "A Free Man's Worship." In *The Meaning of Life*, edited by E. D. Klemke, 71–77. Oxford: Oxford University Press, 2000.

———. *Religion and Science.* Oxford: Oxford University Press, 1997.

Sagan, Carl. *The Demon-Haunted World: Science as a Candle in the Dark.* New York: Ballantine, 1996.

Sartre, Jean-Paul. *Existentialism Is a Humanism.* New Haven, CT: Yale University Press, 2007.

Schliesser, Eric. "Hume's Newtonianism and Anti-Newtonianism." In *Stanford Encyclopedia of Philosophy*, edited by Edward N. Zalta. Stanford, CA: Metaphysics Research Lab, CSLI, Stanford University, 2007.

Shermer, Michael. *Why People Believe Weird Things.* New York: MJF, 1997.

Singer, Peter. *The Expanding Circle: Ethics, Evolution, and Moral Progress.* Princeton, NJ: Princeton University Press, 2011.

Sinnott-Armstrong, Walter. *Morality without God?* Oxford: Oxford University Press, 2009.

———. "Why Traditional Theism Cannot Provide an Adequate Foundation for Morality." In *Is Goodness without God Good Enough? A Debate on Faith, Secularism, and Ethics*, edited by Robert K. Garcia and Nathan L. King, 101–15. Lanham, MD: Rowman & Littlefield, 2009.

Smolin, Lee. *Three Roads to Quantum Gravity.* New York: Basic Books, 2001.

———. *The Trouble with Physics: The Rise of String Theory, the Fall of a Science, and What Comes Next.* Boston: Houghton Mifflin, 2006.

Sorensen, Roy. "Nothingness." In *Stanford Encyclopedia of Philosophy*, edited by Edward N. Zalta. Stanford, CA: Metaphysics Research Lab, CSLI, Stanford University, 2012.

Stanford, P. Kyle. *Exceeding Our Grasp: Science, History, and the Problem of Unconceived Alternatives.* Oxford: Oxford University Press, 2006.

Stenger, Victor J. *God: The Failed Hypothesis—How Science Shows That God Does Not Exist.* Amherst, NY: Prometheus, 2008.

———. *The New Atheism: Taking a Stand for Science and Reason.* Ahmherst, NY: Prometheus, 2009.

Stokes, Mitch. *Isaac Newton.* Nashville: Thomas Nelson, 2010.

———. *A Shot of Faith to the Head: Be a Confident Believer in an Age of Cranky Atheists.* Nashville: Thomas Nelson, 2012.

Susskind, Leonard. *The Cosmic Landscape: String Theory and the Illusion of Intelligent Design.* New York: Little, Brown, 2006.

Taylor, Richard. *Ethics, Faith, and Reason.* Englewood Cliffs, NJ: Prentice-Hall, 1985.

van Fraassen, Bas C. *The Scientific Image.* Oxford: Clarendon, 1980.

Weinberg, Steven. *The First Three Minutes: A Modern View of the Origin of the Universe.* New York: Basic Books, 1993.

Wilcox, Walter. *Quantum Particles and Principles.* Boca Raton, FL: CRC, 2012.

Woit, Peter. *Not Even Wrong: The Failure of String Theory and the Search for Unity in Physical Law.* New York: Basic Books, 2006.

Wykstra, Stephen. "Of Cats, Values, and Cognition." *Logoi* (Spring 2014): 9–10.

Zagzebski, Linda. "Morality and Religion." In *The Oxford Handbook of Philosophy of Religion*, edited by William J. Wainwright, 344–65. Oxford: Oxford University Press, 2005.

Index